POLISH CONTRIBUTIONS TO LATIN AMERICAN CULTURE

Edited by
Edmund S. Urbanski

The American Institute of Polish Culture
Miami, FL 1995

ISBN: 0-930401-97-2

Library of Congress Catalog Card Number: 96-83399

Artex Publishing, Inc.
1601 N. 8th Street
Sheboygan, WI 53081

Table of Contents

Acknowledgement

The publishers and editor wish to express their gratitude to prof. Zygmunt Turski for his assistance in proofreading the content of this book.

PREFACE

Edmund Stephan Urbanski, noted Latinamericanist now residing in the United States, began his career as a journalist in Poland. Born in the first decade of this century, Professor Urbanski first interested himself in Slavic, Scandinavian, and East European affairs.

After studying in Spain, the United States, and Peru, the Professor received his Ph.D. at the National University of Mexico. There followed a long and fruitful academic career. He taught in Latin America for ten years, during which time he published, in Spanish, several academic works on fundamental Slavic problems. For example, **The Slavs Yesterday, Today, and Tomorrow** (1943); **Poland, the Slavs, and Europe** (1944), and **Brief History of Polish Literature** (1946).

His studies in Latin America led him to the conclusion that, unlike the relatively homogeneous Anglo-American culture of the north, Latin America is composed of many civilizations, among which are Hispanic Creole, Mestizo, Black, and Amerindian. As he pointed out in **Among the Indians Mestizos, and Negroes in Hispanic America** (1994), this concurrence of ethnic and cultural groups, biologically diverse, and with distinctive life styles, has generated societies that can be understood only against this pluralistic background.

Professor Urbanski's career took him to the United States, where he taught at Marquette, Notre Dame, Buffalo, Western Illinois, Western Michigan, and Howard University. He concentrated his attention on Spanish American literature, Latin American civilization, and pre-Columbian Indian achievements. Among his publications are **Studies in Spanish American Literature and Civilization** (1964, 1965), **Angloamérica e Hispanoamérica. Análisis de dos civilizaciones** (1965), **Hispanoamérica, sus razas y civilizaciones** (1972), **Hispanic America and Its Civilizations. Spanish Americans and Anglo-Americans** (1978,1981) and (in Polish) **Polish**

Silhouettes in 19th and 20th Century Latin America (1991).

Following his retirement from full time professorship, Professor Urbanski taught several years as visiting professor at the Inter-American Defense College in Washington, D.C.; at the University of Warsaw, and at the Federal University of Paraná, Brazil. In Colombia, he was elected to the Academy of History of Santander, and in Peru to the Peruvian Institute of Human Studies, both great honors. Whereas, P.E.N. of Mexico placed his name in its **Directory of Writers** (1986).

In the present volume, Professor Urbanski presents 23 essays by 16 writers, including four selections of his own, on subjects related to Latin American culture. These Polish-American authors are professional Latinamericanists, so are also these from South America. All of them are dedicated academic researchers, which is a guarantee of their scholarly reliability.

As Dr. Urbanski points out, significant Polish migrations to Latin America began early in the nineteenth century, continued until prevented by World War II and aftermath. The emigrants made substantial contributions in many fields, among them engineering, medicine, the natural sciences, literature, and fine arts.

In addition to providing a valuable information about the contributors and the circumstances under which contributions were made, the volume includes fascinating accounts of the exploits of particularly colorful figures. There is, for example, General-Admiral Krzysztof Arciszewski, who in 1636, in the employ of the Dutch, conquered the coast of Brazil from Recife to Arraial.

Then there is the "incredible" J. Frederic Waldeck, a Polish-born Mayan explorer, the accounts of whose travels, as Professor Urbanski puts it, resemble "those of Don Quixote or Baron Münchhausen." And there is the story of Faustin Wirkus, a U.S. Marine who in 1925 was posted to an island near Haiti, where he was proclaimed king.

It seems that in 1848, another King Faustus had vanished amid prophecies that his namesake would someday come to his throne.

Among these interesting essays is one by Witold Balinski of

São Paulo, who defends the neurological hypothesis of Miguel Osoria de Almeida, that the mind is independent of the brain.. Not less significant were the cultural activities of Dr. Jozef (José) Leonard, who, during his almost thirty years of sojourn in various Central American countries (1880-1908), both, as a counselor to various Presidents and as educator, deeply influenced the intellectual liberalism of that region. Dr. Leonard was also teacher of the young Rubén Darío whom he encouraged to cultivation of poetry, whose recognized master and innovator he became later. As a founder of the known Hispanic Modernist Movement, he is a glory of Latin America!

There were, of course, many more Poles who through their good will and faithfulness to their newly adopted countries, with their scientific or technological activities, contributed to the civilizational progress of Spanish- and Portuguese-speaking America. Following Dr. Urbanski's indication, we may at random mention here a few names: Prof. Ignacy Domeyko, the 19th century pioneer-geologist and Rector of the University of Santiago in Chile; engr. Ernest Malinowski, who in 1870s constructed the trans-Andean Railroad in Peru, the highest in the world; Dr. Piotr Czerniewicz better known as Pedro Chernovich, who published in Brazil his famous **Medical Guide** (Rio de Janeiro, 1841), which described various diseases and medication for them. It was soon translated from Portuguese into Spanish, attaining with its twenty editions a great popularity, especially in Colombia and Mexico; Drs. Szymon Kossobudzki and Juliusz Szymanski, co-founders of the Brazilian Medical School of Parana; Dr. Juliusz Jurkowski, co-founder and dean of the Medical School in Uruguay; naturalists Cz. Biezanko and F. Woytkowski, who operated in various Hispanic countries; Prof. Sophie Jakowska, a pioneer-marine biologist in Santo Domingo; and nuclear physicists Drs. Stanislaw Dolinski, Waldemar Kowalewski, and Leszek Szybisz, who operate mostly in Argentina, and Wanda Las in Brazil.

Altogether, this collective work brings to life not only human activities and historic facts, but also a description of various Hispanic countries, with their fascinating, humanistic and exotic flavor.

In 1993, as recounted by Mariano Kawka in essay number 22, a Congress of Polish Communities in Latin America convened in Buenos Aires and Punte del Este. A distinguished list of attendees participated, both from Latin America and Poland. The meeting resulted in the organization of a Union of Polish Communities in Latin America (USOPAL), with a parallel Federation of Polish Boards of Trade in Latin America (CABIPAL).

The intention is to promote a solidarity of Polish participants in the American countries of their adoption, and a means of collaboration with Mother Poland, as well as strengthening Latin American economy.

As you will see, Professor Urbanski has assembled an excellent book that well illustrates the leavening effect that Polish culture has wherever in the world it may appear.

Lady Blanka Rosenstiel, O.S.J.
President, American Institute of Polish Culture
May, 1995

Early Polish map of the Western Hemisphere drafted by Jan de Stobnica in 1512 in Krakow for his Ptolomy edition. In spite of very limited geographic knowledge of that era, Stobnica clearly distinguished the two oceans that encircled the New World. A. E. Nordenskiold considers this the first complete breaking with the old theory of a single ocean surrounding Europe, Africa and Asia.

85th Anniversary of Prof. Edmund S. Urbanski

J. M. Robbins

Increasing the understanding of Hispanic culture has been the life work of a resident of the Washington, DC, area, Dr. Edmund S. Urbanski. After arriving in the United States after World War II he discovered that there were no text books on Hispanic literature, history or arts. Dr. Urbanski offered to teach these subjects, and his university dean asked him whether Hispanic America had a culture comparable to that of the United States. The dean's ignorance displayed the common impression in 1940s North America that Hispanic culture consisted mainly of mariachi music, Mexican "wetbacks" and bloody Latin revolutions. Dr. Urbanski's efforts have helped to expand knowledge of this rich culture among the people of the United States.

One of the earliest specialists in Latin American culture, Dr. Urbanski observed in 1994 his 85th birthday at his Silver Spring, MD, home.

After earning a doctorate from the National University of Mexico, followed by studies in Peru, Spain and the United States, Dr. Urbanski spent over ten years in Hispanic America.

His teaching activities spanned over forty years. He specialized in Spanish American literature and Latin-American civilization, and he was especially attracted to pre-Columbian Indian achievements. He was also engaged in anthropological comparative research in Anglo-American and Hispanic American civilizations, highlighting cultural differences and similarities within the Western hemisphere and showing how they started during the colonial period in the

Americas and developed afterwards.

Dr. Urbanski's main thesis is that, unlike the relatively standardized Anglo-American culture, Hispanic America possesses many civilizations molded by her various ethnic and cultural groups, biological factors, and distinctive lifestyles, even though all of them have a common linguistic and religious heritage. Thus, we should recognize Hispanic Creole, Mestizo and Black civilizations in addition to the various Indian cultures. All of these cultures developed during the historic process of ethnic mixture or, in the Creoles' case, of its absence. This novel, "pluralistic" theory has been accepted by scholars in most Latin American countries and by Hispanoamericanists in the United States.

Dr. Urbanski's scholarly activities resulted in the publication of ten books in English and Spanish on a variety of Americanist subjects.

Among the most important are: **Studies in Spanish American Literature and Civilization** (1964,1965), **Angloamérica e Hispanoamérica. Análisis de dos civilizaciones** (1965), **Hispanic America and Its Civilizations: Spanish Americans and Anglo-Americans** (1978,1981) and the recently prepared study **Among the Indians, Mestizos and Negroes in Hispanic America** (1995), which is an anthropological quintessence on his studies among these groups. Another work **Od Wikingów do Indian** [From Vikings to Indians] (1987) contains author's reflections on his travels in various Hispanic countries and is now being translated into English and Swedish.

In his colorful life in Latin America, Dr. Urbanski also participated in archeological work in Mexico in the Aztec area of Chimalhuacán and in Peru at the demummification of the Inca Indians at Chankay. Thanks to six research grants, he was able to examine more extensively the most important archeological monuments in Mesoamerica, Colombia, Ecuador, Bolivia, and Peru. In addition, he was active as a foreign correspondent of the Argentine and Brazilian press. He also interviewed the Presidents of Mexico, Ecuador, Costa Rica, and El Salvador.

After retiring from Howard University in 1975, Dr. Urbanski

served as a Visiting Professor at the Inter-American Defense College in Washington, DC, the University of Warsaw, and at the Federal University of Parana, Brazil. He also served as a United States Navy consultant aboard the *USS Nimitz* on the Atlantic. A great honor was his election as a foreign member to the Academy of History of Santandar in Colombia and to the Peruvian Institute of Human Studies. His name was also included in the **Directory of Writers** by the P.E.N. of Mexico (1968). Among his many other honors were two citations of appreciation for his Hispanic American activities that were read into the **Congressional Record** of the 92nd and 95th Congress (1972 and 1977). The professional journal **Hispania** considers Urbanski's various books and over 100 scholarly essays published on both continents as an important contribution to Hispanic studies in the United States.

Prior to his Hispanic American activities, Dr. Urbanski was engaged in Slavic, Scandinavian and East Central European affairs. He was a foreign correspondent for the Polish News Agency A.T.E., traveling extensively in the Balkans and the Near Eastern countries.

Dr. Urbanski's career change from journalism to scholarship in 1939 resulted in the publication of five books on fundamental Slavic problems in the context of European culture, the first to ever appear in Spanish. Among the most important were: **Polonia, los eslavos y Europa** (Poland, the Slavs and Europe) (1944), **Los eslavos ayer, hoy y mañana** [The Slavs Yesterday, Today and Tomorrow] (1943), and **Breve historia de la literatura polaca** [A Brief History of Polish Literature] (1946). The last is so far the only exposition of Polish literary culture in the Spanish language. An unusual feature of this work is that it also contains a chapter dedicated to Polish echoes in the literature of some Hispanic countries, including Polish freedom fighters who fought for their independence.

In 1975, he established at the Polish Institute of Arts and Sciences of America in New York a Polish-Latin American Book Collection which already has about 1500 items in Spanish, Portuguese, Polish, and English. Related archives contain over 4000 documents, scholarly papers, reports, maps, and press clippings illustrating the activities of Polonia in eighteen Hispanic countries and its contributions to their civilizations. This modest but apparently quite important research station already supplies data utilized for papers presented at the discussion section "New Aspects in Polish-Latin American Studies" which meets during annual PIASA meetings. Not surprisingly, some researchers have consulted this collection and archives for academic purposes, including a Latin scholar from California, also a few diplomats.

Despite his age, Dr. Urbanski continues to do research and is currently preparing an extensive monograph, **Polish Contributions to Latin American Culture**, which will present the active participation of Polonia in the humanistic, scientific and technological development of Spanish- and Portuguese -speaking America. In addition, the two volume Polish work **Sylwetki polskie w Ameryce Łacińskiej XIX i XX wieku** [Polish Silhouettes in 19th and 20th Century Latin America] appeared in 1991. He is in the final stage of preparation of his Polish-Latin American Bibliography (with about 3500 entries in Spanish, Portuguese, Polish and English) of considerable importance to historiographers. After all this, as incredible as it sounds, the author considers the completion of that as his academic retirement.

November, 1994
NEW HORIZON, No. 11, Vol. XIX.
New York

Some Polish Scientists and Explorers in XIXth and XXth Century Latin America

Edmund Stephen Urbanski

This essay deals with several Polish XIXth and XXth century naturalists, geographers, geologists and other specialists, who, through their explorations of Latin America, contributed significantly to the general advancement of sciences. Although their range of activities extended from Mexico to the Tierra del Fuego, their scientific or technical research embraced mostly Argentina, Brazil, Bolivia, Chile, Colombia, Ecuador, Mexico, Peru, Venezuela, and Guiana. Our information is based on their own recollections, scattered mostly in reviews, book fragments, some encyclopedic accounts, and even on this author's interviews with a few contemporary explorers during his own sojourn or travel in Latin America during over forty years.

Perhaps the best known Polish scholar is Ignacy Domeyko, who, during his nearly fifty years sojourn in Chile (1838-1889), was active in university lecturing and geological exploration of the Andes, which greatly helped in the development of Chilean mining. He discovered a few until then unknown minerals, one of which bears his name as 'domeykit'. Domeyko prepared and issued the first geological map of the Chilean Andes (1848). His greatest achievement was, however, the discovery of anthracite and silver, thus paving the way for exploitation of that country's mineralogical wealth. He also investigated Chile's volcanic formation and the chemical contents of the country mineral waters for medicinal usage. Domeyko discharged the duties of President of the University of Santiago for sixteen years

IGNACY DOMEYKO
1802 - 1889
PRESIDENT OF THE SANTIAGO UNIVERSITY, GEOLOGIST, DISCOVERER OF MINERAL LAYERS, AUTHOR OF THE MONETARY SYSTEM REFORM IN CHILE, RESEARCHER AND PROTECTOR OF THE ARAUCANS

PAWEŁ M. STRZELECKI
1797 - 1873
GEOGRAPHER, GEOLOGIST, MEMBER OF THE ROYAL SOCIETY, EXPLORER AND DISCOVERER OF MINERAL LAYERS (MINAS GERAIS), INDIAN CULTURE RESEARCHER

ERNEST MALINOWSKI
1815 - 1899
ENGINEER, CONSTRUCTOR OF THE CALLAO - LIMA RAILROAD AND OF THE TRANSANDEAN RAILROAD LIMA - OROYA, CONSTRUCTOR OF THE PORT CALLAO FORTIFICATION

KRZYSZTOF ARCISZEWSKI
1592 - 1656
GENERAL OF THE POLISH ROYAL ARTILLERY, ADMIRAL OF THE DUTCH NAVY, CONQUEROR OF OLINDA AND ARRAYAL FORTRESSES, RESEARCHER OF THE TAPUJA INDIAN CULTURE

JÓZEF SIEMIRADZKI
1858 - 1933
GEOGRAPHER, ETHNOLOGIST, AUTHOR OF "GEOGRAPHIE UNIVERSELLE" RESEARCHER OF POLISH SETTLEMENT IN SOUTH AMERICA, DISCOVERER OF MOUNTAIN RANGES IN PATAGONIA

ZDZISŁAW CELIŃSKI
1847 - 1929
ENGINEER, CONSTRUCTOR OF THE RAILWAY BUENOS AIRES - - SANTA FE AND OF THE PORT GUALEGUAYCHU, EXPLORER OF MATO GROSSO AND GRAN CHACO

CZESŁAW BIEŻANKO
1895 - 1986
NATURALIST, PROFESSOR OF THE CURITIBA UNIVERSITY AND THE AGRONOMIC COLLEGE IN PELOTAS, DOCTOR HONORIS CAUSA OF THE AGRICULTURAL ACADEMY

TADEUSZ CHROSTOWSKI
1878 - 1923
ORNITHOLOGIST, EXPLORER OF THE PARANA'S WILDLIFE, AUTHOR OF "ON SOME RARE SPECIES OF SOUTH BRASILIAN BIRDS"

WŁADYSŁAW KLUGER
1848 -1884
ENGINEER, PROFESSOR OF THE LIMA POLYTECHNIC, DESIGNER OF THE TRANSANDEAN AQUEDUCT, CONSTRUCTOR OF THE ILO - MOQUEGUA AND ARICA - TACNA RAILROADS

(1867-1883), and contributed greatly to the modernization of Chilean academic education. Among his 130 scientific works on various subjects, his manual **Elementos de mineralogía** (Chemical Examination of Minerals) ran several editions; authorized reprint of this work have soon appeared in Mexico and Spain. Declared an honorary citizen of Chile, this "father" of Chilean mining was also awarded an honorary Doctor of Medicine degree by the University of Krakow (1887). An Andean mountain range, a Chilean port and a few Chilean localities were named after him.

Similar were the activities of Prof. Jozef Siemiradzki during his three sojourns in South America. Encouraged by his investigative work on the geological formation of the island of Martinique in 1882, he went in 1883 to Ecuador to conduct geographic-ecological research interwoven with collecting specimens of Ecuadorian fauna and flora, a task in which he assisted Jan Sztolcman. Utilizing his commission to investigate possibilities for Polish emigration to South America, Siemiradzki spent the period 1891-92 in Brazil, Argentina and Chile where he also conducted geographic-geological explorations. Interested in Argentine's pampa and the Patagonian desert, he crossed them on his way to Chile. While traveling through almost untouched land, he was able to correct the cartographic dislocation of the Lihué Kalel mountain range and the nearby lake incorrectly marked in E. Zeballos' military map of 1879. He also discovered a granite spur of a mountain chain, which constitutes a part of the Cordillera de las Angosturas, and described its techtonic qualities. Likewise, Siemiradzki left a geological description of the mountainous regions of southern Brazil explored again in 1896-97 and authored the first geological map of the state of Parana. The results of his South American scientific research were duly utilized by the French geographer Elisée Reclus in his internationally known work **Géographie Universeille** (Paris, 1910-1914).

Known mostly among geophysicists is Prof. Wladyslaw Gorczynski, climatologist and meteorologist who had an international reputation. He untiringly investigated all his life solar radiation in Europe, Africa, Asia, and Latin America, the latter having attracted him more then other continents. Gorczynski utilized for this purpose a "solarimeter" and a "pherhiliometer" of his own construction, scientific instruments which by his permission were used by many Latin institutions. He was specifically interested in Mexico where he conducted research several times, and where he helped to organize the Meteorological and Astronomic Observatory in Tacubaya, D.F. in 1925-26. He felt at his best, as he told me in 1940, in Mexico's desert regions of Chihuahua and Sonora states, because they have the highest degree of insolation. After scrupulous and long investigations, Gorczynski arrived at the conclusion that the best climate in America and in the world, is to be found on the Mexican high plateau (meseta mexicana), also in the coastal zone between Santa Barbara, San Diego and Ensenada (Baja California). The only other Latin American country, important from the climatological viewpoint to Gorczynski, was Peru because of its variety of climatic zones. Since WW II prevented him from going there, he continued his research for the Universities of Florida and California. It was during that time that he crossed by foot California's Death Valley, which was an extraordinary deed. Prof. Gorczynski's master work was his monograph **Comparison of Climate of the United States and Europe** (1945), published by the Polish Institute of Arts and Sciences of America, to which he belonged along with many foreign academies.

Prof. Gorczynski's close associate was Dr. Zenon Lemanski, who also carried for many years meteorological investigations in Mexico, similar to those undertaken by both scholars in North Africa. As an collaborator of the Mexican meteorological Observatory, established with the help of both Poles in Tacubaya in the 1920s. Dr. Lemanski researched individually on the insolation in Ajusco, Tlamacas and Popocatepetl, the result of which was published in Poland and France. Since WW II he acted as a consultant to the Ministry of Public Works in regard to irrigation of vast agricultural areas in Mexico. Dr. Lemanski's Mexican activities span over fifty years.

Also appreciated by the Argentine Meteorological Institute are the activities of Stanislaw Pyzik, known for his uninterrupted service from 1915 to 1955 in the field of meteorology. He invented an "anemometer", a "freatometer", a "perphiliograph" and other instruments. A seismograph devised by him was successfully used in measuring an earthquake which occurred in the San Juan province. Until his retirement, Pyzik was director of the Technical School in Morón, where he lectured and educated two generations of Argentine meteorologists, constantly updating their professional skills.

The traditional Polish interest in natural sciences is obviously responsible for our curiosity about the tropical fauna and flora, They have attracted scholars to exotic Latin America as early as the first part of the XIXth century. Perhaps the best known Polish botanist who systematically researched Latin plants was Jozef Warszewicz, who spent ten years in Latin American countries (1844-1853). Few Europeans, if any, can rival with the achievements of this versatile scholar and plant collector.

Warszewicz undertook two botanical expeditions to Latin America, the first sponsored by the Botanic Garden in Berlin (1844-50) and the second by the Horticultural Society of London (1850-53). His first six-year tour embraced Guatemala, Honduras, Costa Rica, El Salvador, Nicaragua, Panama, Mexico and Ecuador. He collected then a great quantity of plants, among them about 300 species of little grown or unknown flowers, especially orchids, many of which were named after their discoverer - "Warszewicella". They were described by Prof. Reichenbach. Warszewicz's tropical plant collection caused an extraordinary interest within the European scientific circles. Baron von Humboldt personally congratulated the Polish botanist in Berlin, whereas the British Horticultural Society invited him to organize another expedition to South America. Warszewicz accepted, and thus a new four-year tour (1850-53) led him to British Guiana, Colombia, Venezuela, Brazil, Argentina, Bolivia, Chile and Peru. This expedition also rendered splendid results in a great number of rare tropical plants and birds, which enriched various British collections. Some of the birds brought to England by Warszewicz, were named after him. Warszewicz was possibly the only European naturalist who explored sixteen Latin American countries, achieving thus a **sui generis** record which rendered more results than the explorations of Darwin, Humboldt and La Condamine jointly.

Warszewicz's exploratory path was followed by other XIXth century Polish explorer-naturalists, such as Jelski, Sztolcman, Kalinowski, and the already mentioned Siemiradzki. In exchange for stipends they had to furnish Polish and foreign-sponsoring institutions with specimens of both tropical fauna and flora. Thus, they had to frequently combine their botanical with zoological work, collecting plants, especially flowers, as well as animals, birds and butterflies, for scientific purposes and the embellishment of various European, and later, North American museums.

In 1865 ornithologist Konstanty Jelski went to French Guiana with the help of Prof. Deyrolle of Paris, and spent four years in that colony. There he conducted ornithological research and hunted beautiful birds, which he supplied to French collections and after 1868 to the Branicki Museum in Warsaw, from which he had secured a grant. The French and Polish collections were also receiving rare specimens of Guianese flora, especially orchids. Due to the unhealthy climate of Guiana, Jelski moved in 1869 to Peru, where he continued his research and bird hunting for almost nine years. Encouraged by the Italian naturalist A. Raimondi (then in Lima) and by his Polish and Peruvian friends, Jelski accepted the custodianship of the newly established Museum of Natural History in Lima, for which he increased his activities between 1875 and 1878, in both zoology and botany.

Jelski's thirteen years of research and collecting activities in Guyana, Peru and partly in Ecuador were extremely fruitful. He discovered in that period about sixty new species of birds and an Andean mammal which he named "Dinomys Branicki". He also sent around 300 spiders to Poland. According to M. Paradowska, "Jelski discovered many unknown until then South American birds, some of which bear his name as for example a small woodpecker "Picumnus jelskii", two species of colibri "Thalurania Jelskii" and "Mettalura Jelskii", a fly hunter "Ochotoeca Jelskii", etc." Jelski's ornithological South American specimens are displayed in the museum of Lima, Paris, Warsaw and other European capitals. His collections were described by such scholars as Berlepsh, Cabanis, Guenther, the Oberthur brothers, Steindachmer and others. Wl. Taczanowski based his three volume work **Ornithologie du Pérou** (Paris, 1884-88) in great measure on the research of Jelski, as did Sztolcman and other Polish ornithologists.

Jelski's successor in bird collecting in Peru for the Branicki Museum was Jan Sztolcman, who arrived in Lima in 1875. Jelski introduced him to his new job and they jointly made a few expeditions to Peru's interior and even one to Ecuador. On one such joint expedition on the Peruvian coast they caught a sea lion, while on another one Sztolcman secured a number of hitherto unknown birds. They also found a rarely seen hummingbird (Loddigesia mirabills), which is the pride of only a few of the world's museums. Sztolcman hunted humming birds with preference, and once sent twenty-four of them, along with a sizable collection of insects, frogs, lizards and snakes to the Branicki Museum in Warsaw. He also was lucky to find a new species of a fly hunter (in Span. "papamosca americana"), which was later described by Taczanowski. Some of the birds discovered by Sztolcman received names of Polish scholars as for example "Picumnus jelskii" "Dive branickii", "Chrystometris siemiradzkii", "Phoenicothrauppia sztolcmanii", etc. Sztolcman's ornithological collections were described by noted ornithologists such as Taczanowski, Berlepsh, Guenter, Goldman, Peters and others. Some works on this topic also appeared in the **Proceedings of the Zoological Society of London.** Sztolcman spent ten years in Peru and Ecuador.

Sztolcman's work for the Branicki Museum was continued in South America by Jan Kalinowski between 1889 and 1902, and afterwards until 1941, for Peruvian, European and North American collections. During fifty years of work in Peru and partly in Bolivia, Kalinowski gathered thousands of ornithological and entomological specimens, among them about 500 rare species of Andean birds and a great number of insects and smaller animals. Kalinowski's favorite hunting territory was the jungle of Selva Madre de Dios, but he also made expeditions to other regions of the Peruvian interior. He discovered thirty-three species of birds, many of which were named after him. Likewise, a larger rodent bears the name "Dacyprocta kalinowskii", a parrot was named after Branicki, and a rat which lives in water and feeds on fish was named after Sztolcman. Kalinowski's ornithological and entomological collections were described in Sztolcman's Polish work **Peru** (Warsaw, 1912), in the **Proceedings of the Zoological Society of London**, and other foreign scientific papers. Kalinowski was a practical man, for to be independent from the irregular income drawn from foreign museums, he managed his **own** prosperous farm "Cadena", where he also performed his taxidermic work, and where he was visited on occasions by the Amazonian naturalist Witold Szyszlo. His son, Celestino Kalinowski, a US. educated naturalist and authority on Peruvian jungle, follows in his footsteps.

Another Pole who combined ornithology with entomology was Tadeusz Chrostowski, who visited Brazil three times between 1910 and 1923. He made his first expedition to the state of Parana in 1910-11. From his meager savings he built a hut not far from Curitiba and led the primitive life of a trapper engaged in self-supporting farming while hunting Parana's birds and insects.

After returning to Europe, his modest but somewhat representative collection caught the attention of Sztolcman in Warsaw and Prof. K. Hellmayer in Munich. Owing to the latter's intercession, Chrostowski secured a grant from the Bavarian Academy of Sciences in exchange for supplying zoological specimens. It enabled him to undertake another three-year expedition to his favorite state of Parana (1913-15), where his preferred hunting and research ground was the river-basin of Iguaçu. During that sojourn Chrostowski was able to catch a small crawling bird (Leptasthenura setaria), which was the dream of many ornithologists as only two examples of it were at the Natural Museum in Paris. On another occasion he caught an extremely rare species of a Brazilian woodpecker (Picumnus iheringi), the only other example having been found in 1880 in the state of Rio Grande do Sul. Dr. Chrostowski sent six specimens of this bird along with a shipment of other rare birds and insects, which caused great enthusiasm among German ornithologists.

Chrostowski led a team expedition, (1922-23), his third one, to Brazil under the aegis of the Zoological Museum in Warsaw. It also brought rich results in a great number of Brazilian birds, animals, amphibians, bugs and parasites of birds, many of them rare and some unknown in Europe. They were described by Dr. Helmayer, Sztolcman and Dr. Roszkowski. Chrostowski loved Brazil for he loved nature. This was expressed in his book **Parana** (Poznan, 1922), in which he affectionately presented the rich fauna and flora of this state, and in which about 700,000 Polish farmers have settled during the last hundred years.

Scientific predilection for Brazil was displayed by many more Polish zoological explorations, conducted primarily in Parana in the 1920s and 1930s. It was at that time that naturalist Dr. Jozef Czaki, of Marechal Malet, gathered several thousand reptiles, snakes and insects, while entomologist Michalina Isaakowa in the period 1926-28 collected about 13,000 butterflies and insects, which together with supporting research papers enriched Polish collections. In more recent times, ornithologist Arkady Fiedler traveled extensively in Parana, while Prof. Ceslau Biezanko, of Rio Grande do Sul, through his publications and discoveries of new species, made Brazilian butterflies famous all over Europe and Latin America. Also, Rev. Jacek Miesopust, of Santa Catharina, displayed a rare combination of theological preparation with interest in the dendrology of the forest regions of his state.

The best known Polish-Brazilian scientist is, of course, Prof. Ceslau Biezanko, who in a span of fifty years (1930-1980) was uninterruptedly active in research on butterflies and insects, partly combined with botany. He initially lectured at the University of Parana and over three decades at the Agricultural University in Pelotas (RGS). An enthusiastic and practical minded naturalist, in 1952 he introduced the cultivation of soya in the state of Rio Grande do Sul, which, with the passing of time became a major source of agricultural wealth in Southern Brazil. He also devised chemical means of effectively combating tropical parasitic insects. Biezanko is, however and above all, a genuine researcher who discovered and described either alone or with his colleagues, numerous species of butterflies and insects, and their erratic customs. Likewise, he established a new generic classification of butterflies known as Forbesopsis Biezankoi. Two butterfly families were named in his honor: "Biezenkoia Strand"' (1936) and "Biezankoa Skalski" (1974). Eleven entomologic species discovered by him bear his name, Apanteles bezankoi Blanchard (1960), Willistonia biezankoi Blanchard (1960), Archytas biezankoi Guimarães (1961), Lastauropsis biezankoi Carrera e Papaveto (1962), Theridion biezankoi Levi (1963), Ephuta biezankoi Casal (1965), Plusia biezankoi Alberti (1965), Zygaena cynarae biezankoi Alberti (1968), Polyortha biezankoi V.O. Becker (1970), Eupyes subferruginea biezanko Mielke (1972), and Biezankoa biezankoi Skalski (1974).

During his laborious life, (he is now 85 years old), this scholar published over one hundred scientific papers on etnofauna and lepidopterology in Portuguese and Spanish, the result of his findings in Southern Brazil and Uruguay. Biezanko's two well known works are: **Contribuiçao ao conhecimiento da fisiografía do Rio Grande do Sul** (Pelotas, 1958) and **Lepidoptera del Uruguay** (Montevideo, 1966). He also wrote on botany and agricultural chemistry. For his scholarly merits and contributions to the development of agriculture, the Brazilian government bestowed upon him the highest Brazilian decoration "Ordem do Cruzeiro do Sul", the Academia das Ciencias Riograndense elected Biezanko its Vice-President, and the city of Pelotas made him honorary citizen. Among many foreign distinctions, he received the Polonia Restituta order. When I met Prof. Biezanko in Europe in 1973, he urged me to come to Brazil, because as he said "Brazil has the most beautiful butterflies in the world. I agreed, but when I expressed my concern and related my bad experience with termites I had in Mexico, he chuckled, saying, "We also have them in Brazil. They once ate up my piano except for the ivory keys, because they were too hard..."

Always witty and gay, Biezanko fused scholarship with music, finding in it harmony, which may also be seen in the graceful

Prof. **Czesław Bieżanko,** entomologist and recognized authority on South American butterflies. During his teaching and investigative career at Brazilian universities for forty years, he discovered a number of butterflies which were named after him. Decorated with the highest Brazilian order "Ordem do Cruzeiro do Sul" for his scientific and agricultural merits (he introduced soya in Brazil), Prof. Bieżanko was elected Vice-President of the Academy of Rio Grande do Sul, a great honor for a foreign-born scholar.

flight of Brazilian butterflies.

In XXth century Peru, in addition to the previously mentioned Kalinowski, there were two other Polish researchers: Szyszlo and Woytkowski.

Feliks Woytkowski, a humanist by trade and naturalist by vocation, resided mostly in Peru's jungle region of la Montaña (1929-65). There he collected specimens of etnofauna and flora, initially for Peruvian and later North American museums. Between 1942 and 1945 Woytkowski was in charge of Botanical Garden in Lima, also took part in the University of California's expedition to Peru's interior. However, his activities were mostly related to furnishing zoological material to a few US. professors, who utilized it in their research. This arrangement did not always work to his benefit, rather to the scholarly glory of his patrons. Due to his great perseverance Woytkowski undertook numerous expeditions during which he gathered over one thousand insects including butterflies. Among them was a dozen entomological species hitherto unknown to science, several of which were named after him. Even more fruitful was Woytkowski's discovery of about one hundred Peruvian tropical plants, some of them bearing his name as: Aeshna Woytkowski, Monnina Woytkowski, Ectemnostegella woytkowskii Hungerfords Fuchsia woytkowski Macbride, Tipula woytkowskiana Alexander, etc. Many of them were decorative flowers such as orchids and ferns, in which he became an expert.

Encouraged by the American Pharmaceutical Co. CIBA, Woytkowski has for seven years searched for medicinal. plants in the Peruvian jungles which was as difficult as it was dangerous. He conscientiously committed himself to this hardly profitable task, hoping only that through medicinal plants used in drugs, he could alleviate pain or save lives of many people. Owing to his friendly contacts with the "chuncho" Indians, he accomplished in great measure his mission, but it was done at the expense of his declining health. According to a biographer his herbal collection contained about 80,000 plants belonging to five thousand generic families. Engrossed in his work and due to faltering health, he was unable to complete

Lic. **Teodoro Picado Michalski,** President of the Republic of Costa Rica (1944-1948). Possibly, the most intelligent among Chiefs of State of Latin America. Humanist and author of a few historic books, spoke fluently four languages: Spanish, Polish, English and French. Before entering politics, he was director of a college and became Minister of Education. He was also for many years President of the Costa Rican Congress.

LIGIA ESTRADA MOLINA

TEODORO PICADO MICHALSKI

SU APORTE A LA HISTORIOGRAFIA

Tesis de incorporación a la Academia de Geografía e Historia de Costa Rica

V

1967
IMPRENTA NACIONAL
San José, Costa Rica

This book: **Teodoro Picado Michalski, his contributions to historiography** (San Jose, 1967), describes the scholarly contributions of the ex-President of Costa Rica, which was the basis for his reception as a member of the Academy of Geography and History of Costa Rica. It is a rare case where a Latin politician engaged also in scholarly investigations.

cataloguing this valuable collection. Botanical species gathered by Woytkowski during his almost forty years of activities in Peru, are scattered in botanical gardens and herbarium in Lima, the Universities of California and Missouri, and other U.S. academic institutions. A laboratory researcher from Colorado Springs, acquainted with his tragic life, stated that "Woytkowski was a hero in natural sciences."

He was right, because Woytkowski at the age of seventy-three returned to Poland deadly sick and poor. On the basis of his systematically kept notes, a Polish book entitled **Peru, My Not Promised Land** (Peru, moja ziemia nieobiecana) was written in his name by M. Salomea Wielopolska (Wroclaw, 1974).

Less known are the activities of Piotr Paprocki, who, in addition to gathering in Peru entomological specimens for U.S. researchers (1929-1945), was engaged in the cultivation of a jungle plant '"barbasco", whose dried roots are utilized for manufacturing pesticides.

Witold Szyszlo was another naturalists who, from his home base in Lima conducted Amazonian research for almost fifty years. (1915-1963). It was interrupted only by his writing and his lecturing at the Peruvian Catholic University. A geographer and botanist, he undertook twelve exploratory trips to the equatorial regions of Peru, Brazil, Bolivia, Ecuador, Colombia, Venezuela and the Guianas, within the Amazon's basin. During those trips he made useful observations not only on the flora and fauna, but also on ecological and climatic conditions. He brought from there rich botanical collections, being particularly interested in the tremendous variety of ferns, orchids, cacti and palms and in tropical zoology. He utilized that material in Peruvian and foreign reviews, making his name known on both continents. When I met him in Lima in 1959, he showed me with pride a letter from a fellow researcher in England, who congratulated him on the description of some unknown species of Peruvian ferns. I noticed, then in Szyszlo sparks of a romantic scientist, for whom the world was an infinity of mysteries and full of imperfections.

Therefore, I am not sure whether he made as thorough a generic classification of these plants as Woytkowski did and made it available to more botanists, a fact which would have caused naming many more plants after Szyszlo.

Very studious and warm, he was a man with much experience in the tropics. When I inquired how he handled snakes in the jungle, he explained that he avoided them by whistling as they do not like a sharp sound. Szyszlo was also a man with a vision. He propagated the economic exploitation of Amazonia, maintaining that the fertile "humus" left after "inundation" made many highland terrains suitable for agriculture and cattle breeding. Until the middle of the XXth century it was believed that tropical jungle called "green hell" was, useless and dangerous for human and animal life. However, its contradiction was the Jari Agricultural Enterprise, established in the 1970s by the enterprising Daniel K. Ludwig (US.) in the very heart of the Brazilian jungle. It proved Szyszlo's theory to be correct. Szyszlo's master work was his voluminous book in Spanish **Naturaleza de la América Ecuatorial. Observaciones botánicas en la región amazónica del Perú, Brasil, Bolivia, Ecuador, Colombia, Venezuela y la Guyana entre 1904 y 1953, durante doce viajes científicos** (Lima, 1955). It contains much useful data gathered by this distinguished Amazonist, describing over 5000 plants and 900 animals which he found in Amazonia. When I saw him last, this almost eighty year old but sturdy man, was ready to leave for his thirteenth trip to that region.

As we saw, the South American tropics have attracted several Polish scholars. So it was with ornithologist Arkady Fiedler, who made between 1927 and 1979 eight explorations there. He was particularly interested in Brazil and Peru, where the tropical fauna and flora made a strong impact on him as did the native Indians and their customs in these countries. Through his beautiful books of many millions of copies and translations into various languages, Fiedler most probably made South America better known in Poland and Central Europe than any other author. He was enamored with the tropics which he somewhat "humanized" in the way the Ecuadorian Demetrio Aguilera Malta and the Uruguayan Horacio Quiroga treated the subject in literature. He was a great enthusiast of the Brazilian-

VITOLD DE SZYSZLO

La Naturaleza

en la

América Ecuatorial

Descripción de la naturaleza
de la región Amazónica del Perú, Brasil, Bolivia,
Ecuador, Colombia, Venezuela y de la Guayana

Observaciones hechas durante doce viajes
en los años 1904 a 1953

1955
SANMARTI Y CIA.
— Lima, Perú —

Prof. Witold Szyszło's book **Nature in Equatorial America** contains results of his botanic and zoological observations, made during his twelve scientific expeditions undertaken to several Amazonian countries in South America, between 1904 and 1953. Interesting too, are his ecological statements regarding the agrarian utility of some of the Amazonian regions. Prof. Szyszło taught for several years geography at the Catholic University in Lima. As a naturalist he enjoys international reputation. He acted for many years as Consul of Poland in Peru. His son Fernando de Szyszlo is a leading Peruvian artist-painter, who frequently utilizes Indian motifs in his work.

Peruvian Amazonia, to which he dedicated such works as **Bichos, my Brazilian Friends** (Bichos, moi brazylijscy przyjaciele), 1931, **Among Coroado Indians** (Wśrod Indian Koroadów), 1932, **Fishes Sing in Ucayali** (Ryby śpiewają w Ukajali), 1935, **Animals from the Virgin Forests** (Zwierzęta z lasu dziewiczego), 1936, **Conquering the Amazon** (Zdobywamy Amazonkę), 1937, **Rio de Oro**, 1950, and **Beautiful, Frightening Amazonia** (Piękna, straszna Amazonia), 1971. Also, his latest book, **Butterflies** (Motyle) is mostly dedicated to South American entomology, as the author informed us recently. In a somewhat similar vain, Waclaw Korabiewicz described his war-time ornithological trip to the Brazilian jungle in his book **Mato Grosso** (New York, 1946).

Other contemporary authors deserving mention are Burchardt Fularski, Gluchowski, Halik, Dzikowska, Lepecki, Orlowski, Pankiewicz, Pawlowicz, Warchalowski, Wojcik, Zarychta, and a few others. Their works contain mostly elements of adventure but are sometimes interwoven with observations on Indian ethnology of South America. This trend was previously noted in the work of Domeyko, Jackowski, Jelski, Habich, Kluger, Siemiradzki, Szyszlo, etc.

Unique in their field are two biologists: Prof. Sophie Jakowska and Dr. Waclaw Szumkowski. The Sorbonne-educated Szumkowski spent about twenty years in Venezuela (1948-1967), where he was engaged in cotton research and in the fight against cotton-related entomological parasites. He succeeded in introducing the cultivation of long-fiber cotton in the tropical Orinoco region, for which he was awarded the Great Ceres Cross by the Ministry of Agriculture (1964). He authored twenty-five scholarly essays of which perhaps the most important was **El uso y abuso de aplicación de insecticidas en algodón en Venezuela** (Use and Abuse in Application of Insecticides in Cotton in Venezuela), 1967.

Dr. Sophie Jakowska, the U.S. educated biologist, has been intensely active in research of various branches of biological and medical sciences. She lectured in several universities in the state of New York for over twenty-five years, and since 1962 has been

Dr. Piotr Ludwik N. Czerniewicz practiced for fifteen years medicine in Brazil (1839-1854) and through the publication of two scholarly books contributed to the development of medical knowledge in that country, which then lacked physicians. His **Dicionario da Medicina Popular e das Ciencias Accesorias** (Rio de Janeiro, 1842) had six Brazilian editions and was translated from Portuguese into Spanish. Its twenty editions also enjoyed popularity in Hispanic America, especially in Colombia and Mexico. Emperor Pedro II bestowed upon him for these pioneering merits, the highest Brazilian decoration — Cuvalheiro de Cristo.

connected with the marine biology development program of the University of Santo Domingo as its honorary professor. Extremely talented and dynamic, she has to her credit in ichthyology alone the discovery of parasites in electric eels, "protozea" in nervous cells of fresh water fishes, and of antibiotics in sea sponges. Author of over 150 research publications on various aspects of biology, published in English and Spanish, Prof. Jakowska became a staunch defender of sea and land environment. She continues to be active in scholarly pursuits in the Carribean countries from her base in Santo Domingo, where she settled in 1977.

From this kaleidoscopic survey it is hard to omit other Polish contributions to South American culture, especially in the field of exact sciences. From the scarce XIXth century information we know that several Polish physicians were engaged in research or university lecturing. Thus, Dr. Pedro Luiz Chernovich (Czerniewicz), for his meritorious work crowned with his Portuguese language **Dicionario da Medicina Popular** (Rio de Janeiro, 1841),which was a manual for physicians and dealt with treatment of various diseases, received from the Brazilian emperor Pedro II a high decoration of "Cavalheiro da Ordem de Cristo". Dr. Julio Jurkowski was a professor of anatomy and cofounder of the Medical School in Montevideo (1878-84) and later dedicated himself to similar activities in Argentina, where he founded in 1903 a Sanatorium in Córdoba. Dr. Ricardo Sudnik served as professor of pathology at the University of San Luis (1884-1914), was co-founder of the Sociedad Médica Argentina, and published there over sixty scientific papers. The first one was on "El mercurio en el tratamiento de la sifilís", i.e., "Mercury in the Treatment of Syphilis" (1879).

XIXth century Mexico also attracted two Polish doctors who had previously served in Europe as professors of medicine, but had declined to do so in Mexico for political reasons, preferring to lecture in medical associations. One was Dr. Seweryn Galezowski who, as surgeon, enjoyed an excellent practice (1834-48). He published numerous articles related to surgery in the **Journal of the Mexican Academy of Medicine.** The other one was Dr. Wladyslaw Belina

Swiatkowski, an obstetrician. He was interested in blood transfusion and introduced this technique in Mexico with apparatus of his own invention. He practiced there between 1874 and 1890, and published several essays in the Mexican medical press. Both Galezowski and Belina-Swiatkowski were frequently asked to assist their Mexican colleagues in serious operations, being called by them "maestros" i.e. "masters", a title usually bestowed upon distinguished university professors. It was Dr. Xavier Galezowski who, in his famous Ophtalmologic Clinic in Paris, educated two generations of Mexican oculists between 1870 and 1901. Many of his eye operations were described in bulletins of the Mexican University. Activities of these Polish physicians were recorded in Rafael H. Valle's book **La Cirugía Mexicana del Siglo XIX** (Mexico, 1942).

Nor does XXth century South America lack distinguished Polish scientists, especially physicians. Dr. Szymon Kossobudzki and Dr. Juliusz Szymanski were co-founders of the Medical School of Parana. Both were professors there for many years, the first of surgery and the second of ophthalmology. Both have published several research papers in the field of their medical specialties and for their meritorious work were honored with the highest Brazilian decorations. Likewise, outstanding were the activities of the Brazilian-born Dr. Miroslau Baranski, engaged in research and practice of tropical medicine, infectious and parasitic diseases. He was a professor of medicine for over thirty years (1952-1983) and for some time Vice-Rector of the Federal University of Parana. His more than 100 scientific publications earned him high reputation not only in Brazil but also in South America. An expert in physiopathology he helped in drafting the medical curriculum for Brazilian universities.

In the probably incomplete list of Polish physicians in Latin countries, there is one, Dr. Zdzislaw Szymonski, who rendered valuable services as a "jungle doctor" in Peru. He resided in that South American country from 1930 to 1978, and spent several years in the tropical region of Ucayali, where he treated the jungle Indians and mestizo settlers, which won him the gratitude of the Governor of the Amazonian district of Loreto. This Poznan University graduate, authored a Spanish manual **Enfermedades Tropicales** (Tropical diseases), Lima, 1935, a pedagogically important and for some years the only medical work of this type in Peru. He treated this author for "soroche" sickness in Lima in 1959, during his anthropological trip to Peru. Among physicians who, during WW II and after migrated to Chile and achieved there a reputation, we should mention two cardiologist Dr. Mieczyslaw Pawlak, who also lectured at the University of Santiago Medical School; and Dr. Marian Paleczek, known for his rehabilitation therapy treatments in cases considered hopeless by Chilean physicians.

Dr. Seweryn Cytronberg, of Warsaw's Medical School and a cancer expert, practiced in Mexico during WW II and became a research professor at the University of Guadalajara. Popular as gastroenterologist among Mexico City native and foreign residents, Prof. Cytronberg continued his medical research and published a significant essay **"El diagnóstico precoz del cáncer del estomago** (Early Diagnosis of Cancer of the Stomach) in the **Revista de Medicina Pasteur,** Vol. II, No. 5 (Mexico, 1940). Another cancer specialist, Dr. Mieczyslaw Floksztrumpf, was probably the only European physician who, on the outset of WW II, brought to Argentina a half a gram of radium. This permitted him to initiate the radium therapy in Mendoza, where he subsequently became professor at the University of Cuyo and director of its Cancer Institute. He published forty-one scientific essays in Spanish and English in the field of oncology. He earned reputation through his work **Cáncer de cicatrices** i.e. **Cancer with Scars** (Buenos Aires, 1955).

Significant contributions to cancer research were also made by the Batory University scholar, Dr. Leonard Wanke. He conducted it for thirty-two years at the Buenos Aires Cancer Institute. Alone or jointly with other researchers, he published between 1951 and 1980 fifteen extensive essays in Spanish on various aspects of cancer, of which one on "The Anatomic Findings of Cancer in Uterus" was presented at the Gynecological Congress of Parana (Brazil). Likewise, Dr. Wanke's other results of his cancer research were discussed at various Inter-American Oncological Congresses.

Well known for research in astrophysics is the Dobrzyń-born, but Sorbonne and Columbia University educated Dr. Ruth Gall, who since 1962 served as founder, professor and head of the Dept. of Space Research at the National University of Mexico. Prof. Gall authored until 1981 fifty-seven papers on cosmic and galactic rays and her better known works are: **Invariant Magnetic Shells in the Earth Field Distorted by the Solar Wind** (1967) and **Física espacial** (Mexico, 1968). Prof. Gall represented Mexico in many international scientific meetings, some of them in the United States.

A noted Polish-Peruvian ethnohistorian is Maria Rostworowski de Diez Canseco. Between 1960 and 1980 she published over twenty major works on Inca anthropology, highly valued in America and Europe. Her book **Pachacutec Inca Yupanqui.** (Lima, 1953) belongs to anthropological "classics". Significant field research on the Mixtec and Zapotec Indians of Mexico was conducted during World War II by the famous anthropologist, Prof. Bronislaw Malinowski. Known for his previous investigation of aboriginal custom and sexual habits in Melanesia (1914-1918), this Polish-British researcher, while dealing mostly with primitive societies in the Western Pacific, became through his **Magic Science and Religion** (New York, 1925), **A Scientific Theory of Culture** (Chapel Hill, 1944) and other works, a champion of the sociological approach to modern anthropology. Mexico also became a favorite research around for Dr. Alicja Iwanska, who for several years investigated Indian custom in the Valley of Mexico. She left a significant work **Purgatory and Utopia: A Mazahua-Indian Village of Mexico** (Cambridge, 1971) and other monographs. Research On Indians in Mexico and Negroes in Colombia and Ecuador was conducted by Dr. Edmund S. Urbanski, author of essays **Los negros y su idiosincrasia** (Mexico, 1975) and **Los indios y el indigenismo en Hispanoamérica** (Mexico, 1976). Dr. Maria Sten, author of **Codices of Mexico** (Mexico, 1972) on the Nahua Indian prehistory, has been for many years a professor of drama at the National University of Mexico, where she also lectures on pre-Columbian Indian theater.

There are also several ethnologists in Poland, whose research

LIC. JOSE CALERO

•

CRUCES
Y
ALAMBRADAS

LA TRAGEDIA EUROPEA
VIVIDA POR UN MEXICANO

MEXICO, D. F.
1942

Cruces y Alambradas i.e. *Crosses and Barbed Wires* describes the European tragedy of World War II, witnessed by Lic. José Calero. As a Mexican press correspondent, he entered Poland with Hitler's Army and saw the German atrocities committed on the Polish population, as well as the barbarian behavior of the Soviets. As a Christian, he was deeply moved by this brutal conduct of Poland's neighbors, and displays sympathy toward Poles. This testmionial book had three editions and opened eyes on the true personality of the Germans in Hispanic America. Later on, as a diplomat and friend of Poland, Calero served as a councillor at the Mexican Embbassy in Warsaw.

is closely related to Latin American area studies, particularly to Indians and Mestizos. Thus, Prof. Maria Frankowska, of Poznan University, published a few essays on the social organization and acculturation of aborigines in Mexico and Peru, epitomized in her work **The Religious Syncretism of Mexican Indians** (Poznan, 1971). On a variety of pre-Columbian archeology deal the research of Dr. Andrzej Wiercinski, Dr. Andrzej Krzanowski, Dr. Janusz Kozlowski and Dr. Andrzej Żaki. Their topics embrace either the Antilles, Mexico or Peru, regions where they have done their scholarly investigations. No less interesting is the Polish study by Dr. Alexander Posern-Zielinski on **Social and Religious Movements Among Indians of Spanish South America** (Wroclaw, 1974). The same author, in collaboration with his wife, Dr. Miroslawa Posern-Zielinska, produced a well balanced work **Indian Beliefs and Rituals** Wroclaw, 1977). Remarkable are Dr. Maria Paradowska's Polish works: **Among Indians and Mestizos** (1989), **Poles in South America** (1977), and **Poles in Mexico and Central America** (1985), the last two dealing with Polish contributors to Latin American culture and technology.

Unique was the research of an ethnolinguist, Prof. Tadeusz Milewski, author of **The Conquest of Mexico** (Wroclaw, 1959), based on his translation from Nahuatl into Polish of an anonymous Aztec manuscript known as **Codex Florentinus.** He also dealt with the pantheistic elements in the Aztec religion, but is better known for his original contribution on the "Similarities Between the Asiatic and American Indian Languages" (**International Journal of American Languages,** Vol. 26, No. 4, 1960). Whereas, a seasoned anthropologist, Prof. Jan Czekanowski, developed the racial classification of the world. Well known, if somewhat controversial, is his map with the distribution of ethnic groups, including these of the Americas, which has been discussed at international anthropological congresses.

An unusually penetrating contribution to the field of South American sociology and psychology was the work **Parasitism and Subversion. The Case of Latin America** (London, 1966) by Prof. Stanislaw Andreski. This England based scholar, who knows Spanish

HISPANIC AMERICA
AND ITS CIVILIZATIONS

Spanish Americans and Anglo-Americans

by Edmund Stephen Urbanski

Translated from the Spanish by
Frances Kellam Hendricks and Beatrice Berler

Foreword to the English Edition by Carl Benton Compton
Foreword to the Spanish Edition by Manuel M. Valle

University of Oklahoma Press : Norman
1981

The above book **Hispanic America And Its Civilizations. Spanish Americas and Anglo-Americans** appeared in three versions: Spanish, English and Polish. It has been utilized at various U.S., Canadian and Polish universities, attaining ca. sixty favorable book reviews in seven languages in twenty countries. All this was due to the pioneering comparison of Hispanic American and Anglo-American civilizations. The third U.S. edition of this scholarly work is scheduled in 1996.

Americans from his own autopsy, taught in the early 1960's at the National University of Santiago de Chile. A result of a forty year association with Latin America is the study **Hispanic America and Its Civilizations. Spanish Americans and Anglo-Americans** (Norman, 1978, 1981) by Prof. Edmund S. Urbanski, who lectured at the National University of Mexico (1942-1945), in the U.S., Brazil, and Poland. In spite of its title, it is a socio-anthropological comparison of Spanish also American and Anglo-American civilizations, a concept also presented in his other works. Andreski's and Urbanski's books which deal with many "taboo" features of Latin American idiosyncrasies, have also appeared in Spanish editions. There are also two significant works on the historic-legalistic aspects of Spanish America in French, by the Paris-based Dr. Tadeusz Wyrwa: **Le Méxique** (Paris, 1969), and **Les Républiques Andines: Bolivie, Chili, Columbia, Equator, Pérou et Venezuela** (Paris, 1972). These works are known mostly in Europe.

Noteworthy research in Mexican rural communities was conducted by Dr. Witold Langrod, author of **En el Campo de México** (In the Mexican Countryside), Mexico, 1970, who between 1957 and 1970 acted as United Nations expert and advisor to the President of Mexico. Langrod was engaged in a project on a national scale, the "Lerma Plan" encompassing the economic-social integration of six million rural Mexicans. This revitalized a good portion of Central Mexico. Dr. Langrod taught sociology in the 1960's at the Ibero-American University in Mexico City. Outstanding are the activities of Dr. Miguel Wionczek. His research and about twenty books on socio-economic planning and technology of Mexico and Latin Americas, whose consolidation he is promoting, exerted impact on their economies. Since the 1960's, he has been a senior researcher at the prestigious El Colegio de Mexico, belongs to various Mexican commissions and frequently represents Mexico in foreign meetings. A former Polish expert to the U.N., Dr. Wionczek became an influential Mexican economist, whose opinions are closely watched abroad. In 1977 he also became a professor of economics at the Colegio de Mexico.

Mexico has also benefited from the activities of two other Poles, who have been active there since WW II. One was the Argentine-born Dr. Juan de Wyskota Zakrzewski, writer and historian, who since 1964 became a professor at the Ibero-American University. Among his Spanish books one stands out: **San Martin** (Mexico, 1973) on the national hero of Argentina. Highly regarded is the creative work rendered by the well-known concert artist, Henryk Szeryng. As professor of the Mexican National Conservatory, he conducted for fifteen years master classes for a select number of gifted violinists. He included Mexican music in the programs of his world wide artistic tours, and represented Mexico as ambassador in UNESCO for several years. As far as I know, he is the only Polish artist who travels with a Mexican diplomatic passport, thus protecting his valuable Stradivarius...

Of a somewhat different economic nature than Langrod's and Wionczek's activities, was the work of Zygmunt Slawinski in Chile (1953-1978). Acting there as a delegate of the United Nations and International Labor Organization, Slawinski closely watched other South American countries in their daily life. This contributed to his vision of a future integrated economy of Latin America, frequently called "a continent in disruption". He expounded his thesis in two books: **La economía paralela** (The Parallel Economy, Caracas, 1972) and **Nuevas soluciones basadas sobre principios antiguos** (New Solutions Based on Old Principles), Santiago, 1980. Slawinski believes in parallel economies which could be achieved by changing some sectors of the traditional "monoproduction" of articles in most countries into their diversification, which would eliminate mutual competition and assure more economic elasticity. It could be accomplished through some kind of liberal cooperative system of landowners or factory proprietors and workers, on a mutual profit sharing basis. This anti-Marxist, modern economic approach between employers and employees, could bring about the decrease of staggering unemployment in Latin America and promote more economic balance and prosperity. Eng. Slawinski thus established a new school of economic thought, which gained some partisans, but so far without

Prof. Wacław Radecki who for thirty years lectured at Brazilian and Uruguayan Universities (1923-1953), introducing little known experimental and pathological psychology, especially the "discriminacionismo afectivo". For this reason, his and his disciples' teaching became known as "Radecki School of Psychology". Prof. Radecki and his wife Dr. Halina Radecka, who lectured in Argentina, penned a good number of books on related topics in Portuguese and Spanish. They were also dedicated propagators of the Polish culture in South America.

positive results.

Very diversified were the activities of an psychologist, Prof. Waclaw Radecki, who lived in South America for thirty years (1923-1953). Promoter of psychology as a university subject and introducer of clinical psychoterapy, he divided his activities between Brazil, Argentina and Uruguay. Dr. Radecki established in Rio de Janeiro in 1924, the first Institute for Psychic Disorders which he successfully managed for several years. Deeply involved in experimental psychology and psychotherapeutic remedies in child and adult behavior, his methods were then considered innovative by Brazilian medical circles, especially in regard to "discriminacionismo afectivo", which today is of common scientific usage. Radecki's Brazilian research found its manifestation in several publications in Portuguese such as **Tratado da psycología** (Treatise on Psychology), Rio de Janeiro, 1929, republished in Spanish (Bs. Aires, 1961), as well as in some essays. One of them, jointly authored with his Brazilian colleague, Dr. Lucilia Tavares "**Contribuçao a psycología dos juizos**" (Contribution to Psychology of Judgments) in *Anais da Colonia de Psychopatas Engenho de Dentro,* Vol.I, Rio de Janeiro, 1928, is of significant relevance. Between 1935 and 1950 Dr. Radecki held a chair in psychology at the Universidad de la República in Montevideo, interwoven with lecture tours in Argentina. Other scientific interests of Prof. Radecki were paranoia, hallucination and the psychological behavior of airmen, and for the latter he caught the attention of the military authorities in South America.

Radecki left many disciples in the countries in which he taught. One of them, Dr. Allredo Cáceres, published a book on the Pole's scientific work, **La obra psicológica de Radecki: 1910-1935** (Scientific Work of Radecki: 1910-1935), Montevideo, 1935, and a significant essay "**Aporte de Radecki al examen psicológico del aviador**" (Radecki's Contribution to Psychological Testing of a Pilot) in *Revista de Psiquiatría,* Montevideo, 1939. Also his wife, Dr. Halina Radecka, an accomplished psychologist, published several valuable books in Portuguese and Spanish, such as **Exame psicológico da crianza** (Psychological Examination of Children), Rio de Janeiro,

1930, **Psicología social** (Social Psychology), Buenos Aires, 1960, etc. Both Radeckis authored over sixty scholarly publications in Spanish and Portuguese, contributing to what a South American scientist calls the "Radecki School of Psychology". Upon Radecki's death in Montevideo in 1953, a collective work **Homenaje al Prof. Dr. Waclaw Radecki** (Homage to Prof. Dr. Waclaw Radecki), Montevideo, 1953, was issued by his Uruguayan friends. Whereas, Dr. Halina Radecka taught psychology in Buenos Aires colleges almost until her death in 1983.

Another psychologist was the Warsaw-born Dr. Aniela Ginsberg, who for nearly fifty years performed professional duties in Brazil. Interested in youth psychology (1936-1985), she successfully developed research which is perhaps best manifested in one of her basic works **A Comparative Personality Study of Young Men Belonging to Four Groups, in Applied Cross Cultural Psychology** (São Paulo, 1975). In it she deals with the divergent mental attitudes of university students of four ethnic groups: Brazilian, Japanese, Polish and Italian, the last three belonging to the migratory population of Brazil. She has published over fifty essays on different aspects of psychology in Portuguese, English and French. Prof. Ginsberg has taught at the University of São Paulo and the Catholic University of São Paulo, where she introduced new testing techniques and chaired doctoral studies in psychology.

Several Polish philosophers and sociologists were or are scattered in various South American countries. Thus, Dr. Bogumił Jasinowski, author of several treatises e.g. **Saber y dialéctica** (Knowledge and Dialectics) , Santiago, 1957, and **El problema del derecho natural en el sentido filosófico** (Problem of Natural Law in Philosophical Sense), Santiago, 1967, served between 1944 and 1965 as professor of philosophy at the National University of Chile. In that country two other Polish scholars continue lecturing. Since 1949 the Rev. Dr. Michał Poradowski has been teaching sociology and philosophy at the Catholic University of Concepción and is the author of two important books: **El Marxismo en la Teología** (Marxism in Theology), Madrid, 1976, and **La Sociología del Protestantismo**

Dra. HALINA RADECKA

mil años de la
vida cultural de

POLONIA

prólogo del Prof. Dr.
EDUARDO COUTURE

epílogo del Dr.
ADOLFO G. ROCCA

editado por:

el Círculo Arg. 'POLONIA LIBRE"

y A. Uruguaya "PRO POLONIA"

1940

Mil años de la vida cultural de Polonia i.e. *Thousand Years of Cultural Life of Poland* by Dr Halina Radecka is a comprehensive study of this topic. Whereas, her husband Dr. Waclaw Radecki published a similar essay **Rasgos característicos de la cultura polaca,** i.e.Characteristic Trraits of the Polish Culture (1939). They both, as professors of psychology, lectured extensively at Universities of Argentina, Brazil and Uruguay, where they also defended the Polish cause.

(Sociology of Protestantism), Madrid, 1980. Whereas, the Rev. Dr. Bruno Rychłowski, Salesian educator and psychologist, has been lecturing since 1946 at the Catholic University in Santiago; he has to his credit sixteen textbooks on the moral upbringing of youth and on philosophy and theology. A notable achievement was attained by the Brazil-based philosopher Witold Balinski, author of a Portuguese work **Na Procura de Uma Visão do Mundo** (In Search of a Vision of World), Curitiba, 1980. It constitutes a humanistic analysis of philosophical currents of the Western World in their historic dimensions. Prof. João de Scantimburgo considers it "a valuable contribution to philosophical thought in Brazil and in the Portuguese language".

Less known but nonetheless important were the activities of a Lwow scholar, Prof. Mikołaj Altuchow, author of a few Oriental studies in Spanish, who since 1948 has been lecturing on Sanscrit and the philosophy of India at the Uruguayan University of Montevideo. During WW II and many years after, Professors Paweł Siwek, S.J. and Jerzy Zbrożek taught philosophy at the Catholic University in Rio de Janeiro, whereas Dr. Stanislaw Fischlowitz lectured there on sociology, and among his publications left an important historic monograph on **General Christóforo Arciszewski** (Rio, 1959), under whose military command Holland temporarily conquered Brazil in the XVIIth century. The Parana-born sculptor Jan Żak (better know as João Zaco Paraná) has served as professor of painting and sculpture at the Academy of Fine Arts in Rio de Janeiro (1940-1961). Among the creative artists we should also mention Zbigniew Ziembinski, scenographer-director, who became the renovator of the post-War Brazilian theater in Rio, whereas Tadeusz Morozowicz is considered the "father" of ballet in the State of Paraná. Needless to say that the Polish contribution to Brazilian artistic life has an undeniable tradition as it was established in 1931 with the erection by Paul Landowski of the gigantic sculpture of Christ, the Redeemer, on Rio de Janeiro's neighboring Corcovado mountain. And it has been followed by other Polish artists such as Zamoyski, Lewandowski and Dakiniewicz.

Likewise, Argentina may take pride in contemporary artists,

such as Badura, Grocholski (Zygro), Gąssowski, Glett, Fabian, Jurewicz, Pawluczuk and Seyda, to mention but a few. Unusually original art of sculpturing in glass was introduced in monumental works by Feliks Berdyszak in 1950s, a deed which has been duly recognized in Argentina as a new kind of creativity. Whereas, in Peru, Piotr Ostrowski and Fernando de Szyszlo enjoyed artistic recognition, the latter being professor of fine arts at the Catholic University in Lima. Szyszlo's international fame is due to his combining contemporary abstractionism with old Peruvian Indian motifs. Highly rated for portrait paintings in Uruguay was Barbara Tarnowska, who mostly worked in Europe.

The activities of three atomic scientists deserve special attention: Professors Waldemar Kowalewski and Leszek Szybisz, of Argentina, and Dr. Wanda C. Las, of Brazil. The Polish-born but Argentina-educated Kowalewski, has been engaged in cosmic radiation and nuclear magnetic resonance studies since 1948, with additional scientific experimental experience in Sweden, Brazil, Switzerland and Canada. He has to his credit about forty essays on nuclear physics. After lecturing at the Universities of La Plata and Rosario, he was in charge of the Neutron Diffusion Laboratory at the Argentine Atomic Energy Commission (1952-56). Since 1950 until now he has been Professor of experimental physics at the University of Buenos Aires, and from 1964 became principal researcher of the CONICET's Nuclear Magnetic Resonance Laboratory. Prof. Kowalewski received the coveted T. Insardi Award (1971) from the Academy of Sciences in Buenos Aires, and together with Prof. R. Contreras has been leading for many years a group of 20 young Argentine nuclear scientists in experimental work.

The Middle East-born but Argentina educated Dr. Szybisz, engaged in nuclear research since 1966, became professor of nuclear energy at the Univ. of Buenos Aires in 1976. He is also a member of the Argentine Atomic Energy State Commission. After having spent four years of grant-supported research at the Center of Nuclear Physics in Karlsruhe, be became director of exact science research and the promoter of doctoral theses in nuclear physics at the Univ. of

Buenos Aires. Prof. Szybisz authored over forty-five essays on subjects related to nuclear propulsion. Whereas, the Brazil-born Wanda Las owes her professional education to the Univ. of São Paulo and the University of Washington. Dr. Las' research is mainly centered on the thermoluminescent mechanism in ultraviolet radiation and in the effects of the equilibrium concentration of impurities on the reproductability of thermoluminescence. Author of twenty scholarly papers, since 1975 she has been engaged in scientific work at the Institute for Nuclear Energy research in São Paulo. All three, professors Kowalewski and Szybisz and Dr. Las have thus joined the ranks of two Polish American nuclear scholars, Professors Stanislaw Ulam and Stanislaw Mrozowski, known for their activities in the famous WW II atomic "Manhattan Project".

In technological sciences singular activities were displayed by engineers Dr. Teodor Blachut, who performed his skill in Colombia and Peru, and Dr. Janusz Drapinski, who discharged various technical duties during his 37 years' work in Brazil. The Polish and Swiss-educated but Canadian-based T. Blachut was for the last forty years engaged in various branches of geodesy. He invented new systems of fotogrammetric mapping, utilized in measurements of the world's economic resources. Patent-oriented, he is well known for his unique method of radar profiles in basic fotogrammetric operations and analytical "Autograph", useful in various fields, including mapping of cities, regions and icebergs, by means of stereofoto technique. As an internationally recognized authority, Blachut undertook various technological-scientific missions in Colombia (1975) and Peru (1984), and lectured all over Latin America. Author of three geodesic works in English and Spanish, he is particularly known for his famous **Urban Surveying and Mapping** (New York, 1979).

Dr. Drapinski's experience embraced mechanics, hydraulics, industrial pneumatics, and technical organization of factories which he mastered in Brazil's greatest industrial center in São Paulo. Equipped with such a multifacetic experience, since 1970 he has taught for thirteen years these technological subjects at various polytechnic institutions, including the Univ. of São Paulo. Between 1969 and

Engr. **Ernest Malinowski,** who in the 1870s constructed the Trans-Andean Railroad in Peru, the highest in the world! This work also involved construction of a few dozens of mountain tunnels and inter-mountain bridges.

1979 Prof. Drapinski authored five technological textbooks in Portuguese, which according to eng. A. Pereira, filled the then existing Brazilian gap in that field.

Many Polish technological scientists and practitioners contributed to the development of civilization in XIXth century South America. Some of their deeds were quite spectacular as for example, the utilization of a balloon devised by eng. Robert Chodasiewicz during the Paraguayan War (1868-70), when its constructor served in the allied Argentine-Brazilian Armed Forces. It was the first flying object used in South America and Col. Chodasiewicz became the first aviator in the history of Argentina!

Another military engineer Col. Czeslaw Jordan Wysocki has explored the natural resources of Patagonia and during the so called Argentine "Conquest of the Desert" (1870s), devised the first highway, connecting Rio Negro with Puerto San Antonio. Eng. Zdzisław Celiński took part in Argentine exploration of its Chaco province, constructed a railroad between Buenos Aires and Santa Fe, and a fluvial harbor Guakeguaychu on the Uruguay River, displaying a particular interest in the navigability and regulation of Argentine rivers. Construction of Paraguayan war ships was for a few years supervised by Luis Myszkowski, contracted by President Solano López. During the period 1873-1900 architect Juan Luka-Łukasiewicz executed projects of several monumental buildings in Montevideo, where he was Director of Public Works.

In the middle of the XIXth century Polish engineers constructed bridges and highways, as for example Estanislao Zawadzki in Colombia and Alberto Lutowski in Venezuela, both being contracted by the respective governments in Paris. Equally active were some others in Brazil. Thus, military engineer Andrés Przewodowski constructed several public buildings in Bahia, a bridge over Paraguaçu River (866 m.), Canal Ilheus which joins the Itaipe and Itabuna Rivers. During his topographic-geological survey he discovered petroleum, and prepared a project for the port of Bahia. Some of his works in regard to harbor projects were partly continued by his son, Capt. Estanislau Przewodowski, a naval hero of the Paraguayan War and of the famous Brazilian-Argentine incident at Itaqui (1874). Eng. Florestan Rozwadowski, on behalf of the Brazilian Navy, explored the river-basin of the Amazon, and drafted the first hydro-topographic maps of the area. He was also an early advocate of the repopulation of Brazil's enormous interior through his work **Govêrno e colonização** (Rio de Janeiro, 1857). Highly regarded as a mathematician was gen. Roberto Trompowski, professor of ballistics at the Military Academy in Rio de Janeiro, whose son gen. Armando Trompolski became in 1946 Minister of the Brazilian Air Force. Both Trompowskis achieved the rank of marshal in the Brazilian Armed Forces. However, the outstanding deed was the establishment in 1950 by a Polish industrialist Alfred Jurzykowski, of a truck factory "Mercedes Benz do Brasil" in São Paulo. This pioneering feat not only promoted a new industry in Brazil, but also made it independent from foreign car import.

Mountainous Peru attracted several Polish technologists in the XIXth century. One of them, eng. Ernest Malinowski achieved the greatest fame. After having constructed a railroad between Callao and Lima, he undertook a task unique in the history of engineering, the construction in the 1870s of the trans-Andean railroad between Lima and Oroya. Considering the natural topographic obstacles, it was a gigantic deed, for the route led through the high Andes reaching at times 4,800 meters altitude. This compelled Malinowski to excavate a 1200 meter long tunnel and sixty-two smaller tunnels, and to construct thirty steel bridges and viaducts, of which the tallest was seventy meters. In building this highest railroad in the world, Malinowski displayed not only his own genius, but also utilized the mathematical calculations of his colleague eng. Edward Habich, another outstanding mathematician and topographer. This railroad track opened tremendous economic opportunities for Peru, because it connected the Peruvian coast with the fertile Peruvian tropical lowlands. The construction was financed by a U.S. entrepreneur Henry Meiggs, while its extension to Huancayo was finished at the beginning of this century, by the Peruvian Corporation of London.

The activities of the Warsaw-born eng. Edward Habich were

also spectacular. Contracted by the Peruvian government in 1869, he participated in the reconstruction of the city and port of Arica, destroyed by an earthquake; he also devised an irrigation system in southern Peru, and served as a consultant in the enlargement of the cities Ilo and Moquegua. His main deed, however, was the establishment in Lima, in 1872, of the School of Engineering and Mining, the first of its kind in South America! He accomplished this task by inviting from France Polish engineers Tadeusz Stryjenski, Wladyslaw Kluger, and Ksawery Wakulski, who joined forces with their colleagues already working in Peru: Aleksander Babinski, Wladyslaw Folkierski, Aleksander Miecznikowski and Ernest Malinowski. All of them represented various scientific-technological specialties of a high caliber. Habich was a mathematical genius and construction expert, with proven pedagogical experience. A man of great technical culture, he published numerous works on mathematics, civil and water engineering, as well as on Peruvian colonial architecture, in Spanish. To promote the new field of knowledge, he initiated in 1880 publication of a scientific-technological bulletin, the first of its kind in Hispanic America. Eng. Habich was also responsible for devising the first Mining Law and for establishing the Board of Measurement and Weight in Lima, where he established the Peruvian Geographical Society. He directed the Technical University as its President for 37 years, almost to his death in Lima (1909) and was, for his merits, declared an honorary citizen of Peru.

Another Polish engineer, Wladyslaw Kluger, devised a trans-Andean highway between Tacna and the border of Bolivia, which was built in 1878. It is still the main communication tract between Peru and Bolivia. Malinowski's collaborator, Dr. Wladyslaw Folkierski, who coordinated the work of certain sections of his trans-Andean railroad construction, became, in 1883, inspector of northern Peruvian Railroads and Director of Navigation on the Lake Titicaca. Since 1879 he served as professor of mechanics for ten years at San Marcos University in Lima, and finally became Dean of its Department of Physics and Mathematics.

At the outset of the XXth century, very prominent were the

Leszek Zawisza

ALBERTO LUTOWSKI

Contribución al conocimiento de la ingeniería venezolana del siglo XIX

The author of this book, **Dr. Leszek Zawisza**, who for twenty-five years served as professor of urban architecture and environmental aesthetics at the Universidad Central de Venezuela and the Universidad Bolivar, both in Caracas, published several valuable books on Venezuelan architecture and its history. Among them the most important are **Arquitectura y obras públicas en venezuela del siglo XIX** (5 vols., 1992-94) and **Alberto Lutowski. Contribución al conocimiento de la ingeniería venezolana del siglo XIX** (1980). The latter describes the unsually fruitful work of engr. Wojciech Lutowski during his thirty years sojourn in Venezuela (1841-1871). His technological activities consisted in the construction of a network of public highways, bridges, public utility buildings and two churches (one is on the frontispiece of this book). There were, of course, many more Polish architects and university professors of various specialties, working in Venezuela during the last sixty years.

activities of eng. Ryszard Jaxa Malachowski, designer of several monumental buildings in the capital of Peru. Considered an outstanding architect by his Peruvian colleagues, Malachowski was Professor of architecture at Lima's School of Engineering for 32 years. His greatest accomplishments were the designs of Peru's Presidential Palace, the Congressional Palace, the Archbishop's Palace and Lima's City Hall, also a few churches in Peruvian provinces.

Similar are the activities of Dr. Leszek Zawisza, who since 1960 has been professor of architecture at the Central University of Venezuela, being also credited with planning and supervision of several buildings' construction in Caracas. Prof. Zawisza is also the author of a few monographs on Venezuelan architecture, among them of a book **Alberto Lutowski** (Caracas, 1980), which describes Lutowski as a constructor of several XIXth century highways and bridges in Venezuela, also as the builder of two churches and a planner of a spectacular high-mountain railway between Caracas and La Guaira. His son, gen. Alberto Lutowski, a military engineer (1852-1916), distinguished himself as initiator of a navigational channel through the petroleum-rich Maracaibo Lake, who also exercised twice the duties of the Governor of Caracas.

Among Polish engineers who performed scholarly duties during and after WW II in Peru's National University of Engineering, we should mention Jan Nalborczyk, professor of metallurgy, and Gerard Unger, professor of thermodynamics, who became deans of their respective departments. Their busts were erected by the university to honor their professional merits.

Sky-high Bolivia has attracted Polish geological and mineralogical explorations. Thus, eng. Jozef Jackowski, while in charge of bismuth and tin mines in Buen Retire de Tasna, Choroloque and Quechisla (1886-1895) discovered ores of other minerals. Their rich collection, because of it scientific value, received a gold medal at the World Exposition in Paris (1890). Whereas, Dr. Roman Kozlowski, contracted by the Bolivian government, served for eight years as professor of geology at the Mining School in Oruro, of which he became director (1913-1921). Prof. Kozlowski undertook extensive geological and mineralogical explorations in the provinces of Oruro, Potosi and Chuquisaca, the results of which were published in the **Boletin de la Sociedad Geográfica de La Paz** (1920) and also in French and Polish scholarly reviews. Similar were the activities of eng. Marian Tarnawiecki in Peru (1902-1947), who combined railroad construction with successful mining explorations. Notable was, above all, his petroleum discovery in the Loreto and San Martin districts, as well as these conducted in the 1930s in southern Peru, which led to the British oil exploitation. Likewise, effective was his discovery of gold in Pataz, which in a great measure helped the development of the goldsmithing industry in Peru.

Unusual explorations were made by the Polish speleogical expedition in Cuba, in 1961, by ten young men. They explored thirty-five caves in the Oreganos and Sierra Madre mountains, described and mapped them, including many underground lakes and rivers, where they found little known fauna and flora. Altogether, the expedition covered an underground distance of about 100 kilometers. Another, even more dangerous exploration was organized in Peru in 1979 by a Polish kayak expedition composed of five student-sportsmen. Led by Andrzej Pietowski, they explored and chartered several swift Andean rivers regarding their navigability, while describing the ecology of their surroundings. The observations gained from the Peruvian trip were of hydrographic value, as were the results of their previous expeditions to Mexico and the United States.

Another extraordinary achievement was the passing of the Amazon river from its Peruvian source to the Brazilian mouth, by the Polish kayak sportsman Piotr Chmieliński. This unique expedition lasted 175 days and ended on February 20, 1986, establishing a new world record (so described by Guiness Book of Records). During its duration measurements were taken, disclosing beyond doubt that the Amazon has a length of 6,810 km, and not 6,430 km, as previously thought. This was a new Polish geographic and hydrographic contribution to world science.

Recapitulating our findings, we would like to stress the role Poles also played in other fields such as the construction of harbors and the development of aviation industry in South America. Noteworthy was the construction of ports in Peru, Argentina and Brazil. Thus, as early as in the 1870s eng. Edward Habich was charged with the reconstruction of the harbor and city of Arica in Peru, which were destroyed by the earthquake. In the 1850s and 1860s a similar task befell eng. Jerzy Przewodowski and Florian Rozwadowski, who enlarged the Brazilian port of Bahia, having the latter also constructed the Ilheus Channel, which joins the rivers Itaipe and Itabuna, also a large bridge over the river Paraguaçu. At the beginning of the XXth century, the Argentine port of Necochea was constructed under the supervision of eng. Bernard Zakrzewski, also a builder of a water dam and an artificial lake in the state of Mendoza, who for these works received a Gold Medal from the Government of Argentina. In the middle of this century it was the genial eng. Tadeusz Skrzypek, who, combining high technology with industrial initiative, built the Brazilian super-harbor Paranaguá and furnished the port installations in Maceió, São de Maranhao and Belén do Pará. This collective effort was partially shared by eng. Tadeusz Burzynski, specialist in electric installations at various Brazilian factories.

Spectacular was the Polish post-WW II participation in the development of aeronautic industry in Argentina and Brazil. Since 1948 there were in Argentina a few Polish aviation engineers engaged in the construction of airplanes and lecturing at the military Aviation Academies and the University in Cordoba, a city which is the center of Argentine aeronautic industry. Thus, eng. Jan Paczka, after fifteen years of construction work at the factory of military planes, became in 1964 chief of its constructural calculation department; he is also the author of a Spanish manual **Statistics Applied in Aviation Construction.**

Eng. Tadeusz Hajduk, who after lecturing on the flying instruments at the Escuela Superior de Aerotécnica in Córdoba, became in 1958 professor of aeronautical technology and chief of the Aviation Dept. at the University of La Plata. Since 1982 the Argentina-born eng. Enrique Cichocki has been engaged as head in the Industrial Quality Dept. in the construction of the military training plane of the "Pampa" type, and became professor of the Provincial Institute of Technological Education in Córdoba. Whereas, the Polish and British-educated Dr. Jozef Krasiński, conducted since 1948 important experiments related to aerodynamics and thermodynamics at the laboratory of the Instituto Aerotécnico of which he became chief, also serving as a professor at the Escuela Superior de Aerotécnica and the Universidad Nacional de Córdoba. As an aeronautical scientist, Dr. Krasiński is the author of thirty tematical essays in Spanish and English, among them such internationally known works as **Aerodynamics of Compressible Flow** (Córdoba, 1988) and **A Study of Axially Symmetric Base Flow Behind Bodies of Revolution at Supersonic Speeds** (Brussels, 1966).

Similarly, a considerable impact on the Brazilian aviation has been exerted, by the Polish and U.S.-educated Dr. Jerzy T. Sielawa. Interested mostly in space flights, construction of jets and nuclear satellites, his services since 1970s entail experimentation and the scientific-educational field. He serves as a chief of technology at the Technological Institute of Aeronautics, where he is also a professor. He, too, directs the activities of the Brazilian Institute of Space Research in São José dos Campos, overseeing the work of young aeronautical specialists. Prof. Sielawa is credited with fifty studies on aviation and space flights in Portuguese and English, and represented Brazil many times abroad.

In addition to the already mentioned Prof. Sophie Jakowski, a marine research biologist who since the 1970s has been professor at the University of Santo Domingo in the Dominican Republic, we should note the biological activities of Dr. Krzysztof Waliszewski in Mexico, who since 1981 has been connected with the Instituto Tecnológico in Veracruz. Here, as a bionutriologist and professor, he directs its Nutrition Research Dept. of tropical products. Due attention deserve Dr. Jerzy Rzędowski, author of a book **Vegetación de México** (Mexico, 1978), professor of botany at the Universidad de San Luis Potosi and since 1960 at the Instituto Politécnico Nacional, as well as the known philosopher and psychologist Dr. Mieczysław Choynowski, since the 1970 Professor at the Universidad de la Ciudad de Mexico, to mention only a few productive scholars in the Aztec land.

Whether in Argentina, Brazil, Mexico or Peru, Polish settlers, with a few tropical exceptions, rather easily integrated into their respective countries of adoption. This accounts for their willingness to participate in the civilizational development of those lands, even under difficult conditions. To examples previously quoted, a few new ones illustrate this attitude. Thus, it is worthy to mention the construction in Brazil in the middle of the XIXth century of a railroad between São Paulo and Santos by eng. Bronisław Rymkiewicz. It was followed by a construction of a fluvial port of Manaos on the Amazon, also executed by Rymkiewicz, which won him there a statue. Likewise important was the construction of another railroad connecting Curitiba with Paranaguá, built by eng. Teofil Rudzki. It was started by an Italian and continued by a German, but topographic obstacles discouraged them both, so it was finished by the more experienced Rudzki.

In spite of limited Polish immigration to Argentina in the XIXth century, several Poles participated in that country's cultural-scientific development. Feliks Żaba, who lectured on European literature in Buenos Aires from 1862 on; Michał Górski, professor of languages and mathematics at the National College "General Belgrano" in Buenos Aires who became its director (1880-1900); eng. Karol Löwenhard, who was professor of mathematics at the National College of Tucuman, and became its Vice-Rector (1875-1881); and among a few physicians Dr. Ryszard Sudnik, professor of pathology at the University of San Luis, who was one of the founders of the Argentine Medical Society, to mention a few. Prior to WW I, engrs. Bernard Zakrzewski and Eugeniusz Dąbrowski undertook the construction of irrigation canals which enlarged the fruit plantations in the Rio Negro province.

Of considerable importance was the construction by eng. Zdzisław Celiński of a railroad between Buenos Aires and Santa Fe, which became the gateway for Argentina's cultural and economic expansion to its interior. Dr. Rudolf Zuber made later geological exploration for petroleum in the southern part of the country.

The post-WW II influx of Polish immigration was numerically bigger to Argentina than to Brazil, Venezuela, Mexico or other Latin countries. It was composed of ca. 20,000 ex-combatants, among whom, there were about 400 highly skilled engineers, physicians, technicians and other specialists, who were soon absorbed by Argentine life. Many of them who established "Adelphia" Co., were engaged in the electrification of huge parts of Argentina, others in war industry and mechanical enterprises, also in research and university teaching. To the latter categories belong among others: Dr. Leonard Wanke, who for 32 years conducted research in Buenos Aires' Cancer Institute; Dr. Franciszek Płoszaj, who, together with his Argentine colleagues, devised a new system of liver treatment; otolaryngologist Dr. Czesław Czarnowski, ex-Professor of the Univ. of Vilno, continued his research; mineralogist eng. Stefan Wlekliński divided his expertise between the mines of Argentina, Bolivia, Panama and Haiti; eng. Ryszard Białous, who during his forty years of residence in Argentina's little inhabited Patagonia, built and equipped two health resorts Copahué and Caviahué, which made him promoter of balneology. He introduced there Alpine architecture.

A good number of scientific and technological scholars found suitable positions in various Argentine universities or other institutions. A similar situation exists in Venezuela, where Polish architects and construction engineers contributed considerably to the economic growth of the country and, above all, to the architectural outlook of Caracas, the most beautiful hemispheric city which rivals with Buenos Aires. Also, scientists and artists found a good foothold in Venezuelan universities or other institutions. Favorable conditions also prevail in Brazil, where universities in Rio de Janeiro, São Paulo, Curitiba, Bahia and Goias are staffed with several scholars of Polish origin or descendance, while Polish artists enjoy there a traditional reputation. Similar conditions also exist in Chile, Peru and Mexico, known for their high respect for European men of arts and culture.

Participation of the Polish settlers in the civilizational development of their adopted countries in Latin America, as well as their activities there, are recorded in a few monographs in Spanish, Portuguese and Polish. These are: **Los polacos en la República Argentina**

y América del Sur (Buenos Aires, 1966), by Estanislao Pyzik, **Los polacos en el Peru** (Lima, 1979) by Kazimierz Kochanek, **Polonia en el Uruguay** (Montevideo, 1945) by Otokar Jawrower, **Sylwetki polskie w Ameryce Łacińskiej XIX i XX wieku** (with resumé in English), Stevens Point, 1991, by Edmund Urbański, and **Anais da Comunidade Brasileiro-Polonesa** (Curitiba, 1970) by various authors.

Bibliography

Andreski, Stanislaw. **Parasitism and Subversion. The Case of Latin America.** London, 1966.

Barreto, Abellardo. **Bibliografia Sul-Riograndense.** Rio deJaneiro, 1973-76.

Biezanko, Ceslau M. **Contribução ao conhecimiento da fisiografía do Rio Grande do Sul.** Pelotas (RG), 1958.

Bukiet, Albert. **Materiały do Bibliografii: Polonika Ameryki Łacińskiej.** Buenos Aires, 1975.

Breowicz, Wojciech. **Ślady Piasta pod piniorami.** Warszawa, 1961.

Caceres, Allredo. **La obra psicológica de Radecki: 1910-1935.** Montevideos 1936.

Domeyko, Ignacio. **Memorias. Recuerdos de un emigrado.** Santiago, 1946.

Fiedler, Arkady. **Piękna, straszna Amazonia.** Warszawa, 1971.

Fredecensis. **A Polônia na literatura brasileira.** Curitiba, 1927.

Gardolinski, Edmundo. **Imigração e colonização polonesa.** Canoas, 1958.

Gorczyński, Władysław. "El mejor clima del mundo con enfasis especial sobre el de México": **Memorias y Revista de la Academia de Ciencias**: Mexico, D.F. 1948.

Hempel, Antoni. **Polacy w Brazylii. Wrażenia z wyprawy.** Lwów, 1894.

Jawrower, Otokar, Ed. **Polonia en el Uruguay.** Montevideo, 1945.

Kochanek, Kazimierz, Ed. **Los polacos en el Perú.** Lima, 1979.

Krąpiec, M.A. et al. **Wkład Polaków do kultury świata.** Lublin, 1976.

Langrod, Witold L. **En el campo de México.** México, 1970.

Milewski, Tadeusz. **Aztek-Anonim: Zdobycie Meksyku.** Wrocław, 1959.

Paradowska, Maria. **Polacy w Ameryce Południowej.** Wrocław, 1977

Pyzik, Estanislao. **Los Polacos en la República Argentina y América del Sur desde el año 1812.** Buenos Aires, 1966.

Rostworowski de Diez Canseco, Maria. **Pachacutec Inca Yupanqui.** Lima, 1955.

Sarnacki, John. **Latin American Literature and History in Polish Translation** (Bibliography). Port Huron, 1973.

Siemiradzki, Józef. **Szlakiem wychodźców. Wspomnienia z podróży po Brazylii.** 2 vols. Warszawa, 1900.

Skowronski, Tadeu. **Páginas brasileiras sobre a Polônia.** Rio de Janeiro,1942.

Radzymińska, Józefa. **Biały Orzeł nad Rio de la Plata.** Warszawa, 1971.

Sten, Maria. **Las extraordinarias historias de los códices mexicanos.** Mexico, 1972.

Reclus, Elisée, Ed. **Géographie Universelle.** Paris, 1910-1914.

Retinger, Józef. **Polacy w cywilizacji świata.** Warszawa, 1937.

da Silva Carneiro, David. **Galeria de ontem.** Curitiba, 1963.

Szymoński, Zdzisław. **Enfermedades tropicales.** Lima, 1935.

Szyszlo, Witold de. **La naturaleza en la América Ecuatorial.** Lima, 1955.

Taczanowski, Władysław. **Ornithologie du Pérou.** Paris, 1885-1888.

Urbański, Edmund S. "Latin American Studies and Bibliography in Poland": **LARR,** No. 3, Vol. 15. Chapel Hill, 1980.

Urbański, Edmund. **Los polacos en el Notre de Latinoamérica.** Mexico, 1943.

Wójcik, Jan K. **Bibliografia brasileiro-polonesa.** Ms. Porto Alegre, 1960.

Wójcik, Jan K. **Balcerowi następcy.** London, 1975.

Woytkowski, Feliks. **Peru, moja ziemia nieobiecana.** Wrocław, 1974.

Zieliński, Stanisław. **Słownik pionierów polskich kolonialnych i morskich.** Warszawa, 1932.

Collective. **Polacy w Rio de Janeiro.** Rio de Janeiro, 1929.

Collective. **Anais da Comunidade Brasileiro-Polonesa.** Curitiba, 1970-1972.

Collective. **Enciclopedia Universal Ilustrada Europeo-Americana.** Madrid, 1945.

Valle, Rafael H. **La Cirugía Mexicana del Siglo XIX.** Mexico, D.F., 1942.

Historical Sources in the Polish-Latin American Collection at the Polish Institute of Arts and Sciences of America

Sławomir Korzan

Due to the Institute's extensive interest in Polish cultural affairs throughout the Western Hemisphere, PIASA has a unique book collection and archives in Spanish and Portuguese on Polish topics. Established for researchers interested in Polish contributions to Iberian and Latin American culture, this collection of "Polonica" on a variety of topics was organized by Prof. Edmund Stephen Urbanski, upon his retirement in 1975. A professional Latinamericanist, the donor acquired these items during forty years of research and travel in Spanish- and Portuguese-speaking countries of the New World, as well as Spain and Portugal, to encourage scholarship in this as yet little-known domain of Polish-Iberian-Latin-American historiography and literature.

The Collection contains approximately 1,500 books and printed items among them publications by Polish scholars and writers from Argentina, Guatemala, Brazil, Chile, Colombia, Mexico, Peru and Uruguay, some works by Polish immigrant leaders, as well as by Latin American authors, all dealing with Polish culture, history, ethnography, archaeology, sociology, and World War II problems. Of particular interest are books in Spanish and Portuguese concerning Poland during World War II, and its military contributions to the Allied cause. In the attached folders to this Collection-Archives, is material of historic value, including statements about Poland, issued by Latin American foreign ministers at the Inter-American Conference of

DIEGO CAMACHO

EX CATEDRÁTICO DE LA
UNIVERSIDAD DE TRUJILLO

Polonia heróica,
ante el nazismo.

LIMA - PERU
1939

This book by the Peruvian Professor Dr. Diego Camacho **Polonia heróica ante el nazismo** (1939) i.e. *Heroic Poland Facing Nazism* describes the German political acquisitivness toward Poland, the latest proof of which was Hitler's invasion of Poland in 1939, coordinated by similar invasion of Stalin's Soviet Russia. It is a concise and sympathetic overview of the unfortunate Polish history of the last two centuries by a friendly Latin American scholar.

Chapultepec, Mexico, in 1945 (which preceded the establishment of the United Nations), as well as a collection of "war" press clippings in Spanish and Portuguese, which reflect the political attitude of most Latin countries toward then German-Soviet occupied Poland.

A number of pamphlets and some rare bulletins issued by Polish immigrant groups in Mexico and Brazil are also included. Likewise, two MS diaries on WW II experiences: one by Gen. Stanisław Nałęcz Małachowski and another one by Major Mirosław Dziekoński, both written in Chile, belong to this Collection. There is also a diary by Consul Antonio Wiatrak on his long sojourn in Guatemala, and a MS of a Polish unpublished book by Edmund S. Urbanski on "Poles in XIXth Century Mexico, Cuba and Central America", included. Several monographs deal with Polish culture and Polish literary echoes in Latin America and the Iberian Peninsula (Radecki, Skowronski, Urbanski, Zielinski); whereas others with sciences and arts (Biezanko, Cáceres, Domeyko, Gorczynski, F. Gross, Gumplowicz, Jasinowski, Krasinski, Langrod, Malinowski, Radecki, Szymonski, Szyszlo, Znaniecki); while others concern the history of Poland or Polish immigration to Latin America (Halecki, Korbonski, Kochanek, Pobóg-Malinowski, Pyzik, Urbanski, Wl. Wojcik, J. Wojcik); and theological problems and Nazi World War II atrocities (Card. Hlond, Bochenski, Siwek, Wasik).

The native Hispanic-Polish authors are represented by Teodoro Picado Michalski (Latin American bibliography), Miroslau Baranski (tropical medicine), Edmund de Chasca (literary criticism), Enrique Cichocki (aeronautics), Edmundo Gardolinski (architecture), Ramón Pelinski (musicology), the brothers Miguel and Roberto Korzeniewicz (sociology), Piotr A. Ferchmin (biochemistry), Mariano Kawka (linguistics), Hilda Lawinska-Thiesen (musicology), Elena Poniatowska, Ladislau Romanowski, Olga Grechinski Zeni (literary fiction), Edward Szewczak (biochemistry), Edvino D. Tempski (anthropology), Maria Rostworowski de Diez Canseco (ethnohistory), Ruy Chr. Wachowicz and Juan de Wyskota Zakrzewski (history), to mention only those whose writings are in the possession of the Collection. There are, of course, many more in existence.

Useful for researchers in modern European history are works concerned with socio-political situation of Poland under dual Nazi-Soviet WW II occupation. They are represented by Iberian or Latin American and Polish authors: Calero, Camacho, Casanova, Ferrand de Almeida Soares, Kaczmarek, Koc, Jordan, Engel, Matuszewski, Pragier and others. Two rare 19th century Polish books on Spain by Pawinski and Stella Sawicki are included in this Collection. Also, included are two album editions on Stanislaus Polonus' (Polono) XVth and XVIth century publications in Latin, Spanish and Catalan. Polonus was one of the earliest pioneers of printing in Spain. Ornamental types from Polonus printing shop in Sevilla were utilized by J. Cromberger in his printing shop established in 1555 in Mexico City, which was the first establishment of this type in the Western Hemisphere.

Supplementing this Collection are Archives which contain about 4,000 items on similar topics, namely all kind of documents in form of bulletins and minutes of meetings of various Polish organizations, including data on the Polish war-colony in Santa Rosa, Mexico (1943-1945), press clippings on various Polish activities and events in Hispanic America and about 270 xeroxed, early maps of the New World from the XVIth and XVIIth centuries, including the oldest Polish sea chart by Jan de Stobnica from 1512. The greatest assets of this archivistic collection are, however, unpublished materials on the Polish-born Maya explorer and artist, J. Fr. Waldeck in Mexico (1825-1836) in French, English and Spanish; on the activities of Dr. José (Jozef) Leonard, humanist and educator in Spain (1868-1880) and Central America (1880-1908), a personality practically unknown except by a small circle of Hispanists. Also, on Leonard's friendship with his disciple Rubén Darío, future founder of the Modernist poetic movement in Hispanic America. Information on Leonard is in Spanish and English.

By fortunate coincidence the Collection can boast of a few items related to historic Polish-Spanish relations. Thus, it has two valuable volumes of Documenta Polonica ex Archivo Hispaniae in Simancas (Polish Documents from the Spanish Archives in Simancas),

Rome, 1960, compiled by the Rev. Dr. Walerian Meysztowicz. This is a collection of hereto unknown diplomatic documents exchanged between kings of Poland and Spain during the XVIth century. These royal dispatches on a variety of political subjects are written in Latin, Spanish and Italian. Of no less importance are several works on Spanish medieval and Golden Age literature, in annotated editions by Henryk Ziomek and Edmund de Chasca (Trzaska) in our possession. Perhaps we should add here, too, **Literaturas eslavas** (Slavic Literatures), Madrid, 1946, by Jozef Łobodowski, an enthusiastic propagator of Polish culture in Spain. Further manifestations of contemporary Peninsular interest in Polish history were displayed by the following Spanish writers: Sofia Casanova's **Martirio de Polonia** (Martyrdom of Poland), Madrid 1945, and the Duke of Parcent's **El drama de Varsovia, 1939-1944** (The Warsaw Drama 1939-1944), Madrid, 1945, both in our possession.

Among our scarce Portuguese holdings are a few historic essays on Polish-Portuguese relations in the XVIIth century, published by Luis Ferrand de Almeida, historian of the Univ. of Coimbra. They are **O Principe Casimiro da Polônia e os antecedentes da restauração de Portugal, 1638-1640** (Prince John Casimir of Poland and the Antecedents of the Royal restoration in Portugal) Coimbra, 1963; **As Cortes de 1679-1680 e o auxilio a Polônia para a guerra contra os turcos** (Parliament of 1679-1680 and Help for Poland in War with Turkey), Coimbra, 1951, and **Portugal e Polônia** (Portugal and Poland), Coimbra, 1967. Equally important are Adam Zielinski's two French documentary works: **"Les Cartas Regias" Polonaises aux Archives de Lisbonne"** (The Polish Royal Messages in Lisbon Archives) Rome, 1967, and **Repercussions littéraires portugaises des luttes pour l'independence de la Pologne au XIXe siecle** (Portuguese Literary Repercussions of XIXth Century Poland), Rome, 1975. Works of both authors reveal practically unknown details of Polish-Lusitanian relations in the past. Their present moderator is Janina Klawe, author of **Historia Literatury Portugalskiej** (A History of Portuguese Literature), Wroclaw, 1985 .

The other Portuguese-speaking country, Brazil, is better rep-

Dr. Tadeusz Skowronski, Polish Envoy to Brazil (1937-1945), intellectual and very active in Polish-Brazilian affairs, incl. those of over one million of Polish settlers in that country. He published two remarkable books: **Páginas brasileiras sobre a Polônia** (1942) i.e. *Brazilian Pages about Poland,* which brings *Brazilian opinions on Polish* culture and its people, and **Wojna polsko-niemiecka, widziana z Brazylii** (1980) i.e. *Polish-German War Seen from Brazil,* which describes the German aggression of Poland in 1939 and its tragic consequences.

resented in our Collection than Portugal. This is due to the large Polish immigration there, as well as to Brazilian sympathy toward Poles. Its best proof is a unique anthology, **Paginas brasileiras sobre a Polônia** (Brazilian Pages on Poland), Rio de Janeiro, 1942, by Tadeusz Skowronski, who describes the Brazilian cultural and political repercussions of Poland in the XIXth and XXth century literature. Several Portuguese books on a variety of topics were published by Poles or Polish Brazilians, starting with Dr. Piotr Czernowicz's **Dicionário de Medicina Popular** (Manual of Popular Medicine), Rio de Janelro, 1842. It initiated a trend of scientific publications, especially medical, as two Polish physicians Sz. Kossobudzki and J. Szymanski became co-founders of the Medical School of Parana (1913). They were followed by such scholars as M. Baranski, W. Stemski, A. Surgik, H. Szewczak T. Chrostowski, Cz. Biezanko and other intellectuals. Some of them write only in Portuguese, as for example the novelist Ladislao Romanowski and the poet Paulo Leminski.

The existing bilinguism does not interfere, however, with the appearance in Brazil of Polish novels, published by Jan Krawczyk and Roman Wachowicz, who enjoy great popularity there. The colonization of the state of Parana and other Polish achievements are described in **Anais da Comunidade Brasileiro-Polonesa** (Annals of the Brazilian-Polish Community), which started appearing in 1970 in Curitiba.

Polish emigration in Latin America is considerably less numerous (ca. two million) than that in Anglo-America. They are spread out in the vast territories between the Rio Grande and the Tierra del Fuego. This accounts for their less organized social forms, even though some communities have vivid activities. This geographic dispersion and the migratory flow, interrupted after WW II, which could have revitalized the Latin American Polonia, somewhat weakened its initiative. Previously a dozen newspapers were published, whereas only two weeklies survived in our day: **Głos Polski** in Argentina and **Lud** in Brazil, which continue their informative task. There is, however, a good augury of revigoration of that Polonia activities and their unification. This was manifested by the First Polish-Latin American Congress, which met in Buenos Aires in 1993.

ESTANISLAO P. PYZIK

Presidente Honorario de la Unión de los Polacos en la República Argentina

LOS POLACOS
EN LA
REPUBLICA ARGENTINA
Y
AMERICA DEL SUR

DESDE EL AÑO 1812

Algunos antecedentes históricos y bibliográficos con palabras alusivas del Dr. Jorge Castro Nevares y el prólogo del Dr. Manuel V. Ordóñez

Editado por el Comité de Homenaje al Milenio de Polonia

Buenos Aires 1966

Año del Sesquicentenario de la Independencia de la República Argentina y Milenio de Polonia

Stanislaw Pyzik's monograph **Poles in the Argentine Republic and in South America since 1812.** It contains rich information about Polish scientific and technological contributions to the historical development of Argentina, and in a lesser degree about those in South America. Due to a limited accessibility of this monograph in Poland, it is now being translated into Polish by Michał Więckowski of Buenos Aires.

Its noble aim is the coordination of such efforts through a mutual exchange of ideas.

The previously mentioned circumstances and not always benign climatic conditions, did not debilitate, however, the "Polishness" of these migratory centers, as may be seen in a few Spanish-language monographs in our possession. These are: **Los polacos en la República Argentina y América del Sur** (Poles in the Argentine Republic and South America) by Stanislaw Pyzik (Buenos Aires, 1966); **Polonia en el Uruguay** (Polonia in Uruguay) by Otokar Jawrower (Montevideo, 1945), and **Los polacos en el Perú** (Poles in Peru) by Kazimiera Kochanek (Lima, 1979). We may add here the previously mentioned, Portuguese language collective work **Anales da Comunidade Brasileiro-Polonesa** (Annals of the Brazilian-Polish Community), which started appearing in Curitiba in 1970. These monographs are limited to the presentation of Polish activists and events in their adopted Latin countries.

A continental rather than regional character has the two-volume Polish-language monograph **Sylwetki polskie w Ameryce Łacińskiej XIX i XX wieku** (Polish Silhouettes in XIXth and XXth Century Latin America) by Edmund S. Urbanski (Stevens Point, 1991). It contains biographic sketches of 275 Polish-Latin activists from Spanish-, Portuguese- and French-speaking America, also has an extensive topical resumé in English. Its preparation took the author and his 50 collaborators about twenty years, so this monograph may be considered a collective work. Dr. Urbanski conceived the idea of preparing it during his ten year sojourn in various Latin countries, where he conducted research on Hispanic and Indianist subjects. There, he also had close contacts with many Polish-Latin Americans and was impressed with some of their achievements, which inspired him to put them in print. Thus, a voluminous publication emerged complete with 82 sketches from Brazil, 75 from Argentina, 24 from Peru, 20 from Mexico, 16 from Chile, 90 from Venezuela and Colombia, as well as sketches from the remaining Hispanic countries.

Among holdings in our Archives is the information on the activities of the Polish chair at the National University of Mexico,

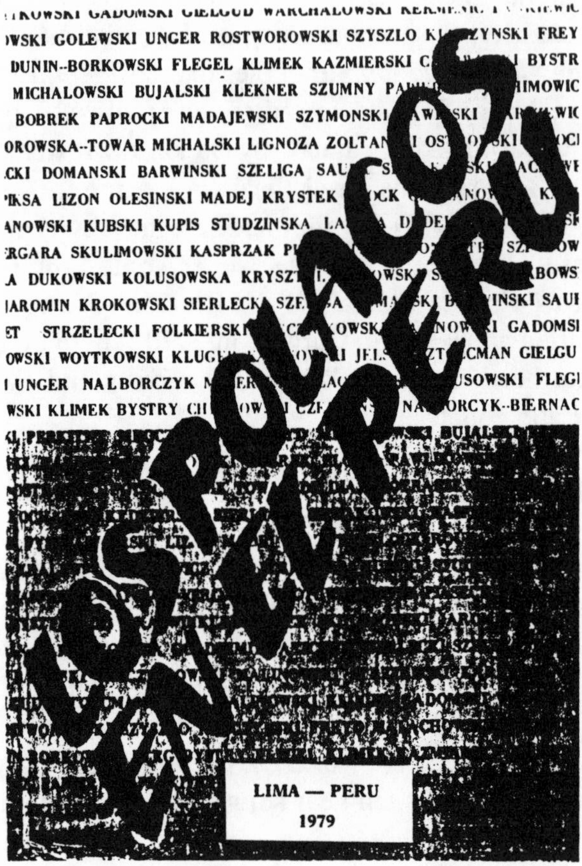

The collective work **Los Polacos en el Peru** i.e. *Poles in Peru,* edited by Kazimierz Kochanek in Lima (1979), contains a good number of bio-bibliographic sketches of Poles, engaged in cultural, artistic and technological activities in 19th and 20th century Peru.

Monograph **Polonia en el Uruguay** *(The Polish Community in Uruguay)*, edited by Otokar Jawrower in Montevideo (1945), where he was engaged in the radio programs called "The Voice of Poland". This work under a Polish patriotic slogan "For Our and Your Liberty" contains a few essays on historico-political topics, including one on Polish-Uruguayan relations rather than biographies.

1945), which with that at the University of Uruguay, were the only Polish academic outposts in XXth century Hispanic America. Of considerable scholarly value are many of the forty-five papers, delivered at the PIASA's Section "New Perspectives on Polish-Latin American Studies" (1979-1994). They constitute a good source of historic and contemporary information on Polish activities in Spanish-Portuguese America and their contributions to the culture of their adopted countries. Similarly informative on the activities of the Brazilian "Polonia" are the Polish-language **Calendars** from various periods, issued in Curitiba, Parana. It is hoped that they may be matched sometime in the future with similar **Calendars** from Argentina.

Our Collection also contains books of a myriad of U.S.-born Hispanists or Latinamericanists of Polish extraction, who are professors of various specialties at American universities: Robert Anderson, Janusz Bugajski, Joseph Chrzanowski, Alicja Iwańska, Edward Kaminski, John E. Kicza, Jeff K. Kowalski, Michael Krzyzanek, Gerald L. Langowski, Bernardine Pietraszek, John Sarnacki, Saul Sosnowski, Dan Stanislawski, John J. Staczek, Edmund Urbanski, Joseph A. Wieczorek, Erik Ziolkowski, Henryk Ziomek and Ann Zulawski. Also, writers Tad Szulc and Frank Tannebaum belong to the same group, as authors of many works on Hispanic America.

Among many other items, our Archives also contain around 350 biographical sketches of known activists, many of whom were not included in Urbanski's monograph **Sylwetki polskie w Ameryce Łacińskiej XIX i XX wieku** (Stevens Point, 1991). They made their names known for their unusual cultural or technological achievements in Latin America, v. gr. Z. Bau and R. Sosnowski in Argentina, H. Siewierski and J. Wścieklica in Brazil, B. Piotrowski in Colombia, G. Szkudlarski and A. Żaki in Peru, Z. Ryn in Chile, and J. Kobylański in Uruguay. Included here are also specialists in Hispanic affairs residing in Poland: M. Frankowska, J. Klawe, M. Sten, T. Łepkowski, M. Paradowska, D. Rycerz, A. Posern Zielinski and A. Wierciński. We also have several books by A. Dębicki, J. Petry Mroczkowska, J. Lipski, E. Skłodowska, E. Urbański and H. Ziomek, professional

Curacas y Sucesiones i.e. *Indian Chieftains and Successions* describes the pre-Columbian indigenous leadership's successions, practised in the northern coast of Peru. The Polish-Peruvian author, **Maria Rostworowski de Diez Canseco**, a noted anthropologist, published between 1960 and 1990 over thirty scholarly books on similar pre-Inca and Inca civilizations, and is frequently quoted by U.S. and European specialists.

Hispanists or Latinamericanists, who work at American Universities and are frequent guest lecturers abroad. Their scholarly contributions are particularly outstanding in the field of Hispanic letters and civilization

Our Collection possesses a good number of Spanish-language "Polonica" on a variety of subjects, from various Hispanic American countries. Among them, most outstanding is the Colombian edition of Krasinski's classic **La no divina comedia** (Nie boska komedia) in a masterly rendition of Inés de Zulueta (Bogotá, 1944). An interesting but not fully explored topic constitutes a work **Visión del Mundo Eslavo** (Vision of the Slavic World) by Ramiro Lagos (Bogotá, 1960). In spite of its many imperfections, it was the first attempt of scholarly evaluation of Slavic historiography by a Hispanic author, in this case a Colombian.

Although pre-WW II Mexico maintained with Poland rather marginal relations, this country displayed since 1939 unusual activities favoring the Polish cause. This may be proved by a documentary book **Cruces y alambradas** (Crosses and Barbed Wires) by a Mexican diplomatic correspondent José Calero, who witnessed the German invasion of Poland (Mexico, 1943). The same war period was likewise covered by Francisco Navarro's **Alemania por dentro** (Germany on the Inside) and Julián Gorkin's **Hitler y Stalin, canibales políticos** (Hitler and Stalin, Political Cannibals), although the last two books are in the Library of Stanford University. Most works dedicated to Polish historiography were, however, published in Mexico by Poles. Such are: Edmund S. Urbanski's **Polonia y el equilibrio europeo** (Poland and the European Balance), 1941, **Los Eslavos ayer, hoy y mañana** (Poland, the Slavs and Europe) 1944, and Juan de Wyskota Zakrzewski's **Polonia en armas** (Poland Under Arms) 1951, **Polonia y sus antecedentes históricos** (Poland and Her Historic Antecedents), 1943, and **Polonia frente a Alemania y Rusia** (Poland Facing Germany and Russia), 1944. The other works on Polish topics are Alfons Jacewicz' **Santa Rosa, osiedle polskie w Meksyku** (Santa Rosa, Polish Settlemet in Mexico), London, 1967, and Witold Langrod's **O niespokojnym życiu i smutnej śmierci**

RYSZARD TOMICKI
TENOCHTITLAN 1521
1984
Wydawnictwo
Ministerstwa
Obrony
Narodowej

R. Tomicki's **Tenochtitlan 1521** is a historic description of the Spanish conquest of the Aztec Empire (1521) of which Tenochtitlan was the capital renamed Mexico City while the country New Spain. Latin American history received considerable attention from such Polish authors as Dembicz, Frankowska, Kieniewicz, Kula, Klave, Langrod, Milewski, Łepkowski, Paradowska, Posern-Zieliński, Smolana, Urbański, Wierciński, to mention a few.

Karola Beneskiego [w Meksyku] (On The Restless Life and The Sad Death of Karol Beneski), Krakow, 1981. Col. Beneski participated in the Mexican War of independence.

Useful for this region's area studies are three other works: a historic monograph **Polska-Meksyk** 1918-1939 (Mexico-Poland 1918-1939) by Tadeusz Lepkowski, Wrocław, 1980, anthrophological monograph **Aztek Anonim: Zdobycie Meksyku** (Aztec Anonymous: The Conquest of Mexico) by Tadeusz Milewski, Wroclaw 1959, and an ethnographic study **Las extraordinarias historias de los codices mexicanos** (The Extraordinary Histories of the Mexican Codices) by Maria Sten, Mexico, 1973.

Hispanic American literature is in contemporary Poland quite popular. Especially popular are the novels of revolution, of social protest and of "Magic realism". This accounts for their frequent translations from Spanish and Portuguese into Polish. Our Collection possesses about 250 such translations, among which Mexican novels occupy a leading place. Among them are ten novels by the Polish-Mexican author Elena Poniatowska, whose radical approach to social problems won her tremendous popularity, also all over Hispanic America. Her so-called "testimonial novels" **Hasta no verte Jesús mío** (1969) which in Polish translation received strange title **Do sępów pójdę** and **La noche en Tlaltelolco** (Noc w Tlaltelolco), 1971 both achieved over fifty editions! On account of a variety of topics and always in defense of human rights, Poniatowska was declared a Hispanic American literary champion, and several of her works were translated into foreign languages. Curiously enough, Mexico "produced" the first translators of Polish authors: Sergio Pitol, Maria T. Dehesa y Gomez Farías de Langrod, and Mario Muñoz, who is also the author of **Breve panorama de literatura polaca contemporánea,** published in the review **La Palabra y el Hombre** (Xalapa, 1976).

The Spanish language works related to Poland during World War II are quite numerous, but they cannot rival the large number of scholarly and scientific books by Polish authors on a variety of topics, Nevertheless, this "war" literature is impressive and originated mostly. in Argentina, Brazil, Chile, Cuba, Mexico, Peru and even the United

States. In addition to books published in Spain and already mentioned, here are the most representative titles: **El terror viene del cielo** (Terror Comes From the Skies) by Boleslaw Kuczynski (Bs. Aires, 1941), **La persecución de los católicos en Polonia** (The Persecution of the Catholics in Poland) by Cardinal August Hlond (Mexico, 1942), **Lo que quiere Polonia** (What Poland Wants) by Ignacy Matuszewski (Bs. Aires, 1942), **Llanto de Vistula** (Weeping of the Vistula) by Abe Engels (Mexico, 1942), **Los primeros que pelearon** (**The First Who Fought**) by Peter Jordan (Mexico, 1944) **Oświęcim, campo de la muerte** (Oświęcim, The Death Camp) by Comité de Polonia Popular (Mexico, 1944), **Los indomables** (The Indomitables) by gen. T. Bor-Komorowski, La Habana, 1946, Selecciones del Reader's Digest), **El caso de Polonia (The Case of Poland)** by Stanisław Mikołajczyk (Bs. Aires, 1948, "La Nación") **Que lo sepa el Occidente** (The West Should Know It) by Jerzy Gliksman (Santiago, 1946), **Warszawa walczy** (Warsaw Fights) by Bronisława Stępniak (São Paulo, 1946), **Sin capitulo final** (Without the Final Chapter) by gen. Władysław Anders (Barcelona, 1948), **Historia de un ejército del país** (History of the Home Army AK) by gen. Bor-Komorowski (Mexico, 1950), **El crimen de Katyn a la luz de los documentos** (The Katyń Crime in the Light of Documents) by Zbigniew Stypułkowski (Mexico, 1955), **En el nombre del Kremlin** (In the Name of the Kremlin) by Stefan Korboński (Mexico, 1965), **Polonia heróica ante al nazismo** (Heroic Poland Confronting Nazism) by Diego Camacho (Lima, 1939), **Imperativos del equilibrio en la politica mundial** (Balance Imperatives in World's Politics) by Tadeusz Kozłowski (Ds. Aires, 1969), **Polonia, país de mil invasiones** (Poland, A Country of Thousand Invasions) by Kazimierz Wiwatowski (Bs. Aires, 1969), as well as a few other publications which missed our Collection.

Those desiring more data on the subject may turn to our bibliographic sources, such as, John Sarnacki's **Latin American Literature and History in Polish Translation** (Port Huron, 1973} by Albert Bukiet's **Materiały do... Polonica Ameryki Łacińskiej** (Bs. Aires, 1975), David Carneiro's **Bibliografía sobre a Polônia**

(Curitiba, 1981), and Luis Ferrand de Almeida's **A imagen de Polônia** (Lisbon, 1992).

The works on the humanistic, scientific and technological topics of Polish contributions to various Hispanic American countries are numerous. Therefore, we indicate here only some selected titles from the XIXth and XXth century, although Polish scholarship starting with Copernicus goes back to the Renaissance, while some scientific achievements as, for example, blood transfusion, the discoveries of the atom, vitamin, anti-typhus serum and hematina, are contemporary.

The most significant in the past century were the publications in the 1840s, of Pedro Czerniewicz's **Dicionário de medicina popular** (Rio de Janeiro) and Ignacy Domeyko's **Elementos de mineralogía** (Santiago de Chile). They were followed by Florestan Rozwadowski's **Govêrno e Colonização, engajamento de estrangeiros do Brasil** (Rio de Janeiro, 1857), Jozef Warszewicz's **scientific reports on tropical plants**, gathered in ten Hispanic countries between 1844 and 1853 for the Berlin and London botanical gardens, on whose behalf he undertook this project, Wladyslaw Taczanowski's **Ornithologie du Péru,** Paris, 1884-88), Jozef Siemiradzki's **La Pampa y la región de Cotto Limary** (Bs. Aires, 1893).

The topical variety of the XXth century Polish scholarly works, originally written in Spanish, Portuguese or Polish is astounding. Although not all are in our Collection, here are some selected titles: Wacław Radecki's **Tratado de Psychología** (Treatise on Psychology), Rio de Janeiro, 1929; Halina Radecka's **Psicología Social** (Social Psychology), Bs. Aires, 1960; Bronisław Malinowski's **Libertad y civilización** (Liberty and Civilization), Bs. Aires, 1948; Bogusław Jasinowski's **Historia filosófica de la cultura** (Philosophical History of Culture), Santiago, 1950; Luis Gumplowicz's **La lucha de razas** (The Fight Between Races), Bs. Aires, 1944; I.M. Bochenski's **La filosofía actual** (The Present Phiosophy), Mexico, 1950; Alfred Tarski's **Introducción a la logica** (Introduction to Logic), Bs. Aires, 1957; Pawel Siwek's **Transformismo antropológico** (Anthropological transformism), São Paulo, 1945;

Adam Schaff's **Filosofía del hombre, Marx y Sartre** (The Philosophy of Man, Marx and Sartre), Mexico, 1968; Witold Balinski's **Na procura de una visão do mundo** (In Search of the World's Vision) Curitiba, 1950; Zdzisław Szymonski's **Enfermedades tropicales** (The Tropical Diseases), Lima, 1935; Miroslau Baranski's **Estado clínico de amebiase intestinal** (Clinical Conditions of Intestinal Amoeba Sickness): Curitiba, 1952; Mieczysław Floksztrumf's **Sarcoma de utero** (Sarcoma of the Uterus), Bs. Aires, 1986; Władysław Słucki's **La cibernética** (Cybernetics), Bs. Aires, 1956; Witold Szyszlo's **La naturaleza en la America Ecuatorial** (Nature in Equatorial America), Lima, 1955; Miguel Wionczek's **Integración de la America Latina** (The Integration of Latin America), Mexico, 1964; Pedro Pablo Kuczynski's **Toward Renewed Economic Growth in Latin America**, Washington, 1987; Dana Markiewicz's **Ejido Organization in Mexico**, Los Angeles, 1980; Leszek Zawisza's **Colonia Tovar-Tierra Venezolana** (Tovar Colony - Venezuelan Soil), Caracas, 1980; Ceslau Biezanko's **Contribução ao conhecimento da fisiografía do Rio Grande do Sul** (Contribution to the Physiographic Knowledge of Rio Grande do Sul), Felotas, 1958; Ruy Christovam Wachowicz's **Historia do Paraná** (History of Parana), Curitiba, 1977; Andrés Karcz's **Electrometría** (Electrometry), Bs. Aires, 1968; John J. Staczek's **On Spanish, Portuguese and Catalan Linguistics,** Washington, 1988; Stanislaw Andreski's **Parasitism and Subversion. The Case of Latin America,** London, 1966; Edmund S. Urbanski's **Anglo-América e Hispanosmérica. Analisis de dos civilizaciones** (Anglo-America and Hispanic America. Analysis of two Civilizations), Madrid, 1965; and **Hispanic America and Its Civilizations**, Norman, 1978, 1981; and Elżbieta Skłodowska's **Testimonialism in Spanish American Poetry,** Philadelphia, 1992.

We have previously mentioned Dr. Jozef Leonard's close intellectual relationship with the Nicaraguan poet Rubén Darío. This contact influenced Darío's youthful writings. Our Archive has a sizeable documentation in this regard in Darío's own **Antología**, also in the works of E. Guzman, M. Maldonado, D. Martinez Sanz, T. Picado, E. Torres, M. Jover, R. Lagos, and Charles Watland.

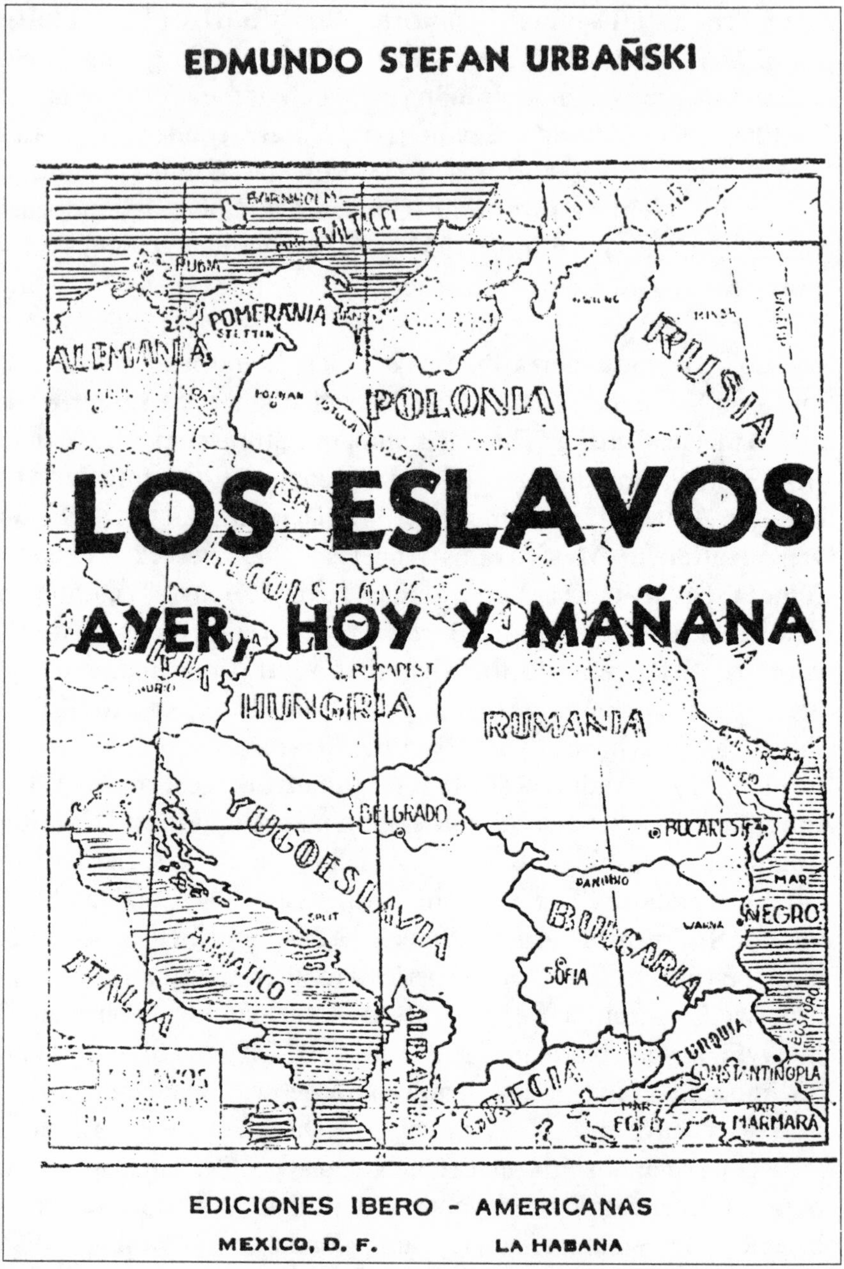

These Spanish-language books on the Polish and Slavic cultures, as the first ever published in Hispanic America, facilitated their knowledge to Hispanic readers. They were also utilized by the Polish Chair at the National University of Mexico (1942-1945), and by other Hispanic educational institutions, press and radio.

EDMUNDO STEFAN URBAÑSKI

POLONIA LOS ESLAVOS Y EUROPA

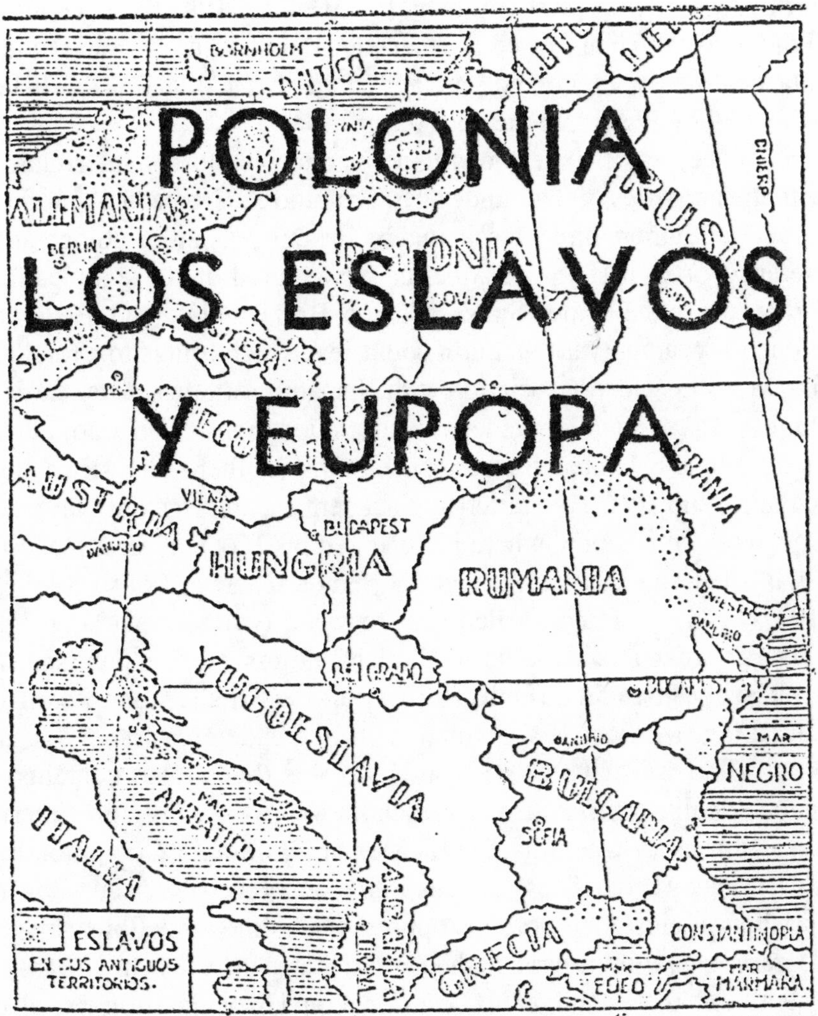

EDICIONES IBERO-AMERICANAS
MEXICO, D. F. LA HABANA

Nearing its completion is E. S. Urbanski's monograph **Polish-Latin American Bibliography**, with about 3,500 entries in Spanish, Portuguese, Polish and English. It covers mostly XXth century "Polonica" which appeared in Hispanic America, the Iberian Peninsula and partly in Poland. As a part of this Collection, will be published by PIASA in the near future.

The establishment of this Collection is closely interrelated with the activities of its founder, Dr. Edmund S. Urbanski. A professional Latinamericanist, fascinated by the cultural anthropology and literary works of Hispanic America, he lectured on these topics for forty years in the United States, Mexico, Brazil and Poland. He lived about ten years in various Latin countries, which brings to a total of fifty years his close association with Hispanic America. After earlier studies in Poland and Sweden, he continued them in Mexico, Peru, Spain and the United States, specializing in Ibero-American and Indianist subjects. He started his academic career at the National University of Mexico, where he received his Ph.D. degree. He also established and conducted for four years a Chair in Polish Studies (1942-1945). This compelled him to write two Spanish-language university manuals in Slavic and Polish cultures. He also published a book **Breve historia de la literatura polaca** (Brief History of Polish Literature), Mexico, 1946, which is now considered a "rare book".

The unusual feature of this work is that it also contains a chapter dealing with Polish echoes in literature of such Latin American countries as Argentina, Brazil, Mexico, Colombia, Cuba, Honduras and Nicaragua. These are favorable accounts of various Polish uprisings against their political oppressors, unknown to Polish historiographers! After moving to the United States in 1946, Dr. Urbanski in addition to his university lecturing on Hispanic subjects, also became interested in and conducted research on Anglo-American civilization in comparison with that of Hispanic America. This resulted in the publication of his **Studies in Spanish American Literature and Civilization** (WIU Press, 1964, 1965), and two other books mentioned before. He issued in 1987 another book **Od Wikingów do Indian** (From the Vikings to the Indians), which is a curious combination of scholarly essays on Indians and of cultural reflections about Hispanic America and the United States, where he lived over fifty years. The PIASA Collection is constantly growing, due to its founder's addition of new items.

Polish Historical Contributions to Latin American Medicine

Stanislaw Rola-Szustkiewicz

The Polish contributions to Latin American medicine are multifarious and they span mostly the XIXth and XXth centuries. They embrace the pedagogical field as well as medical practice of various kinds. The most prominent pioneer of Polish medicine was the internist, Dr. Piotr Czerniewicz, who spent fifteen years in Brazil (1839-1854), practicing in Rio de Janeiro and publishing there two important medical books in Portuguese. Both were considered valuable vademecums for physicians and patients, and thanks to their Spanish translation became popular also in Hispanic America, especially in Colombia and Mexico, where they were reissued. Czerniewicz studied in Warsaw, but because of his participation in the 1831 insurrection against Russia, was compelled to leave Poland and finished his studies in France. After a few years practice, he migrated to Brazil. There, he found neglected social hygiene, which prompted him to the publication of two basic works with the description of various diseases and their treatment. One, published in 1841 was titled **Formulario e Guía Médico.** The other one was **Dicionário da Médicina popular e das Ciencias accessorias** i.e. Dictionary of Popular Medicine and of Accessory Sciences, also published in Rio de Janeiro, in 1842. Because of their intrinsic value, Dr. Czerniewicz won the highest Brazilian decoration "Cavalheiro de Cristo" and a membership in the Brazilian Academy of Sciences, which is even more significant for Brazil did not have then her own Medical School.

However, the most important Polish contribution to Latin American medicine was that prominent Polish physicians participated actively in the establishment of Medical Schools in Brazil and Uruguay, where they also served as faculty members. There were also professors of medicine, at various times, in Argentina, Chile, Mexico, Brazil and Venezuela. This we present in due course in our exposition.

Professor Dr. Czeslaw Czarnowski, laryngologist, was living in Argentina for over sixteen years. Born in Warsaw in 1883 he studied medicine at Moscow and Petersburg Academies. During World War I, he served as ordinator in military hospital in Russia and after 1920 returned to Poland and he settled in Wilno. There, besides his medical practice, he became Professor at the Batory University. In 1939 the Soviets sent him to Siberia to a slave labor camp. When General Anders organized in Russia the Polish Army, he joined it and served as an ordinator in the military hospitals in Iran, Iraq, Palestine, Egypt and England. In 1948 Dr. Czarnowski emigrated to Argentina where the contract from the Ministry of Health allotted him an only limited practice of medicine. Therefore, most of his operations were performed almost clandestinely, in which he utilized methods little known in Argentina. He published an interesting treatise in Spanish "Auscultacion pectoral" (osłuchanie klatki piersiowej) in **La Semana Médica** (No. 20) 1955 in Buenos Aires. Dr. Czarnowski returned to Poland where he died in 1983, at the age of over one hundred years.

Dr. Mieczyslaw Floksztrumpf, a Warsaw onclogist and specialist of radiumtherapy, upon his arrival in 1939 in Buenos Aires was not allowed to revalidate his diploma and therefore, worked in the province of Mendoza, as a medical technician. There, after many years he became a Professor at the University of Cuyo and Director of the Cancer Research Institute at the same university. Because of his meritorious scientific work, that Institute was named after him. Prof. Floksztrumpf published over forty papers dealing with research on cancer, radiumtherapy and the cancerimmunology, among them a significant treatise, "Cancer de cicatrices" (The Cicatrized Cancer) published by **Semana Médica** (No. 10) 1955 in Buenos Aires. The memory about this Polish doctor-radium therapist is still alive among the inhabitants and scholars of the province of Mendoza, the proof of which was a celebration of his contribution by a special act on the twenty-fifth anniversary of his death.

Another Pole who made a considerable contribution to Argentinian medicine in the XIXth and at the beginning of the XXth century was Dr. Ryszard Sudnik, a specialist in physiotherapy. He was born in 1845 in Poland and started the study of medicine at Warsaw University, but, because of his active participation in the 1863 insurrection, he was forced to leave Poland and went to France. In 1872, he received his title of Medical Doctor and immigrated to Argentina. In 1880 he joined the Faculty of Medicine in San Luis and in 1884 started lecturing there on Experimental Pathology. Dr. Sudnik published more than sixty scientific papers in Spanish and French. In 1879 he passed his Argentine nostrification by presenting a thesis titled: "The Mercury in the Treatment of Syphilis" in which he described different methods of curing venerial disease in the local Hospital for Men. Prof. Sudnik was the promoter and one of the founders of The Medical Association of Argentina where he was the member of the Committee of Nervous Diseases and of the Forensic Medicine. He was also the delegate at many Congresses of Electrotherapy where he presented his papers. That is why his name is quoted in contemporary Argentine medical text books. Besides his professional occupation he was also the co-founder of the Polish Society in Buenos Aires in which he was active until his death in 1915.

Distinguished physician of Polish origin, Dr. Miroslau C. Baranski in Brazil, was born in 1918 in Curitiba. He received his doctorate at the Federal University of Parana in 1940 with "summa cum laude." From 1946 to 1952 Dr. Baranski practiced as an internist in the states of Parana and Santa Catarina. In 1952 he published a paper titled, "Clinical Study of Intestinal Amebiasis" in Curitiba. In 1952 he attained professorship of infectious and parasitical diseases in the Medical School of the Federal University of Parana. In 1978 he was elected a member of the Parana Medical Academy. As an experienced scholar, Prof. Baranski was a consultant in the field of therapy of infectious and parasitical diseases to a number of international pharmaceutical factories, such as Merck-Pfizer, Schering, Beechan and others. Prof. Baranski is the author of over one hundred treatises and essays written in Portugese, Spanish and English. Besides, he is the co-author of over thirty university manuals. In 1960-1977 he was the editor of the yearbook titled: **Anais de Medicina da Universide Federal do Paraná.** He was also the member of the Polish Association of Internal Medicine and a correspondent of the Polish Medical Academy in Warsaw. He also represented Brazil at various International Medical Congresses, delivering lectures in Buenos Aires (1971), Warsaw (1968), Cracow (1973), Florence (1981) and Miami (1981). Prof. Baranski died in Curitiba on April 17, 1983.

Dr. Szymon Kossobudzki, a supreme surgeon, spent nearly thirty years in Brazil, and for eighteen years he was the Professor of Surgery at the Medical School of Parana of which he was the co-founder in 1913. Born in Plock in 1869, he completed his medical study in Poland and Russia, and then he practiced in Warsaw. Engaged in political conspiracy against Russia he was sent for five years exile to Siberia. In 1907 he settled with his wife Halina in Curitiba, where he soon won great reputation due to his innovative surgical techniques. At the Medical School he conducted lectures on the propaedeutics of surgery, and during eighteen years of his professorship he educated the first generation of surgeons in Parana. He was deeply engaged in research. In 1897-1902 he published five interesting papers in the field of *surgery* in the Russian Review **Medycina.** Later, ten more treaties on his specialization were published in Brazilian medical journals such as **Brasil Médico, Paraná Médico** and **Revista Médica Paraná** (1919-1932). He was also the administrator of the Santa Casa Misericordia Hospital in Curitiba (1914-1934) and was responsible for adding a new surgery ward there. Prof. Kossobudzki paid a visit to Poland (1922-1923) where he delivered lectures on Brazil and epidemiology and hygiene in the tropical countries, at the Society of Polish Physicians in Warsaw. A good deal of his income went to finance Polish-Brazilian press, publishing Polish books and education. For his professional and cultural merits he was awarded high Brazilian and Polish decorations.

Professor Dr. Julian Szymanski, was a well known

opthalmologist and lecturer on opthalmology at the Medical School of Parana of which he was the co-organizer together with Professor Sz. Kossobudzki. Prof. J. Szymanski was born in Kielce and completed his medical studies at the University of Kiew with honors in 1896. Because of his conspiratorial activity he had to leave Russia and he settled in Chicago, where he was lecturing on ophthalmology at the Rush Medical School. Engaged also in patriotic activities, he was the founder of the Polish Peoples University in Chicago. He moved to Brazil in 1907 and practiced several years in Parana. He was offered in 1913 in Curitiba a position of departmental head of ophthalmology at the then organized Medical School of the University of Parana. He was very successful in his professional work after opening his own eye clinic, the first of this kind in Parana. Engaged in research, he published a number of scientific books in Portugese, English and Polish, such as **Resume das Licoes da opthalmología** (Curitiba 1917); **Fundus Oculi** (Chicago 1919); **Ophotypus** (Curitiba 1919); **Opthalmología para estudantes** (Curitiba 1920) and **Okulistyka w skróceniu** (Curitiba 1920). In 1919 Prof. Szymanski moved to Poland where he became honorary Professor at the Batory University. He also opened his own ophthalmological Clinic in Wilno where he did not charge the poor for his services. Like in Brazil, he was also engaged in research in Poland where he published many scientific books such as: **Anatomical-Pathological Atlas** (Wilno 1927), **Corpus tabularurn ophthalmicarum** (Wilno 1930) which were also published in French and German. His other scientific essays are: "Operation Anti-glaucoma-half-Elliot; "The Clinical Picture of Trachoma, simple and complicated, tuberculosis of Eye." Important are his three-colored **Oculistic Atlases,** etc. Altogether, Prof. Szymanski authored over one-hundred scientific papers, which won him international recognitions, many foreign honorary doctorates and high Brazilian and Polish decorations. He died in 1958.

After World War II a few Polish physicians immigrated to Chile. Two of them were a cardiologist, Dr. Mieczyslaw Pawlak and Dr. Marian Paleczek, a specialist in traumatological rehabilitation. Both were medical scholars. Dr. Pawlak, due to his changing fortunes, completed his medical studies at Madrid University, and married a Chilean lady and moved to Chile. He started his work as a cardiologist in José Joaquín Aguirre Hospital in Santiago. He later opened his, own clinic called "Centro Integral de Cardiología" which he successfully managed until his death on March 17, 1981. His professional work was interwoven with lecturing on cardiology at the University of Santiago. On the other hand, Dr. Paleczek an experienced Warsaw physician, who for a long time was denied nostrification of his diploma in Chile, was privately engaged in physical rehabilitation of people, considered hopeless by Chilean physicians. His successful twenty year professional work won him a great popularity and official recognition.

Dr. Seweryn Cytronberg, of Warsaw's Medical School and cancer expert, practiced in Mexico during World War II and became a research professor at the University of Guadalajara. At the same time he continued his medical research and published a *significant* essay "El diagnostico precoz del cáncer del estómago" (Early Diagnosis of Cancer of the Stomach) in the **Revista de Medicina Pasteur,** (Mexico 1940).

Dr. Zdzislaw Szymonski, physician and researcher of tropical diseases was working in Peru for over 40 years. Born in Moscow in 1902, he completed his medical studies at Poznan University and soon after he became a head of tuberculosis ward in a hospital in Warsaw. In 1928 he was sent by Polish authorities to Peru to organize health care for Polish immigrants there and to study the tropical diseases in the Amazon region called "la Montaña." The Peruvian physician Dr. Carlos Enrique Paz Soldan published a paper in the journal **La Reforma Médica** (Lima 1934) in which he praised Dr. Szymonski's five years of activities in the basin of the Ucayali and Marañón rivers, during which period he not only observed tropical diseases but also treated the Indian and Mestizo population. Dr. Szymonski's Peruvian experiences constituted the basis for his book published in Peru under the title **Enfermedades Tropicales** (Lima 1935) i.e. Tropical Diseases, which for many years was used by Peruvian medical students. The same book was also published in Polish, being thematically the first work of this type in Polish medical history. Dr. Szymonski enjoyed the reputation of a "jungle doctor," a title which was later shared also by Dr. Antoni Goscinski, a Poznan-educated gynecologist who also practiced surgery in Belize (1950-1986).

Dr. Juliusz Jurkowski, a surgeon, was working in Uruguay for nearly thirty years. He was the co-founder of the Medical School in Montevideo, and he held there the position of a professor of anatomy (1876-1884). Born in Kujawy, he started his medical studies at Warsaw University, but because of his participation in the 1863 insurrection he had to leave Poland and went to France. There, he completed his studies at Montpellier University with the title of "Officer de Santé", and soon after he moved to Uruguay in 1867. After passing a state examination in Montevideo and getting the license to practice, he started his work as a surgeon in a hospital in Isla de Flores. In 1876 the first in Uruguay, Faculty of Medicine in Montevideo was established. Professor Jurkowski was selected as the head of the anatomy department and in this way, he became the co-founder of the Uruguayan Medical School. He also served as Dean of the Medical School for six years. After eight years of university work in Montevideo, Dr. Jurkowski moved to Argentina in 1895, and together with his friend Laudanski, he opened a sanatorium for tuberculosis patients in Cosquin, Argentina. A few years later he moved to the woodland province of Misiones where he treated Polish settlers for over ten years.

He died in the city of Apostoles in December, 1913.

Bibliography

Urbanski, Edmund Stephen. "Iberian and Latin American Studies in Poland: A Bibliographical Essay." **The Polish Review,** Vol. XXVII, Nos. 3-4. New York, 1982.

Urbanski, Edmund Stefan. **Sylwetki Polskie w Ameryce Łacińskiej w XIX i XX Wieku.** Stevens Point, 1991. 2 vols. ca. 500 pp. With extensive summary in English and extensive bibliography in Spanish, Portugese, Polish and English.

Interactionism: Mind-body Relationship A Philosophical Hypothesis

Witold Baliński
(Brazil)

The problem of mind-body relations can be correctly considered as pertaining to the core of philosophical investigation. The admission of the existence of the mind, independent from physiological processes governing the body, opens the possibility to consider the spiritual factor as a part of the reality of the world.

Without this admission all the principles of the Christian and in general all the theist philosophy would lose their basis. It would be also necessary to renounce all purely ethical norms and deny their importance in governing the human behavior. Indeed, the acceptance of such ethical norms depends on individual decisions to obey the divine command. Even if ethics would be considered only as a conjoint of norms necessary to sustain the social order, there is a need to understand the importance of this order, and such a comprehension is unattainable without mind's participation. Without the mind able to govern his behavior, man is devoid of the means to proceed accordingly to the ethical existencies.

The exclusively materialist philosophy admits the existence of the mind considered scarcely as an epiphenomenon due only to the complexity of the physiological organism. Accordingly to this opinion, mental processes are devoid of independence and destined to perform activities similar to those of a computer directing the functions of a machine. Everybody who does not approve this opinion ought to acknowledge the existence of the mind with the power to influence sometimes decisively, the observable man's behavior.

These observations about the importance of the mind-body relations problem obviously do not pretend to be exhaustive. Furthermore, we omit the examination of all possible opinions searching the solution of this problem. So we do not quote the theses of parallelism or many other ideas created to attain the understanding of mind-body relationship. It would be a task impossible to perform in a brief exposition of the examined problem.

Only one remark is necessary. If one admits that all this examination will lead to a conclusion, no philosophy, that does not refute metaphysics, can be conceived without confirmation of the following postulate: the human mind has the capacity to influence acts performed by the human body. One may have a firm conviction that the above quoted postulate is obviously right, but some doubts emerge in further analysis of reality.

Many times this postulate is ignored, because of an obstacle consisting of arguments that seem impossible to be refuted. One may well ask: how is it possible that the mind, not being matter nor energy, can influence the body, indubitably composed by matter? The answer seems, indeed, impossible to find. This difficulty has led many thinkers to admit that the mind ought not be considered as an element independent from matter, but as a phenomenon which is a result of material processes, existing in living bodies. Many scientists approve this opinion and the general appreciation of science's merits contributes to amplify the recognition of materialist tendency in the philosophy of our days.

The actually rising crisis in philosophy is a result of the conflict between the materialist and other opinions. It is perhaps unnecessary to add that not all philosophical trends, even when they do not have a materialist characteristics, represent a truly spiritual thought. There are also philosophers who do not appreciate the importance of science and, entering into the field of pure speculation, they consider nothingness as the essence of all that exists.

Neither the materialists nor the existentialists will approve our ideas. Perhaps many scientists will also reprove us, considering that

Science is an adversary of metaphysics. We do not believe that it is a just judgment. The reproving of metaphysics by many scientists has its source in the materialist interpretation of reality, introduced into the modern philosophy of science.

In our century Science dared to postulate theses that, at first sight, seemed paradoxical. The theory of Louis de Broglie proved that light has characteristics of waves and simultaneously also of particles, though this statement seems to be logically unsound. Accordingly to Einstein, the universe is finite, though without borders. His theory remains solid independently of the choice of one of the two possible previsions: either an eternal expansion or future collapse of the universe. Consequently, scientists these days should not be scared by something seemingly paradoxical, but they ought to seek some possible solution not conflicting with the accepted laws of nature and scientific principles.

There is already a hypothesis that reveals the possibility of an explanation of mind-body relations. This hypothesis was formulated immediately after the end of the Second World War, but, unfortunately, remains generally unknown. The man who created it died before ending his work intended to present it in an adequated form and proving that it is scientifically acceptable.

Only once in his life he spoke about his ideas with reference to the mind-body problem. It happened in 1946, when the "International Center of Synthesis" reassumed its activities interrupted during the war.

The "Center", created by French scientists in Paris, was particularly active in the decade of the thirties, when every year a "Week of Synthesis" was organized. Leading thinkers of international renown gave then their lectures.

Among them can be mentioned the generally most known names, such as (in alphabetical order): Émil Borel, mathematician, specialist in probabilistic calculus; Louis de Broglie, physicist (Nobel Prize, 1929); Léon Brunschwig, philosopher; Maurice Halbwachs, sociologist; Pierre Janet, psychologist; Adolphe Landry, orientalist; Marcel Mauss, anthropologist; Jean Rostand, biologist; Edouard le

Roy, philosopher and mathematician; and Henri Wallon, psychologist. Sometimes representative foreign scientists were invited, as, for exemple: Max Born, a German physicist (Nobel Prize, 1954) or Gugliermo Fortoro, an Italian sociologist and historian.

Needless to say, the lecturers of the "Week of Synthesis" in 1946 were also professors with the highest qualifications.

The entire texts of each conference were recorded and also were all the words of greetings pronounced at the opening of the "Week of Synthesis" by Henri Berr, the director of the "Center", and all that was spoken by the members, when after each lecture a discussion was opened, All this material was later put together in form of a book edited in 1949 by the "Presses Universitaires de France" entitled **The Energy in Nature and Life** (L'Énergie dans la Nature et dans la Vie). This was, indeed, the matter discussed at the "Week of Synthesis" of 1946.

Given the public character of the reunion and the "Center's" intention to discuss science, no copy-rights had been reserved and everyone is authorized to reproduce the parts of the book.

Among the lecturers a Brazilian was present: Miguel Osório de Almeida. He spent many years of his life in France, studying and working in the fields of biology, physiology and psychology, and collaborated with other "Center's" member, Pierre Janet.

Henri Bert, the "Center's" director gave him a warm welcome, saying: "Mr. Osório de Almeida is coming to us, in France, proceeded by a worldwide reputation. He is an honor to the science of his country - he is an honor to the Science in general". Almeida pronounced his conference in French, the language that he mastered with perfection. The title of his conference was: **Le Système Nerveux"** (Nervous System).

There is no need to reproduce here all the theses and explanations exposed on this occasion. Only one sequence of Almeida's ideas is connected with the possibility of formulating a hypothesis about the influence that the human mental processes can have on the human behavior.

Almeida approached this problem with a description of an observation of someone "who is raising his arm and tells us that he is doing it simply because he was wishing to do it." (1) "We can say then", continued Almeida, "that he has accomplished a voluntary movement. Really, there is a discharge of nervous influxes issued from some part of brain's cortex that comes to the arm, where these influxes provoke a contraction of appropriate muscles. We know that these influxes ought to be provoked by impulses, i.e., by something physical or chemical."

"How then", asks Almeida, "the idea of wishing to raise the arm does excite the brain's cells? Or, even if this idea did not create the excitement, how could it guide the impulses - the already existing impulses - giving them the efficiency to follow a determined purpose?"

Almeida reminds subsequently that the living organisms do not create new energy nor destroy the energy existing in the world.

It would be, therefore, reasonable to affirm that there is "a psychic energy" created "ex nihilo" by a living organism. All organisms are submitted to the general laws of nature and their existence cannot abrogate the law of conservation of energy. Living organisms are also submitted to the laws of biology; they have their own structure on the condition, however, of not contradicting the laws of physics.

Continuing the presentation of his theses, Almeida comes to mention the experiences of Atwater and others who have proved the strict equivalency between the quantities of energy received by an organism and the quantities of energy spent in the mechanical work, including the loss of organism's heat, etc.

Atwater's observations gave, however, also other results: he stated that the metabolism of the nervous system at rest is relatively intense, but when the observed man is working intellectually, no increase in this metabolism can be detected. Consequently, Almeida states, intellectual activity is not accompanied by any complementary expense of energy.

Almeida also takes note of the opinion expressed by Fessard and Durup. These scientists affirmed that the attention's concentration in the observation of something that is raising the interest of the observer is to be considered as a result of a canalization, i. e. of directing nervous impulses towards specific centers. One can say that, in case of an effort connected with the task of solving a difficult problem, the process is identical.

These statements allow to raise the following hypothesis: the thinking, as well as every voluntary act, consist of giving orientation and adequate canalization to the nervous influxes. These influxes, being in continuous movement, are transmitted along the ramifications of the nervous system and, then, they begin to flow in determined directions to provoke, as a result of their impulses, the desired and observable performance of some concrete activity. Therefore, the execution of acts that are physical events depends from an agent that directs the impulses, i. e, from mental processes.

Almeida concludes his conference with these words: "It would be an exaggeration to claim that there is an immediate explanation for the mechanism of this "canalization", I do not think convenient to invoke the phenomena of inhibition and "facilitation" in the nervous system as a starting point for further psychological investigation. Both of these phenomena are dependent on excitations, so the problem would be only displaced. But I'll remind you that the most rigorous physicians are familiar with "Maxwell's demons" whose task was nothing more but to command, without spending energy, the passage of molecules gas dividing them in conformity with their velocity. The choice of channels in the nervous system may be equally independent from the consumption of energy as is independent from it the choice of more rapid molecules inside a vessel filled with gas. Let us hope that Psychology and Physiology of he future will be able to solve their problems without help of any sort of "demons"."

There are not many scientists whose knowledge is not limited to the field of their specialty. Almeida has given a proof of his extraordinary capacity when, in a conference full of analysis of physiological matter, he could include an exact definition of the "Maxwell's demons" concept. This concept represents an idea conceived by James C. Maxwell who. in 1871 perceived for the first time the connection existing between the notion of information and basic notions of energetics. L. Boltzmann made this connection more easily understood by developing the concept of entropy and defining it as a logarithm of the possibility of the formation of a given configuration among a set of other possible configurations. However, it was L. Szillard who consciously introduced the notion of information in the field of energetics.

In 1929, he quoted the "Maxwell's demons" thesis and proved the reduction of entropy equal to K log 2 in the receptor (receiver's system), while the system furnishing information suffers a growth of energy in the same proportion.(2)

The "Maxwell's demons" paradox became more generally known only after it has been mentioned by Norbert Wiener in his book **Cybernetics and Society**, edited in 1948. Therefore, Almeida, in 1946 when he pronounced his conference, had no possibility to read the Wiener's statement: "Just as entropy is a measure of the organization, the information carried by a set of messages is a measure of organization."(3)

Almeida had also no possibility to know the definition of machine, formulated afterwards by Walter Ross Ashby: "The essential characteristics of a machine as a physical systems linked to the "variation", i.e. to the quality of the information transmitted notwithstanding the existence of disturbances called "noise". It becomes evident that for complex machines "information" has the same meaning as "energy" for ordinary physical systems."(4)

These two above quoted statements, based on the knowledge made accessible by cybernetics, allow us to reflect on a completion of Almeida's ideas, perhaps possible, considering the Progress of Science.

We can note that in the light of these statements there is an essential difference between the organized systems and other parts of world obedient to the natural trend of entropy, i.e., to the disordered dispersion of energy.

Furthermore, we can note that this difference is not an effect of intensity of disponible energy, but of an adequate distribution of energy obtained from the ambient world. This idea finds its confirmation in the following Wiener's words: "If we wish to use the word 'life' to cover all phenomena which locally swim upstream against the current of increasing entropy, we are at liberty to do so."(5)

One can, then, formulate one more conclusion: the living organism functions well when the effects of entropy do not destroy the information necessary to direct the adaptation of its behavior to the conditions reigning in the ambient world. In other words, the living organism functions accordingly to the information they receive. These information can be received in different ways. One part is received by the sense organs, other part is transmitted by the genetic code, directing the instinctive reactions. One cannot, however, exclude other sources of information. For example, experience and training furnish information how to react in specific situations. Some artificially imposed training as the applied to Pavlov's dogs can determine the desired reaction. Indeed, these dogs react to the determined stimuli as if they were motivated by a concrete information.

Still another source of information is created by mental process.

One can say that, the human behavior consists of different kinds of reactions. One might divide them in two different groups, in conformity with the following scheme: reactions provoked by "signals for", and provoked by "signals of". The term "signal for" is here used to describe a signal that can be followed by a reaction originated by mental processes. So, this is a signal that motivates a conscious reaction. This reaction is meaningful, and the process of responding to the signal constitutes a subjective experience in the individual life of a human person.

When the other signal, the "signal of" is received it constitutes barely a motivation for an automatic adoption of a certain behavior.(6)

The statement that the mental processes are able to develop their activity as an independent source of information can be considered as a postulate authorizing to specify the terms of a hypothesis concerning mind-body relations without entering in conflict with Science.

The general outlines of this hypothesis were certainly conceived by Almeida and may be formulated in the following terms: the mental processes constitute a source of information endowed by its own nature with a certain amount of energetic value (so as all forms of information) which without creating new energy (something obviously impossible) is able to regulate its distribution. This activity of information sources can always take place depending on only two necessary conditions: the functions of the entire nervous system as receiver of information, ought to be performed perfectly and, therefore, ought to be able to decodify without distortions (caused by mental illness or other reasons) all the received signals, and, furthermore, the nervous system ought not to be disturbed by exterior impulses furnishing false information (as in cases when the in brain implanted electrodes are emitting artificially conceived commands).

It is not easy to understand why Almeida's conference did not provoke a broad repercussion. One could expect opinions sustaining his ideas and, on the other hand, severe criticism. Neither of these expectations was fulfilled. The scientists present at his conference remained silent. They were strictly positivists and the problem did not work up their interest. So, they did not sacrifice their time to discuss Almeida's ideas.

Almeida, himself, could tend to make his theses more generally known but, obviously, he wanted to elaborate them well before publishing some serious work, dedicated to the main problem of his conference. His current occupations caused that he could not undertake the writing of his work immediately after his conference in 1946. Some months after the "Week of Synthesis" he was appointed by the Brazilian Government as representative of Brazil to the Executive Council of UNESCO. After his return to Brazil he assumed the function of director of the "Osvaldo Cruz Institute", dedicated to the study of serotherapy.

The Brazilian Government wished to take advantage of the capacities of an illustrious scientist who already in 1923 was elected secretary of Brazilian Academy of Sciences. Almeida could not decline but even overworked, he began to write an extensive treaty of physiology.

His ideas about mind-body relations were ready to be presented in this work. Unfortunately, he had no time to bring his task to the end.

He died in 1953, and his treaty, incomplete as it was, was not published and his ideas remained in oblivion.

It is true that many years already elapsed since Almeida held his conference in Paris, in 1946. There is no reason, however, to desist from trying to convince the world's opinion that the Almeida's ideas do merit a serious examination, able to transform the proposed hypothesis into a generally accepted theory of great scientific and philosophical importance.

Nevertheless, some previous reflections can be of some utility as an introduction to the scientific examination of this hypothesis.

The acceptance of the hypothesis about mind-body relations is conditioned by the result of the examination of a serious criticism that could be constructed with reference to one of the postulates admitted by Almeida. We have already noted his affirmation that the mental processes do not cause an additional, spending of energy. Many scientists do not agree with this thesis. They state that the mental processes are a cause of an outlet of energy more intense than the observed when other organism's activity is taken into account.

The weight of the brain represents only about 8% of the weight of all the human body, but the quantity of oxygen needed by the brain represents about 80% of the quantity needed by the whole of the human organism. It seems that the mental processes are promoted by the brain's work. Therefore, one could say that every intellectual effort ought to be accompanied by spending of energy.

One cannot ignore the opinions of physiologists who present their serious writings, objectively based on experience. Consequently, a doubt surges about the exactitude of the observations made by Almeida. To admit this and, thus, to admit that the mental processes provoke the energy spending is the same as not a scientific explanation, conceived accordingly to the objective observation of reality.

The doubts about the possibility of a reasonable justification of Almeida's ideas seem to gain yet more strength in face of a simple statement that the brain is a body's organ and, therefore, by its own nature it cannot function without spending energy.

To confront these seemingly logical and objective opinions,

opposing the Almeida's theses, we need to analyze some propositions, accepted generally by the scientists who are defending the above exposed opinions. One, maybe the most important of these propositions, is the following: every mental process is also a cerebral process (brain's process). In other words: if one approves this proposition, there would be no difference between these two categories of processes, because they are identical in their nature.

There is no possibility to convince the thinkers who are sustaining the above quoted statement. They consider mind as a form of the brain's activity that is to be considered as an expression and consequence of the physiological brain processes, and not an independent factor. Therefore, they deny the possibility of speaking about mind-body interaction, because there is no interaction if mind and cerebral processes do not differ.

This statement is not new. On the other hand, it was many times refuted. Recently, it was once more refuted by the words of a great American philosopher, Mortimer J. Adler: "We do not think with our brains, even though we cannot think without them."(7) We ought to, indeed, consider the brain as a source of the adequate interpretation of information about the world, but not as a source of ideas in general.

The significance of the word "idea" is in this context different from the significance given to this word by Locke. "Idea" can mean also "a conjoint whole of concepts" and it is what we have in mind using this word.

The cerebral processes are capable of operating with ideas, but they cannot create them.

An analogy between the brain and a computer is certainly admissible. A computer can work with the data it receives and, performing its activity accordingly with the laws of physics, it can duly connect them, but is not able to create new concepts. Its activity is regulated by the program that is ready to direct its functions, but no computer can create a new program on its own and independent initiative, because such an initiative does not belong to its capacities.

By analogy, the brain is not able to create new concepts, and it operates only with what may be considered as an "input" furnished by the mind or other sources of information. Therefore, the activity of the mind can be compared with the creation of programs to be prepared for the computer.

In this analogy, the mind can be compared to an autonomous agent, not able, however, to obtain observable events without the participation of an instrument, i.e. the brain.

A difficulty seems, however, to arise, when one considers that some part of "the program" which directs the brain does not proceed from mental processes. The cerebral processes are also subject to the influence of what is sensually perceived. Their activity is many times directed by the call of instincts and by the obedience to the schemes of behavior learned by training and consisting of automatic reflexes. In these cases, the human reaction is not of the same nature as it is, when it represents a conscious response exacted by a given situation. Indeed, the instinctive reactions and the condition reflexes are not consequences of an aberrant evaluation and understanding of perceived elements of a situation provoking the reaction.

The difference between these two kinds of reaction was here already summed up in our description of the different reactions to the "signals of" and the "signals for". It could be, perhaps, admitted that these signals are source of the "perceptual thought" in the first of these cases, and the "conceptual thought" in the second case.

This admission allows us to see the conformity of our opinion with the adopted by Mortimer J. Adler. In his already here mentioned book he criticizes the negligence, or the ignorance, of the scientists who do not understand "the difference between perceptual and conceptual thought."(8)

The conceptual thought is something more than putting together the disponible information. If it were no more than this, it could be a product of brain's activity, not demanding the participation of mind processes. The conceptual thought englobes a free evaluation of the worth of concepts, performed many times without computable data.

The consciousness has in this process an essential and decisive importance. The word "consciousness" is subject to be understood in different ways, because its definition varies in conformity with its different interpretations.

The materialists attempted to demonstrate that the term "consciousness" is devoid of significance. "The psychology without consciousness", obedient to the scientism, tried to prove it in existence.

With the progress of psychology the influence of the primitive positivism diminished and in our days existence of consciousness in human psyche is generally admitted. Nevertheless, the materialist trend continues strong and, unable to deny the reality, sustains its efforts to reduce the importance of consciousness. Therefore, many psychologists consider the consciousness as a natural trait of a living organism, so complex in its structure as it is in man.

The modern "neuropsychology" wishes to consider the consciousness as a way in which the identification of all what is perceived is performed. So, the brain, even without the participation of the mind, would be able to carry out this task, necessary for the adaptation to the life conditions.

Another definition of consciousness, more extensive, can also be admitted without conflicting with the neuropsychologist ideas. Thus, it could be said that the consciousness is a way to identify all the categories of information, i.e., not only obtained by senses, but also furnished by memory, volition impulses, etc.

The neuropsychologists use the argument that the destruction, even when only partial, of the brain can cause profound modifications of the psychic reactions and can provoke mental illness, introducing a complete disorder in all mind activities. If it happens, say the neuropsychologists, the consciousness disappears, and it is a proof that consciousness is a product of brain's activity.

Examining this opinion, one can remark that the consciousness is indeed a way to identify all that is perceived or recorded by the memory. Obviously, when the brain injured by the illness is no more able to furnish to the mind the elements necessary for identification of objects or events existing in the world, then the mind suffers a pathological state of confusion. Even when one considers the consciousness as effect of mental, not only cerebral, activity, there is a necessity to concede that its activity must be affected by the injuries inflicted to the brain.

Consequently, it is necessary to defend the opinion that the definition of consciousness given by the neurologists is defective. It is true that a simple identification of that what is perceived can be performed by the brain programmed by the genetic code. This program is still insufficient to cause such reactions as these that appear in consequence of a program brought on by the mental activity. This very program that is an achievement of the activity of consciousness is able to supply the brain with information based on concepts created by consciousness itself.

It is not an easy task to give an exact definition of consciousness. How to put adequately into words the idea that was adopted by Descartes as a base of all his reasoning: "Cogito, ergo sum"?

Man knows that he can think and that he is something that exists. This "he knows", this knowledge, is the essence of consciousness. Maybe then, one can say that consciousness is a way of knowing one's own thoughts and ideas, images, feelings and judgments produced by one's own mind.

So, consciousness is mainly "endodynamic" — directed by the mind towards the contents of man's own self. The self-consciousness is, then, an endodynamic form of consciousness. It seems that nearly all the consciousness is really endodynamic. Consciousness consists not only in identification of all that can be perceived — it is also the identification of the act of perceiving.

The brain identifies the wave-length of the light perceived by the eyes, but it is the task of the conscious mind to decode the received message and, then, to "know" that this act of perception ought to be interpreted as an act of perceiving a certain given color and not any other. So, consciousness identifies the meaning of all what can be perceived and, consequently is leading to understanding the significance of the received information.

The brain proceeds in the same way as a computer, putting together all the admissible possibilities. A computer cannot distinguish any differences among various classes of possibilities which are, consequently, admitted as equal in their importance. It can, at best, distinguish the degree of probability of their appearance. A computer has no criterion to judge the uncomputable qualities.(9)

A machine is able to perform its task working with computable data. The consciousness does not ignore algorithmic relations, but is able to take into account the uncomputable. That is the cause of some mental attitudes which may assume a very informal aspect.

Consequently, one can state that opinions, judgments and convictions concerning such problems as ethical or esthetical, and also acts inspired by intuition are not effects of computable causes and they are themselves uncomputable. Therefore, they cannot be originated exclusively by cerebral activity.

The consciousness has an intuition of itself which allows the conception of self-criticism, something that is inaccessible to any machine nor to any physiological organism.

In accordance with Husserl, the empirical intuition shall be intensely experienced, but shall be also "put in parentheses", To lay aside the "atomic facts", to proceed to a "phenomenological reduction", to suspend the judgment ("epoquê") and, using this method, to get at a "residue" — it all is the right way to conquest the "eidetic intuition" the intuition of what is essential. (10)

It is not necessary to agree completely with all Husserl's phenomenologist theory in order to admit that intuition does exist in our consciousness. It is, however, one more base to sustain the thesis that there is a difference between mental and cerebral processes.

The brain's participation in the "exodynamic" (not directed towards the inside of the self) activities of consciousness is not to be denied. In the acts of gaining knowledge of the surrounding world it is sometimes not easy to state which activity, mental or cerebral, is performed. Even if one admits that the difference between these two kinds of activities is in those acts more difficult to be observed, it has no great importance, considering that this difference is undeniable if one takes in account the analysis of the essence of "endodynamic" consciousness.

Therefore, one can state that mental processes, independent from cerebral processes, can be considered as a source of information able to direct ("canalize") the energy of organism and in this way they can determine the acts following a previously formulated idea.

It seems that nowadays the scientists are beginning to perceive the necessity of explaining some processes ignored by the philosophy of science influenced by the positivism of materialist origin.

As an example one can note the words of Prof. Carol Sonnenreich included in his lecture **"Cerebral and Psychical Processes"**, delivered on the occasion of a meeting organized by the Brazilian Society of Psychobiology on May 28th, 1982, in Atibaia (Brazil). (11)

The lecturer quoted E. Wignet, scientist (Nobel Prize, 1963) who "applies his own way of speaking to say that the consciousness can influence brain's proper activities, and that our will can act on the matter". Among other scientists quoted by prof. Sonnenreich we can find the name of Pribram who expressed his opinion in following words: "The spirit is an emergent property, result of the elaboration of information performed by the mind".

The Pribram's definition of spirit was, probably, influenced by the theory "of psychoneural identity" or "materialist theory of mind".

This theory, as it is examined by Prof. Raul Marino, is a corollary of the so-called "emergentist materialism" preached by M. Bunge.(12) According to this theory "the condition of the mind and the mind processes, even though they are cerebral activities, are not exclusively of physical, chemical or cellular nature; they are complex activities of neural system. Therefore, the mind functions can be considered as specific functions of CNS (Central Neural System), emergent above the level of what is of physical nature (they are not purely physical processes)."

Prof. Marino finds that Darwin was one of the adherents of emergentist materialism. It can be said that the followers of this opinion are considering the evolution as able to provoke the transformation of inanimate matter into living organisms, everlastingly more complex, till the human level, when there occurs the emergence of mental processes and even of that what may be called spirit.

Therefore, in conformity with this opinion the spirit would be considered as created by the matter, in opposition to the belief that the matter was created by spirit. It seems that we are confronting a dilemma: in what to believe - in the creative power of spirit or of matter?

If, indeed, there is no other solution ("tertium non datur"), we are compelled to have faith in one of two possible miracles: either God created matter or matter created the spirit. The atheistic convictions of materialists clearly exclude the first of these two eventualities.

Strictly speaking, from the point of view of interactionism the solution of this problem has no decisive importance. If mental processes are no more considered as phenomena of physical nature, but, even so, they can influence the brain, the interaction between physical and no physical events can be logically admitted.

The analysis of the above exposed problems may be completed by two observations. First, the idea of emergence is not new.

An extensive elaboration of this idea is due to two English philosophers, C. Lloyd Morgan (1852-1936) and Samuel Alexander (1859-1938). It may be, perhaps, convenient to quote some observations containing one of possible appreciation of the Morgan's theory and, consequently of the Bunge's ideas: "The theory of emergency is an acceptable description of the evolution's processes. It does not present, however, its exhaustive explanation actually necessary. It does not demonstrate the existence of any rules or laws that would direct the process of "emergence". Therefore, it limits itself to a specific description of the evolutionary process, and does not contribute in a significant way to enlarge our understanding of this process." (13)

The theory of emergence elaborated by Samuel Alexander was presented in his work **Space, Time and Deity.** This work seems to begin with an exposition of a spirit-matter dualism that, in following pages, seems to give up its place to a prevailing influence of pantheistic monism. The speculative character of the emergence theory is clearly noticeable in Alexander's work.

Secondly, it can be noted that the approbation of principles of materialist emergentism leads, in its consequences, to appreciate ethics based on basic different from the one adopted by the spiritualists. The theory of evolution accepts the principle that the survival of living organism depends on its degree of adaptation to the conditions in which it lives. The survival of the most apt was the cause of evolution accompanied by a growing complexity of organisms. The living beings began to behave accordingly to what was understood as convenient or necessary. This understanding had its origin in the capacity of identifying what was perceived, and it is what the neuropsychologists are now calling consciousness. In conforming with their opinions, there is a necessity of joining the individual efforts in common activity of a society, and it is the reason of the formation of a new characteristic of human being. The followers of the theory of emergence in its recent form call this new trait spirit.

This set of arguments allows to stress the importance of information exchange as a decisive factor of social life, a necessary condition to form and to sustain the mental activity. The social life in organized community, being the very source of mental activity, commands consequently the ethical norms of human behavior. All other reasons to establish these norms could be, therefore, ignored. So such motivations as search of perfection, the observation of canon law and all spiritualistic deep love and respect of goodness could be disregarded.

It is, therefore, no wonder that the materialists are prone to demonstrate some complacency when they examine the "spiritualism" of neuropsychologists and the ideas of the emergentist theory.

In spite of the critical appreciation of these ideasn one cannot deny the existence of some difference between the new approach to the problems of the nature of consciousness and the more simple-minded opinions of materialists prevailing some decades ago.

It can be stated that in our days a very significant fact is recognized as real: the existence of something physically inexplicable in the structure of human personality.

The general consent to admit this fact ought to be followed by its logical consequence. If something non-physical exists as active factor in man, then the interaction between this factor and the human organism can be considered as undeniable. So, the thesis of Miguel Osório de Almeida concerning the capacity of mind processes for directing and canalizing energy can be accepted as a scientific explanation of the way in which this interaction is performed.

The postulates of pure materialism lose their basics in confrontation with the reality inaccessible to the positivist thinking. The influence of materialism has still strength enough to suggest some definitions not perfectly conceived. It is possible that in the future these definitions will undergo a reform to give them satisfactory meaning.

We hope that this will happen and that Almeida's hypothesis will be admitted as a generally approved scientific theory.

---

(1) The quotations from Almeida's conference are given in conformity with our translation of the text included in the book **L'Énergie dans la Nature et dans la Vie.** The indication of page numbers is omitted, considering that the entire text of Almeida's conference is only of 31 pages.

(2) Cf. História Geral das Ciências (General History of Sciences) Vol. 11 — **A Ciência no Seculo XX** (Science in the XX-th Century), Ed. Difusora Europea do Livro, São Paulo, 1971, p. 109; translation from **Histoire Generale des Sciences — Le XX-e Siècle,** edited in France by Presses Universitaires de France, Paris.

(3) Norbert Wiener, **The Human Use of Human Beings – Cybernetics and Society,** Ed. Doubleday & Company, Inc., p. 21 .

(4) Ross Ashby, **A Aplicação da Cibernética á Psiquiatría**, translated from **The Application of Cybernetics to Psychiatry,** edited by Journal of Mental Science, 100-114, 1954. The text of this Ashby's work in its Portuguese version is included in the book **Cibernética e Comunicação** organized by Isaac Epstein, Ed. Cultrix, São Paulo — Editora da Universidade de São Paulo; Cf. op. cit. p. 192.

(5) Norbert Wiener, op. cit. p. 32

(6) The terms "signal for" and "signal of" are sometimes used by other authors with a different signification.

(7) Mortimer J. Adler, **Ten Philosophical Mistakes,** Macmillan Publishing Company, New York – Collin Macmillan Publishers, London, p. 53.

(8) Mortimer J. Adler, op. cit. p. 75.

(9 Cf. W. Balinski, **Na Procura de uma Visão do Mundo** (In Search of a World-Vision), Ed. Beija-Flor Ltda, Curitiba, 1980, p. 187.

(10) Cf. W, Balinski, op. cit. p.184.

(11) The texts of this and other lectures given on that occasion were not published in form of a book; they are available in manuscript form.

(12) Raul Marino Jr., **O Problema Cérebro-Mente uma Incursão no Monismo Emergentista de Bunge** (The Brain-Mind Problem - A Glance at Bunge's Emergentist Monism), Revista da Psichiatria Clínica. (Clinical Psychiatry Review), N° 14 (1-2), 1987, p. 36-41.

(13) Cf. W. Balinski, op. cit. p. 201

Ethno-Cultural, Social and Political Interpretation of Spanish American Personality in Joseph Conrad's *"Nostromo"*

Marian Hillar

Story-telling and story-writing is the favorite preoccupation of mankind. It developed into structured and formal disciplines which we call "literature" *(Belle lettres)* and "religion". The former attempts to recreate social life in the form of aesthetic images and evokes emotional states. The latter attempts, in addition, to satisfy our curiosity and explain existential questions through the stories we call "myths." There may be substantial overlap between the two, but both activities are fictitious and belong to the non-rational part of the human psyche.

On the other hand, when we ask questions and try to develop rational answers to them, we practice philosophy, that in a broad sense of the word includes also scientific inquiry. Philosophy "is not," if we quote Seneca, "an occupation of a popular nature, nor is it pursued, for the sake of self advertisement. Its concern is not with words but with facts. It is not carried on with the object of passing the day in an entertaining sort of way and taking the boredom out of leisure. It molds and builds the personality, orders one's life, regulates one's conduct, shows one what one should do and what one should leave undone, sits at the helm and keeps one on the correct course as one is tossed about in perilous seas. Without it no one can lead life free of fear or worry."

Conrad was a wonderful story-teller recreating in artistic way human situations. His stories should not be analyzed as philosophical treatises, but as aesthetic images, his personalities — as composites of human characteristics, often exaggerated for artistic purpose. His social *milieu* is an artistic representation of the human society. In one word -- a story is a fiction in which everything is decided by its author. The best way we can do is to enjoy it if it satisfies our aesthetic and moral sensitivities.

The novel **Nostromo**, written in 1904, is considered one of the best if not the best novel of Joseph Conrad (1857-1924). The setting for the story is an imaginary, "generic" country of South America, Costaguana. Conrad himself, describes how he got the idea about writing the novel: "The first hint for **Nostromo** came to me in the shape of a vagrant anecdote completely destitute of valuable details." In the preface to the novel, Conrad alludes to a story he heard in the Gulf of Mexico, during his voyage in 1875-1876, about a man who stole a shipment of silver during a revolution in South America. The story slipped out of his mind until many years later when he came across "the very thing in a shabby volume picked up outside a second-hand book shop. It was the life story of an American seaman written by himself." The literary sleuths were able to track down this: book to be **On Many Seas: The Life and Exploits of a Yankee Sailor** by Frederick Benton Williams (pseudonym of Herbert Elliot Hamblen) and edited by William Stone Booth (1897). In the book the thief is a sailor named Nicolo who, after murdering the other two crew members of the freighter, scuttled the boat and then slowly enriched himself with the cargo of silver. Though the tale of the thief was very brief in Williams' book, Conrad found here his theme for his own story of the silver and transformed the villain into **Nostromo**. **Nostromo** too, slowly grows rich, but rather than a thief he is a victim of the silver for whom wealth becomes a trap when he momentarily relinquishes his sense of himself.

Conrad also used many other sources and he actively deceived the reader by creating a fiction within fiction. For example, he says in the preface that he sojourned on the Latin American continent for about two years, and that he depended for the history of Costaguana on the'manuscript of the History of Fifty Years of Misrule which was supposedly written by one of the characters Don Jose Avellanos. This deception is a literary license similar to that practiced by Isabel Allende who mentioned in an interview that she places her novels in an unnamed country to avoid the necessity of being historically correct in details. The factual sources of Conrad were traced to George Frederick **Materman's Seven Eventful Years in Paraguay** (1869). from which, Conrad drew the names of his chief characters: Decoud, Mitchell, Gould, Fidanza (Nostromo), Corbelan, Barrios, and Monygham. Other borrowings came from Edward B. Eastwick book entitled Venezuela, from which he applied the names such as Sotillo, Ribiera, Antonia, and Guzman Bento. The descriptions of the port Cabello in Venezuela he applied to the topography of Sulaco. The general folklore was picked up from the works of Cunningham Graham who traveled extensively in Central and South America.

Conrad's biographers tried to explain the secrecy of Conrad in revealing his sources. They assumed a certain compulsion "to make his every situation or condition appear worse than it actually was." Thus, Conrad would appear to be in command as if "from the bridge." Furthermore, drawing heavily from the experience of Conrad's parents as conspirators and national revolutionaries, they tried to ascribe to the writer a kind of genetic conspiratorial trait. Finally, drawing from a pseudo psychoanalysis of Conrad's personality, they decided that his personality of withholding information or disguising his tracks must be reflected in his method of literary métier: "Conrad," they write "had become a gigantic container of goods, and nothing must be wasted or lost." And since Conrad felt that a serious writer was a lonely person they deduced: "What could be more natural than for this marginal being to shut off all access, become hermetic, turn back upon himself so that he recreates himself only in his own work."

Conrad began the work on *Nostromo* in February of 1902 and continued working for two and a half years. Originally, he planned a short story of about 25,000 words; however, he built a vast story of about 500 pages upon only a very brief personal experience in Latin America. He had only short glimpse of this continent in 1876 when he sailed on Saint-Antoine. The first mate of the ship, Dominic Carvoni, was to be one of the model for *Nostromo* . Conrad himself wrote about his Latin American experience: "All my memories of Central America seem to slip away. I just had a glimpse, 25 years ago — a short glance." And he continues: "[as] to Nostromo. If I ever mentioned 12 hours it must relate to Porto Cabello where I was ashore about that time, **La Guayra** [sic] as I went up the hill and had a distant view of Caracas, I must have been there 2 1/2 to 3 days. It's such a long time! And there, were a few hours in a few other places on that dreary coast of Venezuela."

The novel is divided into three parts: "The Silver of the Mine," The Isabels," "The Lighthouse." It begins with the description of the harbor town of Sulaco and its region know for "heaps of shining gold," lying in the precipices of the peninsula. Those who exploit it are foreigners like the two gringo adventurers who perished in the search of treasures and the foreign capital that is partially operating the silver mine San Tomé. The silver mine becomes the main source of income for the country, and the Sulaco region becomes important in politics. This silver mine was operated in the past but was abandoned as it was not profitable. After the war of independence, the English company obtained the right to it, but native miners rose against the English chiefs and the mine was nationalized.

Eventually, the Gould family obtained concession for the operation. Charles Gould, a native Costaguanero, became the Director of the mine and operated it efficiently with the American financier and capitalist named Holroyd. Foreign capital also builds the railway line in the country. The working people in the mine are local Indians in the construction of the railway, mostly imported Italians and Basques; and in the port, local people of mixed blood. In the time of Conrad Holroyd epitomized the domination of the capital, and he predicted the leading role for North America.

"The Costaguana Government shall play its hand for all it's worth, and don't you forget, Mr. Gould. Now, what is Costaguana? It is the bottom-less-pit of ten-per-cent loans and other- fool investments. European capital had been flung into it with hands for years. Not ours, though. We in this country know just about enough to keep indoors when it rains. We can sit and watch. Of course, some day we shall step in. We are bound to. But there's no hurry. Time itself has got to wait on the greatest country in the whole of God's Universe. We shall be giving the word for everything: industry, trade, law, journalism, art, politics, and religion, from Cape Horn clear over to Smith's Sound, and beyond, too, if anything worth taking hold of turns up at the North Pole. And then we shall have the leisure to take in hand the outlying islands and continents of the earth. We shall run the world's business whether the world likes it or not. The world can't help it — and neither can we, I guess."

Idealistic Charles Gould, however, believed that he had to follow the policy of his father and for him wealth was only a means for social progress and not an end:

He [Charles Gould's father] did not like to be robbed. 'It exasperated him,' said Charles Gould. 'But the image will serve well enough. What is wanted here is law, good faith, order security. Anyone can declaim about these things, but I pin my faith to material interests. Only let the material interests once get a firm footing, and they are bound to impose the conditions on which alone they ran continue to exist. That's how your moneymaking is justified here in the face of lawlessness and disorder. It is justified because the security which it demands must be shared with an oppressed people. A better justice will come afterwards. That's your ray of hope.'"

Nostromo, as he was called by the English, really was named Giovanni Battista Fidanza and he is the central character of the story, in which, by the word of Conrad himself, he is a representative of the people. He left the Italian ship at the advice of his compatriot, Giorgio Viola, an old incorrigible republican refugee from Italy after the fiasco of Garibaldi, who ran a hotel and a café in Sulaco. Nostromo was employed by captain Mitchell as a foreman of the longshoremen (in Spanish his title was Capataz de Cargadores). Being a foreigner he did not have fixed ties to their conventions, and he did not aspire to be a leader. He enjoyed, nevertheless, a prestige and power among the cargadores and local people due to his inherent qualities. He was a man of character, faithful and reliable in his duties and able to control crowds. He was described by the terms: "feared," "dreaded," "magnificent," "wonderful," "invaluable," "a prodigy of efficiency in his own sphere of life," "incorruptible fellow," and "disinterested, and therefore trustworthy"; and in words of Dr. Monygam: "The fellow was unique. He was not 'one in a thousand'. He was absolutely the only one." He never lost touch with his class. In spite of his aloofness, he was able to condescend "to make jocular remarks to this man or other." Later, when he became captain Fidanza, he visited and supported the surviving family of the cargador killed during the riots. The only thing he seemed to care for was his reputation, and for this reason, he got involved in the events he was skeptical about. He was "a man for whom the value of life seems to consist in personal prestige."

Nostromo, makes history in the story three times. Around these three events, Conrad develops the three parts of his novel. In the first part Nostromo saved life of the old President-Dictator Don Vincente Ribiera, during the riots. In the second part, he saved the shipment of silver first from the looters and then from the troops of the ruling regime by hiding it on the Great Isabel island. The silver was to be used for the cause of the Sulaco revolution. In the third part, Nostromo saved the revolution itself by bringing the soldiers of general Pablo Ignacio Barrios back to Sulaco to combat the new aspiring dictator and the former War Minister Montero. Captain Mitchell calls these events historical occasions: "It was history, sir! And that fellow of mine, Nostromo, you know, was right in it. Absolutely making history, sir." In the process of saving the silver, Decoud saw it as a political action; however, for Nostromo what mattered and all that he expected was glory, and to be well spoken of: "They will talk about the Capataz of the Sulaco Cargadores from one end of America to another." And he hoped for his exploit: "It shall be talked about when the little children are grown up and the grown men are old."

But then, quite naturally and credibly, after having saved securely the silver on the Isabel island, Nostromo "felt the pinch of poverty for the first time in his life." "He remained rich in glory and reputation. But since it was no longer possible for him to parade the streets of the town, and to be hailed with respect in the usual haunts of his leisure, this sailor felt himself destitute indeed. He realized that "Kings, ministers, aristocrats, the rich in general, kept the people in poverty and subjection; they kept them as their keep dogs, to fight and hunt for their service." He realized for a moment that he had been used, that his fidelity had been taken advantage of, and that he had been betrayed. Thus, Nostromo had a change of heart and decided to use the silver for his own enrichment. But since then he became a different man. "A transgression, a crime, entering a man's existence, eats it up like a malignant growth, consumes like a fever. Nostromo had lost his peace; the genuineness of all his qualities was destroyed. He felt it himself, and often cursed the silver of San Tomé." Only at the point of death do we learn that the ultimate reason for his act was his pride: "And Decoud took four. Four ingots. Why? Picardía! To betray me? How could I give back the treasure with four ingots missing? They would have said I had purloined them."

And for this last event captain Mitchell used a different term: "Sir, that was no mistake. It was a fatality. A misfortune, pure and simple, sir. And the poor fellow of mine was right in it — right in the middle of it! A fatality, if ever there was one — and to my mind he has never been the same man since."

In the political situation in Costaguana, Conrad certainly recreates the Polish past: "In all these houses she [Mrs. Gould] could hear stories of political outrage; friends, relatives, ruined, imprisoned, killed in the battles of senseless civil wars, barbarously executed in ferocious proscriptions, as though the government of the country had been a struggle of lust between bands of absurd devils let loose upon the land with sabres and uniforms and grandiloquent phrases." The country is in constant political turmoil where one regime replaces the other. We learn of the "barbarous general Guzman Bento" who destroyed the old system of Federation in the country, shot the elected President of the province of Sulaco, uncle Harry of Charles Gould, and became himself "Perpetual President, famed for his ruthless and cruel tyranny." Now the political party in power in the Union were the so-called Blancos, the Oligarchs "the families of pure Spanish descent" under the leadership of the "President-Dictator, a Blanco of the Blancos."

But the rule of the enlightened tyrant Vincente Ribiera did not last for long because his Minister of War together with his brother Pedro Montero plotted a military revolt in the name of national honor. As a pretext, they claimed that the Ribierits had plotted to deliver the country as prey to foreign speculators. In fact, Montero planned to exploit the mine himself. Sulaco organized a Patriotic Committee with a respected statesman Don José Avellanos as the chairman, and Don Martin Decoud, a local journalist, "an idle boulevardier," as the executive member of a small-arms committee. Decoud represents the typical intellectuals who inspire revolutionary movements by their ideas. His "life, whose dreary superficiality is covered by the glitter of universal *blague*, inspired in him a Frenchified — but most un-French — cosmopolitanism, in reality a mere barren indifferentism posing in intellectual superiority."

Of his own country he said: "Imagine an atmosphere of *opéra bouffe* in which all the comic business of stage statesmen, brigands, etc., etc., all their farcical stealing, intriguing, and stabbing is done in dead earnest. It is screamingly funny, the blood flows all the time, and the actors believe themselves to be influencing the fate of the universe. Of course, government in general, any government anywhere, is a thing of exquisite comicality to a discerning mind; but really we Spanish-Americans do overstep the bounds. No man of ordinary intelligence can take part in the intrigues of *une farce macabre*. However, these Ribierits, of whom we hear so much just now, are really trying in their own comical way to make country habitable, and even to pay some of its debts."

The plan was to separate the whole Occidental Province from the rest of the country. In the attitude of Decoud, Conrad may have represented his own realism and contrasted it with the idealism of Gould: "The natural treasures of Costaguana are of importance to the progressive Europe ... just as three hundred years ago the wealth of our Spanish fathers was a serious object to the rest of Europe — as represented by the buccaneers. There is a curse of futility upon our character: Don Quixote and Sancho Pancha, chivalry and materialism, high sounding sentiments and a supine morality, violent efforts for an idea and a sullen acquiescence in every form of corruption.

We convulsed a continent for our independence only to become the passive prey of a democratic parody, the hopeless victims of scoundrels and cut-throats, our institutions a mockery, our laws a farce — a Guzman Bento our master! And we have sunk so low that when a man like you [Don José Avellanos] has awakened our conscience, a stupid barbarian of Montero — Great Heavens! — becomes a deadly danger, and an ignorant, boastful *indio* like Barrios, is our defender. Furthermore, Decoud had to come to grips with the eternal issues a politician has to face: the nature of his commitment, the conflict between an ideal and the personal motives or gain expected. He described his motives to Mrs. Gould: "Think also of your hospitals, of your schools, of your ailing mothers and feeble old men, of all that population which you and your husband have brought into the rocky gorge of San Tomé. Are you not responsible to your conscience for all these people? Is it not worth while to make another effort..."

And he explains: "... I am not a sentimentalist, I cannot endow my personal desires with a shining robe of silk and jewels. Life is not for me a moral romance derived from the tradition of a pretty fairy tale ... I am practical. I am not afraid of my motives." But Decoud remains pessimistic: "No, the whole land is like a treasure-house, and all these people [Decoud means foreign interference] are breaking into it, whilst we are cutting each other's throat. The only thing that keeps them out is mutual jealousy. But they will come to an agreement -- and by the time we've settled our quarrels and become decent and honorable, there'll be nothing left for us .... We are a wonderful people, but it has always been our fate to be ... exploited." Decoud's death "from solitude and want of faith in himself and others" is less believable though psychologically quite possible. "The brilliant 'Son Decoud,' the spoiled darling of the family, the lover of Antonia and journalist of Sulaco, was not fit to grapple with himself single-handed." He "lost all belief in the reality of his action past and to come." Conrad needed it, however, as a literary device for the final point of the story.

In *Nostromo*, Conrad shows himself to be a skillful dialectician — the events and characters are structured on conflicting opposites: appealing skepticism and cynicism of Decoud, Nostromo's kind of "natural man," Gould's idealism, and Viola's infallible faith in the ideal created by Garibaldi. If Gould had not been corrupted in his judgment by the mine concession, "he might have known that Ribierism could never come to anything." Yet these characters in some way are irrelevant to the events and are motivated by self-interest, except Viola -- the personification of idealism. Even for Padre Corbelan, who was rewarded for his activity by being nominated the first Cardinal-Archbishop of Sulaco: "The idea of political honour, justice, and honesty ... [consisted] in the restitution of the confiscated Church property. Nothing else could have drawn that fierce convertor of savage Indians out of the wilds to work for the Ribierist cause! Nothing else but that wild hope!." Nostromo himself was suspected erroneously by Decoud to "not exercise his extraordinary power over the lower classes without a certain amount of personal risk and a great profusion in spending his money .... that he had come to here to make his fortune." Conrad saw how crime and corruption were at the basis of the politics on the Latin American continent: "Meantime, the ignorant were beginning to murmur that the Ribierist reforms meant simply the taking away of the land from the people. Some of it was to be given to foreigners who made the railway; the greater part was to go to the padres." Conrad presented the workings of the political process in which the entire population is involved, in which no political act separates government from the people. Those "ranks of poor peons and *indios,* that know nothing either of reason or politics" always remain in the background, and they become a real force when they are "incited to kill and to die." Conrad's artistic ending of the story on the positive note with creation of a separate Occidental Republic is an optimistic solution, though a utopian one -- but what else could be expected from a realist if one wants to be optimistic?

Bibliography

Lucius Annaeus Seneca, **Letters from a Stoic. Epistulae morales ad Lucilium.** Selected and translated with an introduction by Robin Campbell. (Harmondsworth, Middlesex, England: Penguin Books, 1987).

Frederick R. Karl, **Joseph Conrad. The Three Lives.** (New York: Farrar, Straus and Giroux, 1979).

Joseph Conrad, **Nostromo.** First published in 1904. (Harmondsworth Middlesex, England: Penguin Books, 1994).

Mexico: Interior of the Polish salt mine in Wieliczka. Its beautiful color stained glass adorns since 1909 the interior of the Geological Institute in Mexico. A few Polish scientists were engaged in geological research in Mexico, including vulcanology (Dr. Habdank Dunikowski), contributing thus to the knowledge of this little developed science.

Some Polish Émigré Writers In Spanish- and Portuguese-speaking America During World War II

Edmund Stephen Urbanski

This paper deals with Polish émigré fiction writers and travel-memoir writers in Latin America during World War II. We will consider the variety of their literary productions, which in many cases embraced Polish rather than local topics, thus affirming that they all considered their sojourn in Latin America to be a temporary one. Because of the limited scope of this paper, our enumeration of the various authors and their topics is presented in a telegraphic manner.

Two prominent writers who arrived in Mexico were Teodor Parnicki and Elena Poniatowska. Parnicki came to the Aztec land on a diplomatic mission in 1944 and remained there as a political exile for twenty-two years. Parnicki is known for his historic novels: **Aecjusz, ostatni Rzymianin** (Aecius, the last Roman), 1937, and **Srebrne Orły** (The Silver Eagles), published during the war in 1944-45. Of his thirty works, fifteen were composed in Mexico. Parnicki's novels set most often in the early Middle Ages while making frequent references to the Greco-Roman antiquity and the Byzantine epoch, evolve around these topics. They are compositions of historiosophical tendency interlaced with cultural, religious, and political reflections on the value of human life and the fate of nations. Since Parnicki fuses history with legends and facts with literary fiction, his compositions have the character of half-fantastic tales rather than historical novels. However, some of his works contain rational ideas such as the equality of nations. He is a master of dialogue, based either on Socratic deduction or Byzantine argumentation. However, the excessive length of his dialogues, his Baroque-like verbosity and his frequent employment of the "flashback" technique also qualify his works for the genre of "magic realism", sometimes found in Hispanic America. In spite of his long stay in Mexico, Hispanic motives are only occasionally invoked in one novel, **Nowa Baśń** (The New Tale). While living in Mexico, I encouraged Parnicki to write a novel on the morganatic wife of Hernán Cortés, Malinche, also called doña Marina, who played a considerable role in the Spanish conquest of the Moctezuma empire. To my regret, he did not undertake the project, even though he displayed toward it great enthusiasm.

The Paris-born Elena Poniatowska, of Polish-French-Mexican origin, arrived in Mexico in 1942 and still remains there. In spite of her aristocratic ancestry, this newspaperwomen and writer has long displayed an interest in lower and middle-class matters, showing her democratic spirit. She has published seven books in Spanish, which are a mixture of the novel and newspaper "reportage" and deal with the social and political matter of her milieu. She started with a novel **Lilus Kikus** (1954), which describes and sharply contrasts Mexican customs and modes. Her **La Noche de Tlatelolco** (1970), which deals with the atrocious governmental suppression of the Mexican student riots in Tlatelolco in 1968, in which her brother Jan died, is a hard-biting work, standing in strong opposition to the government's despotic measures. Poniatowska's greatest popularity comes from her novel **Hasta no verte Jesús mio** (Until I see you my Jesus), 1969. In spite of its religious title, it is a secular novel, which registers a strong social protest against certain Mexican customs and ways of life, including the deceitful practices of various Mexican revolutionaries of the past. This book was based on the unfortunate experiences of Jesusa Palancares, a simple, uneducated peasant woman. Palancare's life-story is so dramatically portrayed and moved readers so much that it appeared in over sixty editions in two years! It was translated into various foreign languages including Polish, with a quite strange title **Do sępów pójdę** (1976), meaning "I Will be Devoured by Vultures". This and other novels put Elena in the frontline of Mexican contem-

Lima, 1990

Lawinska's book **Italian Presence in Republican Peru** is a factual description of the various contributions to the development of Peruvian civilization, with special attention to scholarship, fine arts and mass media.

porary authors. Poniatowska owes this extraordinary success to her usage of the street-like "spoken language", with its racy expressions, very popular among the village and urban Mexicans. Prof. Abreu Gomez considers Poniatowska an authentic Mexican writer. She won several literary prizes and is listed as a member of the PEN CLUB of Mexico.

The Argentine-born, European-educated writer Juan Wyskota Zakrzewski published several short stories, based on Mexican and South American legends in Mexican magazines and Polish-American newspapers.

Guatemala, the largest country of Central America, was for fifteen years the home for Andrzej Bobkowski (1947-1961). He developed his literary talent in postwar France and published his war memoirs there: **Szkice piórkiem** (Sketches with a pen), 1957, preceded by his **Dziennik podróży** (Travel Memoirs). The latter describes his trip from France to Guatemala and was published in installments by the Krakow-based **Tygodnik Powszechny** (1949-50). He displayed in these works literary dynamism and a wealth of observations ranging from intellectual to political life in France and Europe. It was followed by **Czarny piasek** (The Black Sand), a three-act play based on native Indian motives from the Central American West Coast (Paris, 1955). However, his most important Guatemalan work was a collection of short stories **Coco de Oro** (The Golden Coconut), Paris, 1970. This is a lively description of Indian customs and beliefs, with fictional stories of United States pilots and Polish sailors interwoven. T. Terlecki believes that Bobkowski's writings were strongly influenced by Joseph Conrad's exoticism. Bobkowski admired him greatly and called him "Kosmopolak", i.e. cosmopolitan Pole, a nickname sometimes extended to Polish literary figures active abroad.

During World War II Argentina had several Polish refugee authors. Among the best known were Witold Gombrowicz, Janina Surynowa-Wyczółkowska, and Florian Czarnyszewicz. Gombrowicz arrived there in 1938 after his literary debut of **Ferdydurke** (1938), a strange mixture of pseudo-sociological contemplation, bordering on what one critic called, "metaphysical infantilism". Capricious and cynical, his intellect was primarily egocentric. During his twenty-five year sojourn in Buenos Aires (1938-1963), Gombrowicz dedicated himself mostly to writing memoirs, i.e. **Dzienniki,** which are really autobiographical novels. They contain reflections on the Argentine cultural and social life. Some of his observations are true, but many more, strange and unfounded. Presumptuous and feeling culturally superior toward Argentine as well as Polish writers, he established a peculiar kind of new "existentialism", which consisted of opposing traditionalism in literary forms, and advocated cultural primitivism. Living in intellectual limbo, he tried to impart his strange ideology to some young, lower-class Argentines, and managed to find a few followers. With his antagonism toward established culture, which he wanted to "improve", he considered himself a new Polish literary titan, but was not recognized as such. Argentine writers considered him some kind of "intellectual anarchist". His literary controversy made him, however, quite well known. His satirical novels **Transatlantyk** (1953), **Pornografia** (1960) and **Cosmos** (1967), deal in a grotesque way with social problems of the pre-war generation, whose mentality and myths he severely criticized. Nevertheless, as thought-provoking works, exposing psycho-pathological frailties, they have sociological value. A sarcastic tone is displayed in his stage plays **El matrimonio** (The Marriage), 1948, and **Opereta** (Operette), 1966, whereas his historic play **Yvonne, princesa de Borgoña** (Yvonne, the Princess of Burgundy), 1968, was less controversial. Some of them were staged in Poland. Gombrowicz's greatest ambition was to be published and to receive the Noble Prize. While he never achieved the latter ambition, but received a literary prize in France, some of his works were translated into foreign languages, mainly Spanish and French.

Janina Surynowa Wyczółkowska was a seasoned writer who came to Argentina riding on the glory of her elegantly written prewar novels about Warsaw's high-society life: **On i jego kobiety** (He and His Women) and **Egoizm we dwoje** (Double Egoism). During her nearly forty-year stay in that country (1948-1985), she combined her essay work for Polish émigré magazines in Europe and Argentina with writing a cycle of novels of customs titled **Gringa,** which in Spanish means "foreigner" in not the best connotation. Their titles are **Lato Gringi** (The Summer of Gringa), **Jesień Gringi** (The Autumn of Gringa), and **Teresa, dziecko nieudane** (Teresa, the Unfeign Child). These works of fiction deal with the complex problem of Polish acculturation into the Argentine milieu, the difference of ethnic customs and shock between two civilizations. Teresa is subject to these conditions for her personality is torn between her parents. Her mother is a Pole inclined toward supreme sacrifice for Poland, while her half-German and half-Czech father during the war, lives abroad to make money. Teresa is, thus, a bearer of two contrasting ideologies. A subsequent personification of similar mutually excluding personality traits is Barbarita, Teresa's daughter, born in a mixed Polish-Argentine marriage. The process of assimilation - with all its psychological, cultural, and racial ingredients - is presented by Surynowa Wyczółkowska in quite a dispassionate way, confirming the analytical agility of the authoress. Her work may equally interest cultural anthropologists.

Worthy of attention are the novels of Florian Czarnyszewicz, who was a self-made writer, with the flare for authenticity. Three of his Argentine novels deal with the life and fate of the Polish population on the eastern borderlands (the region he came from) under Russian, and later Soviet occupation. The forth, titled **Pasierby** (Stepchildren), 1958, describes the hard experiences of a Polish immigrant-laborer in Argentina, resembling Czarnyszewicz's own life story of forty years in that country. It is a kind of epopee in prose, which takes the reader to the various chores performed by the protagonist, be it in the "pampa" where he sometimes worked with Indians, be it in the slaughterhouses, or as a railroad worker, moving from region to region. Everywhere, he works assiduously in order to support his family, and he is always nostalgic for his far away fatherland. He and his family feel like stepchildren of the country that could not assure them of a life existence. These vivid pictures are presented in a simple, vernacular style, with the addition of a Polish-

La Victoria del Vístula

Estudio histórico por

TEODORO PICADO MICHALSKI

1931

SAN JOSE, COSTA RICA

América Central

IMPRENTA GUTENBERG

Picado Michalski's historic **La Victoria del Vistula** i.e. *The Vistula Victory* is a detailed description of Polish military victory over the invading marxist Russia, which in 1920 stopped Communism from its extension over Western Europe and, thus, saved the Western Civilization. A similar, politico-ideological "invasion" occurred also in 1945, with the naive U.S.-British consent trusting USRR good will in her domination of Eastern Europe. Fortunately, this communist movement was defeated by the Polish "Solidarity" movement and caused a politico-social turmoil in Soviet Russia. It contributed to the termination of the so-called "Cold War" in 1989.

Argentine lingo, which gives this story a somewhat exotic flavor. Anecdotal veracity goes hand in hand here with narrative gracefulness, which confirms the fictional ability of the writer. It is not the language, however, which is flawed in composition, but the originality of topic which makes Czarnyszewicz's work so remarkable.

A prolific writer was Roman Dabrowski, who during his over twenty-five year stay in Argentina (1948-1974) was engaged mostly in editing **Głos Polski** (La Voz de Polonia) of Buenos Aires. Before the war he served as a foreign correspondent, visiting Europe, North Africa, the United States, Cuba, and Mexico. Under the pen name of Marek Romanski he published about fifty sensational novels classified as "roman policier", which were read by intellectuals and chamber maids alike. Of those a few appeared in Argentina e. g. **Pan y vino** (Bread and Wine), 1952, and **Sto dni Mussoliniego** (A Hundred Days of Mussolini), 1952, described the Italian-Ethiopian campaign of 1935; another one **Szpieg z Falklandów** (A Spy from the Falkland Islands), 1930, is set in South America. When I met him in 1966 in Buenos Aires, this well-humored man told me about an amusing encounter with Melchior Wankowicz in Mexico, the country Dabrowski adored because of its rich Indian-Mestizo folklore. Dabrowski's novels were written in flawless Polish, which cannot be said of some contemporary authors of the Polish Popular Republic.

Józefa Radzymińska was a controversial writer. After the downfall of the 1944 Warsaw Uprising in which she participated, she was taken prisoner of war to Germany. Afterwards she spent a few years in Italy and England, and arrived in Argentina in 1948. In addition to newspaper work, she published a few minor compositions in Buenos Aires, crowned by a patriotic poem **Czerwony mak, elegie o Ojczyźnie** (Red Poppy. Elegies about the Fatherland), 1955. It was an emotional paean about the Polish military heroism at the famous battle of Monte Cassino and the martyrdom of Poland under Nazi-Soviet war occupation. It also appeared in Spanish as **Amapola purpurea. Elegias a la Patria**, which brought her literary recognition among the Spanish-speaking nations of South America. Unexpectedly, her patriotic exaltation - possibly through marxist propaganda -

Jan Kiepura, a famous Polish artist-singer, who performed on three continents in five languages and became popular in Latin America, where he also sang in Spanish. Here, Kiepura appears in an original Polish mountaineer outfit from the Carpatian region, which by many foreigners was considered exotic...

changed into sympathy toward the communist system of Poland, which made her in 1962 to return to her motherland. There, Radzymińska published a few books under the red censorship. They dealt with the Polish immigrant colony in Argentina, which frequently was presented in a rather critical light. Such work as quasi-monographic character were **Biały Orzeł nad Rio de la Plata** (The White Eage Over the River Plate), 1971, and especially **Czternascie lat zmroku** (Fourteen Years of Darkness), 1978, the latter referring to her personal life in Argentina. Thus, she cut her ties with the Polish Argentines, but she also complained to her friends that she did not feel happy in communist Poland either. Like Gombrowicz, Radzymińska was apparently discontented on both sides of the Atlantic.

During and after World War II Uruguay was the host country to Czeslaw Straszewicz. Known for his fine prewar fiction and journalistic essays, Straszewicz was engaged in both diplomatic work and Polish radio programs in that country. In 1953 he published a novel under the suggestive title **Ludzie z bocianiego gniazda** (Men From the Stork's Nest). It consists of two subplots. One narrates the fate of Polish sailors who left their ship in Montevideo and chose freedom, and had to make the uneasy adaptation to living as political refugees in Uruguay. Fortunately, this process was eased by the social symbiosis with older Polish settlers there, who helped them secure jobs. The other subplot concerns the social conditions in the communist-dominated port city of Gdynia, which these sailors left when embarking on their trans-Atlantic voyage. The economic mess, tricks and dishonesty as well as drunkenness are general social features, including graft of the communist police chief's family. He, a martinet, upon seeing once an offensive sign against Stalin made with excrements on the wall, removes it with his own hands. The tragico-comical situation shows the unpopularity of the "red power" in Poland, sacrificed by the Anglo-Saxon allies to the Soviet Union after World War II. Such and other scenes are presented by the simplistic sailors with sincerity and grim humor. When analyzing their behavior, Straszewic observed their lack of initiative, a consequence of the communist regime complete state control of labor. This new Polish post-war idiosyncrasy, presented in anecdotal form, is worthy of our attention. Written in a graceful but ironic way and in classic Polish, **Ludzie z bocianiego gniazda** is possibly one of the best Polish novels from Hispanic America of the present "Diaspora" period.

Due to its attractiveness in natural sciences and its Polish immigrant colony there, Portuguese-speaking Brazil always drew the attention of Polish writers and travelers. Suffice it to mention Arkady Fiedler, Mieczyslaw Lepecki, and Bohdan Pawlowicz with their numerous books on Brazil, along with stories on the Polish-Brazilian settler's life by Jan Krawczyk, Ladislau Romanowski, and Roman Wachowicz, that appeared during the between-wars-period and later.

Among the better known authors who arrived in Rio de Janeiro after the outbreak of World War II, were the poet Julian Tuwim and the prose writers Jerzy Kossowski and Waclaw Korabiewicz. During his short stay in Brazil Tuwim composed a lyrical-elegiac poem "Kwiaty polskie" (Polish Flowers), which on account of its beauty reminded us of the "Skamander" poetic group to which he belonged. Korabiewicz described his jungle adventures in his **Mato Grosso**, named after the hunting state of the same name; it appeared in Polish (1947) and English (1954). Kossowski - already known from his pre-war realistic novels - was the most productive. He wrote a trilogy on the life of a few Polish volunteers from Brazil who joined the Polish Army in France during World War II. He described their travel adventures in the Brazilian bush of the state of Espiritu Santo, before leaving Rio de Janeiro, their military fate in France and after her downfall, their political quandry. The title of this trilogy is **Ta krew nie plami** (This Blood Does Not Stain), and its three parts were named: **Wici w puszczy** (Call to Arms in the Jungle), 1954, **W Wogezach straszy nocami** (It Haunts at Nights in the Voguezes Mountains), 1955, and **Wracać? Dokąd?** (Return? Whereto?). These novels are pleasantly written in simple and correct Polish. Their straightforward style with patriotic pathos betray autobiographic traces of the author, who during the war changed his pen into a rifle as did other writers. The Kossowski war trilogy resembles Wankowicz's trilogy **Bitwa o Monte Cassino** (Battle of Monte Cassino), 1945-47.

Famous Polish pianist **Witold Małcużyński,** considered the best interpreter of Chopin's music. In frequent artistic tours he was warmly applauded by the Latin American listeners from Mexico to Argentina.

Kossowski was also a translator and a manager of a Brazilian press agency. He also undertook the translation of my **Historia de la literatura polaca** (Mexico, 1946), the only History of Polish Literature which so far appeared in the Spanish language. His untimely death did not permit him to finish its translation into Portuguese.

We cannot close this brief and incomplete survey without mentioning the activities of Polish émigré writer-travelers, who earned an international reputation through their sophisticated Spanish description of Latin America, for the pleasure of readers anywhere. From among them we have to single out two: Antoni Halik and Wiktor Ostrowski. Halik covered an enormous area from Mexico through Brazil to the Tierrra del Fuego. He described it in his book **180,000 millas de aventuras** (180,000 Miles of Adventures), in which he included his exotic hunting expeditions in the South American jungles. As a movie maker, he also released several movie travelogues and published numerous topical articles in various American and European countries (France, Poland). Whereas, Ostrowski, a sportsman-alpinist, after conquering the highest peaks of the Argentine-Chilean Andes, described his fascinating experiences in a book **Más alto que los condores** (Higher Than the Condors), 1954. He also made a remarkable kayak expedition on the tricky Parana River from Argentina through Paraguay to Brazil, which he described in a book **La vida en el Gran Río** (The Life on the Great River), 1975. Books of both authors also appeared in Polish.

Polish émigré activities, relating to Latin American current events also were and still are manifested in the work of two Polish foreign correspondents. One is Maciej Feldhuzen, who, after his war stint with the Polish Army fighting on the side of the Allied Forces in Europe, migrated to Brazil and then became South American correspondent for the London-based **The Daily Telegraph** and the New York-based **Nowy Dziennik**. After similar activities in Europe and Argentina, Zdzislaw Bau became United States correspondent for the Buenos Aires-based daily **Clarin** and collaborator of the Paris-based Polish review **Kultura.** Their articles also occasionally appear in the Polish weeklies **Lud** of Curitiba and **Głos Polski** of Buenos Aires.

The Polish-Brazilian Literature

Mariano Kawka
(Brazil)

When the massive emigration of the Polish peasants to Brazil began in the second half of the 19th century, the landowners in Poland were upset by the idea that the whole country would eventually be depopulated. This was a threat against their interests, because the movement represented a substantial reduction of the cheap amount of workers they could reckon with. Their preoccupation originated the need to send special envoys to this Latin American country in order to personally ascertain the attractions by which so many humble and poor people were allured.

Such was the cause of the true deluge of publications about Brazil that broke out in Poland and persists until nowadays. Writers, journalists, or simple globetrotters, all of them have contributed with their impressions, reports, fictional writings or research works to create a rich literature, as well as to give life to a legend, to a powerful myth about a land as vast as a continent and as mysterious as a sphinx.

One of the first journalists and writers in Poland to investigate the causes of the emigration and the attractions of the new world upon the emigrants was **Adolf Dygasiński**, who in his time was a popular writer and a specialist in social problems. He traveled to Brazil in 1890 and explored the regions of great migratory intensity, examining sheds and provisional inns where immigrants and humble people sought shelter, especially immigrants from Italy, Spain and Poland. He established friendly relations with several Brazilian intellectuals, as the writer and politician Benjamin Constant, and published long and alarming reports in the Polish press, depicting the misfortunes and

Original cover of the Polish-Brazilian calendar for 1971, published by the Polish-Brazilian weekly "Lud" in Curitiba (it recently changed its title to "Nowy Lud"). The 1971 calendar is dedicated to the 100th anniversary of the Polish immigration in Brazil.

the misery of the Polish emigrants. A fruit of his stay in Brazil was the publication of the books **Listy z Brazylii** (Letters from Brazil) and **Na złamanie karku** (At a Breakneck Speed). The former contains the impressions of his trip to Brazil and the latter is a fanciful narrative about the emigrants who abandon their homeland and try to establish in Brazil.

Many others followed the track opened by Dygasinski. One of the most outstanding among them, because of his sincerity, frankness and objectivity, was **Dr. Stanisław Kłobukowski**, a special envoy of the Geographic and Commercial Society of Lwow. Fluent in several European languages, he had no difficulty in approaching the Brazilians, including conspicuous people in the political and cultural world, with whom he discussed the problems of emigration, including the advantages of the Paraná state being colonized by European peasants. The observation contained in his book **Za Emigrantami** (Following the Steps of the Emigrants) deserves special attention of the researchers, since we find there descriptions of various regions of Paraná, analyses of its land and climate, and the future advantages of its economical exploitation.

Then other names make their appearance, as for example **Siemiradzki** whose purpose in traveling to Brazil was the same as Klobukowski's and Dygasinski's. Father **Chełmicki** travels through Southern Brazil, were imitated also by **Antoni Hempel**. While some of them had a glance of the Polish colonies in Paraná and Rio Grande do Sul in passing, others remained for a longer time or even felt fascinated by the new world, as for instance Klobukowski, who returned from Poland to Brazil and lived for several years in Paraná, where he died near Palmas.

Many others traveled through the inland of Brazil, leaving their observations in books of several kinds: personal impressions, reports, memories, notes, researches or general considerations. There were journalists as **Jan Hempel** or **Paweł Nikodem**; professors as **Eugeniusz Gruda** or **Jan Gauze**; merchants as **Kazimierz Warchałowski** or **Marian Hessel**; scientists as **Tadeusz Chrostowski** or **Michalina Issakowa**, or even single adventurers in search of impressions and emotions.

In later years the Polish-Brazilian literature developed in other fields as well, including fiction and poetry. Therefore, in order to make a more exact appreciation of this literature, we shall divide it in three different sections: 1) personal or general reports; 2) fiction; and 3) poetry.

1) Reports

The "Brazilian fever", the name given to the massive migratory outbreak to Brazil by the end of the 19th and the beginning of the 20th century, compelled some economic and social institutions (as for example the Geographic and Commercial Society) to dedicate a special attention to this problem. This was the origin of researchers and explorers (Klobukowski, Siemiradzki, etc.) who made for Brazil in the name of these institutions or financial groups. The opinion prevailed — and with some reason — that Brazil had no conditions to shelter and give adequate assistance to thousands of families that sold their possessions in a hurry, anxious to reach as soon as possible the "Promised Land".

The representatives of the Polish institutions sent detailed accounts of the conditions the emigrants found in the new country. Some of those accounts were decidedly pessimistic, as those of Dygasinski. Others, as Klobukowski, were more optimistic in their view of the situation.

Having traveled to Brazil with the same objective and having observed the Brazilian reality, Chelmicki and Siemiradzki put in evidence the advantages and disadvantages the Poles would have in facing the Brazilian land. **Aleksy Kurcyusz**, for several years a teacher in the Polish private schools in the inland of Paraná, wrote a work in two volumes entitled **Brazylia** (Brazil), in which he depicts accurately the country in those times.

A special attention must be given to **Mieczysław Lepecki**, who lived in Belo Horizante for several years as a merchant of precious stones. From time to time he traveled through the inland of

Brazil, where he spent months in the inhospitable jungles. As a writer and former official of the Polish army, he visited all the countries of South America before settling in Minas Gerais. He wrote several books reporting his trips and impressions, facing with the same seriousness both the Brazilian Indians and the emeralds and diamonds, without forgetting to make considerations about the Polish settlers in Paraná. In 1957 he returned to Poland, devoting himself exclusively to literary creation.

Another kind of literature about Brazil was the creation of the young and promising writer **Zbigniew Uniłowski** (he died in his twenties), whose book **Żyto w dżungli** (Rye in the Jungle) provoked excited criticism and comments among the Polish settlers in Paraná. As an independent and keen observer he did not feel enthusiastic about the accomplishment of his fellow countrymen in Paraná. He also made a detailed report (270 pages) of a trip on horseback he made from Guarapuava to Londrina in 1935.

A special kind of literature is represented by the memories or remembrances written by several people who visited Brazil or established definitely in the country. The most prominent among them is **Sebastian Edmund Wos Saporski**. Without any kind of emotions, sometimes in a very simple and superficial manner, he recounts his ups and downs since he left Poland and sailed to Montevideo, and afterwards to Santa Catarina and Paraná, where he settled definitely in Curitiba. When he wrote his **Memoirs** he had in mind to leave a remembrance of his travel and toils to his descendants. Today his work is a historic document testifying the difficulties the first 32 Polish families that left Santa Catarina and established in Pilarzinho (Curitiba) had to confront.

The remembrances of **Eugeniusz Gruda, Apoloniusz Zarychta** and **Władysław Wójcik** are useful to illustrate the period of the more intense social, and cultural life of the Poles in Brazil, between 1920 and 1938, when hundreds of cultural and educational societies, private and semistatal schools, amateur theatres and several newspapers in Polish language flourished with rare vitality in the three Southern states, until this activity was interrupted by the nationalizing acts of Getúlio Vargas in 1938.

In the same period appeared the memoirs of several Polish emigrants in Brazil, which were published in a thick volume entitled **Pamiętniki Emigrantów** (Memoirs of the Emigrants) in Poland in 1939. The second volume with the same title was published in 1965. Both volumes constitute a valuable dossier not only of the personal adventures and misfortunes, but also of the time in which their characters lived.

We find an entirely different group of writers in the works of **Arkady Fiedler** or **Wacław Korabiewicz**, whose stay in Brazil (Fiedler five or six times; Korabiewicz two times) was due to their profound passion for the luxuriant nature and the picturesque primitiveness of the Brazilian inland. We can find the same words of enchantment in **Michal Rusinek** and **Antoni Olcha**, who visited Brazil as single tourists.

There are many other names, of course. The list below intends to present only the most representative names of this group:

Adamczewski, J. (Rev.): **Łazarzu, wstań... Sprawy społeczne i oświatowe w Ivaí** (Lazarus, get up... Social and Cultural Questions in Ivaí), 1935.

Adamski, Józef: **Polacy jako producenci bananów w Brazylii** (Poles as Producers of Bananas in Brazil), Warsaw 1938.

Arciszewski, Krzysztof: **Pieśń Polaka dyssydenta sławnego w wieku XVII, rządcy w Brazylii** (Song of a Famous Polish Dissenter in the 17th Century, Governor in Brazil), Lwow 1863.

Arnens, Sebastian: **Przygody w Brazylii** (Adventures in Brazil), Cracow 1934.

Azembski, Mirosław: **Mój kapitan** (My Captain), Warsaw 1964; **Inny Świat** (A Different World), Warsaw 1966; **Powrót do Rio** (Return to Rio), Warsaw 1967.

Barański, Jan: **Pamiętnik** (Memoirs), in **Zmagania polonijne w Brazylii**, vol. 2, Warsaw 1987.

Barański, Stefan: **Z naszego życia w Paranie** (From Our Life in Paraná), Curitiba 1923.

Barciszewski, Stefan: **Na szlaku sławy, krwi i złota** (On the Path of Glory, Blood and Gold), Warsaw 1928.

Basiński, Euzebiusz: **Polonia brazylijska wobec kraju przodków** (The Brazilian Polonia Facing the Forefathers' Country), in **Emigracja polska w Brazylii**, Warsaw 1971.

Bayer, Franciszek: **Paraná** (orig. title), Warsaw 1912.

Belczak, Leopold; Jeziorowski, Konrad: **Stan Parana** (The Paraná State), Curitiba 1930.

Beniowski, Maurycy: **Historia podróży i osobliwszych zdarzeń** (Tales of Travels and Interesting Events), Warsaw 1802.

Bochdan-Niedenthal, Maria: **Ucayali — raj czy piekło nad Amazonką** (Ucayali — Paradise or Hell on the Amazon), Warsaw 1934.

Borkowski, Janusz; Stępowski, Stefan: **Dwanaście tysięcy mil morskich na "Darze Pomorza"** (Twelve Thousand Sea Miles on the "Dar Pomorza"), Warsaw 1935.

Breowicz, Wojciech: **Ślady Piasta pod piniorami** (Footprints of the Piasts under the Pine Trees), Warsaw 1961; **Ochotnicy polscy z Ameryki Łacińskiej** (Polish Volunteers from Latin America), in **Emigracja polska w Brazylii**, Warsaw 1971.

Bronny, Ludwik (Rev.): **Parana wczoraj i dziś** (Paraná Yesterday and Today), in **Kalendarz Ludu** 1957, also in **Emigracja polska w Brazylii**, Warsaw 1971.

Bryla, Stefan Władysław: **Ameryka** (America), Lwow 1921.

Brzostek, Stanisław: **Brazylia** (Brazil), in **Zmagania...** 2, Warsaw 1987.

Budrewicz, Olgierd: **Pozłacana dżungla** (The Golden Jungle), Warsaw 1967; **Spotkania z Polakami** (Meetings with the Poles), Warsaw 1969; **Zobaczyć znaczy uwierzyć** (To See Means to Believe), Warsaw 1969.

Bujwid, Oto Dr.: **Stosunki zdrowotne w Brazylii** (Health Conditions in Brazil), Warsaw 1936; **Rozpowszechnianie się trądu w Brazylii** (The Spreading of Leprosy in Brazil), Cracow 1932.

Caro, Leopold: **Emigracja i polityka emigracyjna** (Emigration and Its Policy), Poznan 1914.

Cebula, Stanisław (Rev.): **Murici — kolonia polska w Brazylii 1878-1928** (Murici — a Polish Colony in Brazil 1878-1928), Curitiba 1928.

Chelmicki, Zygmunt (Rev.): **W Brazylii** (In Brazil), Warsaw 1892.

Chrostowski, Tadeusz: **Paraná** (orig. title), Poznan 1922.

Cieszyński, Nikodem (Rev.): **W cieniu palm i piniorów** (In the Shadows of Palm Trees and Pine Trees), Warsaw 1935.

Czarnota-Bojarski, Michał: **Stosunki handlowe polsko-brazylijskie i ich obecna organizacja** (Polish-Brazilian Commercial Relations and Their Present Organization), Warsaw 1934.

Czykiel, Walerian Szczepan: **Wspomnienia z pobytu w Ameryce Południowej w latach 1913-1924** (Remembrances from a Stay in South America in the Years 1913-1924), in **Zmagania...** 2, Warsaw 1987.

Denega, Kornel: **O emigracji polskiej w Santa Rosa — Rio Grande do Sul** (About the Polish Emigration in Santa Rosa — Rio Grande do Sul), in **Kalendarz Ludu**, Curitiba 1967; **Tułaczym szlakiem** (A Roving Trail), in **Emigrancja polska w Brazylii**, Warsaw 1971.

Dębicki, Tadeusz: **Z dziennika marynarza** (From the Diary of a Sailor), Warsaw 1934,1946.

Dmowski, Roman: **Wychodźstwo i osadnictwo** (Emigration and Colonization), Lwow 1900.

Dranka, Franciszek (trans. Aleksander Krajewski): **Stulecie epopei wychodźcy polskiego w Paranie** (Centennial of the Epopee of the Polish Emigrant in Paraná), in **Emigracja polska w Brazylii**, Warsaw 1971; orig. in "Diário do Paraná", 1.17.71.

Drapiewski, Teodor (Rev.): **Ks. Karol Dworaczek** (Father Charles Dworaczek), Olsztyn 1936.

Durski, Hieronim: **Pamiętniki** (Memoirs - manuscript in Portuguese), 1885.

Dworecki, Tadeusz (Rev.): **Ośrodki działalności polskich**

Werbistów (Activity of the Society of the Divine World), in **Zmagania...** 1, Warsaw 1980; **Polonijne problemy** (Problems of the Polish Emigration), in **Zmagania...** 1, Warsaw 1980.

Dygasiński, Adolf: **Czy jechać do Brazylii?** (Does it Pay to Travel to Brazil?), Warsaw 1891; **Klawiszewski and Rózia** (Mr. Klawiszewski and Little Rose), 1891; **Listy z Brazylii** (Letters from Brazil), Warsaw 1891, 1953; **Opowiadanie Kuby Ciełuchowskiego o emigracji do Brazylii przez...** (Tale of Kuba Cieluchowski about the Emigration to Brazil by...), Warsaw 1892; **W brazylijskim piekle** (In the Brazilian Hell), in **Pisma wybrane**, Warsaw 1949-1952.

Federowicz, Władysław: **Z biegiem rzeki Tocantins** (Navigating on the Tocantins River), Curitiba 1927; **Miernik w interiorze** (A Geometer in the Hinterland), in **Emigracja polska w Brazylii**, Warsaw 1971.

Ficinska, Maria: **Za ocean do Parany** (Beyond the Ocean to Paraná), Warsaw 1938; **Dwadzieścia lat w Paranie** (Twenty Years in Paraná), Warsaw 1938.

Fiedler, Arkady: **Bichos, moi brazylijscy przyjaciele** (Bichos, My Brazilian Friends), Poznan 1931; **Wśród Indian Koroadów** (Among the Coroados Indians), Poznan 1932; **Ryby spiewaja w Ucayali** (Fishes Sing in Ucayali), Warsaw 1955; **Rio de Oro** (orig. title), Warsaw 1956; **Wyspa Robinsona** (Robinson's Island), Warsaw 1958; **Zdobywamy Amazonkę** (Conquering the Amazon River), Warsaw 1959; **Orinoko** (orig. title), Warsaw 1960; **Spotkałem szczęśliwych Indian** (I Met Happy Indians), Warsaw 1968; **Zwierzęta z lasu dziewiczego** (Animals from the Virgin Forest), Poznan 1969.

Gadomski, F.: **Organizacja kolonizacji w Argentynie i Brazylii** (Organization of the Colonization in Argentina and Brazil), Warsaw 1930.

Gajewski, Antoni: **Z dziejów Brazylii** (From the History of Brazil), Warsaw 1969.

Gardolinski, Edmundo (trans. Jan Wojcik): **Osiemdziesiąt sześć lat kolonizacji polskiej w Rio Grande do Sul** (Eighty-six

Years of Polish Colonization in Rio Grande do Sul), in **Kalendarz Ludu**, Curitiba 1960; **Polska grupa etniczna w "Região Missioneira"** (The Polish Ethnic Group in the "Região Missioneira"), in **Kalendarz Ludu**, Curitiba 1958; **Szkoły polsko-brazylijskie w okolicach Dom Feliciano** (The Polish-Brazilian Schools in Dom Feliciano), in **Kalendarz Ludu**, Curitiba 1964; **Polacy w Rio Grande do Sul** (The Poles in Rio Grande do Sul), in **Kalendarz Ludu** 1958, also in **Emigracja polska w Brazylii**, Warsaw 1971.

Gauze, Jan: **Na przełaj przez dżunglę** (Across the Jungle), Warsaw 1961; **Brazylia mierzona krokami** (Brazil Step by Step), Warsaw 1961.

Gittlin, Jan: **Do zobaczenia, Brazylio** (Goodbye, Brazil), Warsaw 1956; **Opowieści z dżungli, pustyni i pampsów** (Tales from the Jungle, the Desert and the Pampas), Warsaw 1957.

Giżycki, Kamil: **Hevea płacze kauczukiem** (The Crying Rubber Tree), Katowice 1962.

Glinska, Anna: **Gdzie mój dom?** (Where is My Home?), Warsaw 1968.

Głuchowski, Kazimierz: **Wśród pionierów polskich na antypodach** (Among the Polish Pioneers in the Antipodes), Warsaw 1927.

Gozdzikowski, Władysław: **Wspomnienia z Brazylii** (Reminiscences from Brazil), in **Zmagania...** 2, Warsaw 1987.

Grabias, Józef: **Alfonso Pena** (orig. title), in **Kalendarz Ludu** 1955, also in **Emigracja polska w Brazylii**, Warsaw 1971.

Grabowski, Franciszek: **Wspomnienia osadnika o rewolucji brazylijskiej w latach 1893-1894** (Reminiscences of a Settler about the Brazilian Revolution in the Years 1893-1894); **Z Mateusza do Lapy — Polacy w rewolucji 1893-1894** (From São Mateus to Lapa — The Poles in the Revolution of 1893-1894), in **Emigracja polska w Brazylii**, Warsaw 1971.

Grabowski, Tadeusz Stanisław: **Dla Chleba** (In Search of Bread), Wilno 1937; **Brazylia i jej dzieje** (Brazil and Its History), Cracow 1947; **Brazylia** (Brazil), in **Polska i Polacy w cywilizacjach świata**, Warsaw 1939.

Groniowski, Krzysztof: **Polska emigracja zarobkowa w Brazylii** (Polish Emigrants Looking for a Living in Brazil), Wroclaw 1972; **Gorączka brazylijska** (The Brazilian Fever), in **Kwartalnik Historyczny** 74 (2).

Gruda, Eugeniusz: **Gęsi za wodą** (Geese across the Water), Warsaw 1965; **Dziennik niekapitański** (Not a Captain's Diary), Warsaw 1969.

Gruszecki, Artur: **Na drugą półkulę** (To the Other Hemisphere), Warsaw 1904; **Przygody chłopca w Brazylii** (Adventures of a Boy in Brazil), Warsaw 1912; **W kraju palm i słońca** (In the Land of Palm Trees and Sun), Cracow 1928.

Hajduk, Ryszard: **Loksodroma Śląsk — Brazylia** (Loksodroma Silesia — Brazil), Katowice 1969.

Hempel, Antoni: **Polacy w Brazylii** (The Poles in Brazil), Lwow 1893.

Hessel, Marian: **Na pionierskim szlaku** (On the Trail of the Pioneers), in **Pamiętniki Emigrantów**, Warsaw 1965.

Hessel, Stanisław: **Pamiętniki emigranta w Brazylii** (Memoirs of an Emigrant in Brazil), in **Zmagania...** 2, Warsaw 1987.

Issakowa, Michalina: **Polka w puszczach Parany** (A Polish Woman in the Jungle of Paraná), Poznan 1937.

Iwaszkiewicz, Jarosław: **Listy z podróży do Ameryki Południowej** (Letters from a Trip to South America), Cracow 1954; **Dziela** (Works), Warsaw 1958-1959; **Opowieści zasłyszane** (Heard Tales), Warsaw 1955.

Jaczewski, Tadeusz Dr.: **Polska wyprawa zoologiczna do Brazylii** (A Polish Zoological Expedition to Brazil), Warsaw 1925, Curitiba 1928; **Pamięci Tadeusza Chrostowskiego** (The Memoirs of Tadeusz Chrostowski), Curitiba 1923.

Jankowski, Placyd: **Krzysztof Arciszewski** (Christopher Arciszewski), Wilno 1843.

Jeziorowski, Konrad: **Kolonia Jagoda w Paranie** (The Jagoda

Brazil: A miniature sculpture of "happy family", made by **Irena Godlewska-Morgensztern,** a Polish artist who resides in São Paulo. Due to the originality of her work, she achieved a great popularity in southern Brazil.

Colony in Paraná), Curitiba.

Jurkiewicz, Stanisław: **Polski ruch migracyjny** (The Polish Migrating Movement), Warsaw 1929.

Kajsiewicz, Hieronim: **Listy z drugiej podróży amerykańskiej do braci i przyjaciół** (Letters to Brother and Friends from the Second Trip to America), Lwow 1872.

Karman, Rafal (Pinior): **Kurytyba — sławne miasto w Brazylii** (Curitiba — a Famous Town in Brazil), in the **Lud** newspaper, Curitiba 1962; **Z Apostoles przez Posadas do Kurytyby** (From Apostoles through Posadas to Curitiba), in **Lud**, Curitiba 1956; **Dni chwały imienia polskiego** (Days of Glory of the Polish Name), in **Lud**, Curitiba 1963.

Karwowski, Adam: **Na pokładzie "Kanclerza" i "Itapariki"** (On Board the "Kanclerz" and the "Itaparica"), Warsaw 1900.

Kawka, Mariano: **Polacy wśród pionierów Północnej Parany** (The Poles among the Pioneers of Northern Paraná), in **Kalendarz Ludu,** Curitiba 1967.

Kempa, Adam: **Tak bylo** (So it Was), in **Emigracja polska w Brazylii**, Warsaw 1971.

Klobukowski, Stanisław: **Za Emigrantami** (Following the Emigrants), Lwow 1895; **Opis stanu Parana** (Description of the Paraná State), Lwow 1895; **Wycieczka do Parany** (An Expedition to Paraná), Lwow 1909; **Wspomnienia z podróży po Brazylii, Argentynie, Paragwaju, Patagonii i Ziemi Ognistej** (Remembrances from a Trip to Brazil, Argentina, Paraguay, Patagonia and the Fire Land), Lwow 1898.

Kowalski, W.: **Organizacja wychodźstwa polskiego w Brazylii** (Organization of the Polish Colonization in Brazil), Warsaw.

Korabiewicz, Wacław: **Mato Grosso** (orig. title), Cracow 1948, Warsaw 1968.

Kraushar, Aleksander: **Dzieje Krzysztofa z Arciszewa Arciszewskiego** (The History of Christopher from Arciszewo Arciszewski), Petersburg 1893.

Krawczyk, Jan: **Nad Gauibą** (On the Guaíba), in **Zmagania...**

2, Warsaw 1987; **Dziki Zachód** (The Wild West), in **Zmagania...** 2, Warsaw 1987.

Kruczkowski, Andrzej: **Listy spod równika** (Letters from the Equator), Warsaw 1959.

Krul, Tadeusz: **Spod Lublina do Parany** (From Lublin to Paraná), in **Zmagania...** 2, Warsaw 1987.

Krzesimowski, Romuald: **Jak brać się za bary z lasem parańskim** (How to Face the Jungle in Paraná), Warsaw 1937.

Kubina, Teodor (Bishop): **Cud wiary i polskości wśród wychodźstwa polskiego** (A Miracle of Faith and Patriotism among the Polish Emigrants), Czestochowa 1935; **Wśród polskiego wychodźstwa w Ameryce Południowej** (Among the Polish Emigrants in South America), Potulice 1938.

Kula, Marcin; Kula, Witold: **Listy Emigrantów z Brazylii i Stanów Zjednoczonych 1890-1891** (Letters of the Emigrants from Brazil and the United States 1890-1891), Warsaw 1973

Kurcyusz, Aleksy: **Brazylia** (Brazil), Warsaw 1911.

Kurnatowski, Eryk: **Wspomnienia z Brazylii** (Remembrances from Brazil), in **Zmagania...** 2, Warsaw 1987.

Kurowski, Aleksander: **Przewodnik dla wychodźców do Brazylii** (A Guide for Emigrants to Brazil), Warsaw 1924.

Lago, Juliusz: **Polska — Brazylia** (Poland — Brazil), in **Zmagania...** 2, Warsaw 1987.

Langanowski(Langowski?), Stanisław: **Kolonie polskie w Paranie** (Polish Colonies in Paraná), Warsaw 1912.

Lapiński, Jan: **Powrót z Brazylii** (Return from Brazil), Wloclawek 1891.

Lepecki, Bohdan Teofil: **Czarni Brazylianie** (Black Brazilians), Warsaw 19??; **W krainie piniorów** (In the Land of the Pine Trees), 1936; **W miastach i puszczach Ameryki Południowej** (In the Towns and Jungles of South America), Warsaw 1934.

Lepecki, Mieczysław Bohdan: **W krainie jaguarów** (In the Land of the Jaguars), Warsaw 1925; **Na cmentarzyskach Indian** (In the Indian Cemetaries), Warsaw 1926; **W sercu czerwonego lądu** (In the Heart of the Red Land Continent), Warsaw 1928; **Opis stanu Parana** (Description of the Paraná State), Warsaw 1928; **Polskie tereny kolonizacyjne w Ameryce Południowej** (The Regions of Polish Colonization in South America), Warsaw 1931; **Ameryka Południowa** (South America), Warsaw 1936; **Drogą korsarzy i zdobywców** (On the Path of Corsairs and Conquerors), Warsaw 1933; **Na Amazonce i we wschodnim Peru** (On the Amazon River and in Eastern Peru), Warsaw 1931; **W dzikich ustroniach** (In the Wild Land), Warsaw 1933; **Od Amazonki do Ziemi Ognistej** (From the Amazon to the Fire Land), Warsaw 1958; **Z gwiazdy na gwiazdę** (From Star to Star), Warsaw 1959; **Opis stanu Espirito Santo** (Description of the Espírito Santo State), Warsaw 1931; **Po bezdrożach Brazylii** (Astray in Brazil), Warsaw 1961; **Parana i Polacy** (Paraná and the Poles), Warsaw 1962; **Niknący świat** (A Dwindling World), Warsaw 1968.

Lewandowski, Zenon: **Wychodźstwo polskie — stan Paraná w Brazylii** (Polish Emigration — The Paraná State in Brazil), Poznan.

Lewestam, Fryderyk Henryk: **Brezylija, Brezylija** (Brazil, Brazil), Warsaw 1860.

Ludkiewicz, Stanisław: **Ameryka Lacinska** (Latin America), Warsaw 1961.

Lapinski, St. J.: **Powrót z Brazylii** (Return from Brazil), Wloclawek 1891.

Los, Stefan: **Przygody w Serra do Mar** (Adventures in the Serra do Mar), Warsaw 1932; **Czarny Wojtek** (The Black Wojtek), Warsaw 1932.

Łyp, Franciszek Feliks: **Brazylia — kraj, ludzie, stosunki** (Brazil — the Country, the People, the Environment), Warsaw 1930.

Makarczyk, Janusz: **Nowa Brazylia** (The New Brazil), Warsaw 1929; **Widziałem i słyszałem** (I've Seen and I've Heard), Warsaw 1957; **Przez morza i dżunglę** (Through Seas and Jungles), Katowice 1970.

Maliszewski, Stefan: **Ilustrowany przewodnik po Brazylii**

Brazil: A miniature sculpture of a "united family", made by **Irena Godlewska-Morgensztern**, a Polish artist who became famous in São Paulo, Brazil. Head details of these miniature figures are not always visible.

(An Illustrated Guide to Brazil), 1910.

Mazurek, Czesław: **Droga emigranta w nieznane** (The Way of an Emigrant towards the Unknown), in **Lud**, Curitiba 1986; **50 lat w Brazylii** (Fifty Years in Brazil), in **Zmagania...** 2, Warsaw 1987.

Migasiński, Emil Lucjan: **Polacy w Paranie współczesnej** (Poles in the Contemporary Paraná), Warsaw 1923.

Młynarski, Marian: **Wśród żararak i grzechotników** (Among Jararacas and Rattlesnakes), Warsaw 1962.

Modzelewski, Henryk: **Pamiętnik z pobytu w Brazylii 1972-1973** (Memoirs from a Stay in Brazil in 1972-1973), in **Zmagania...** 2, Warsaw 1987.

Morawski, Zdzisław: **Listy z podróży do Ameryki Południowej** (Letters from a Trip to South America), Cracow 1886.

Nast, Janusz: **Polskim żaglowcem do Brazylii i Afryki** (By a Polish Sail to Brazil and Africa), Warsaw 1934.

Nestorowicz, Stefan: **W Brazylii i Argentynie** (In Brazil and Argentina), Warsaw 1891.

Nikodem, Pawel: **Guaíra** (orig. title), Warsaw 1930; **Pół wieku osadnictwa polskiego w Brazylii** (Half a Century of Polish Colonization in Brazil), in **Gazeta Polska w Brazylii**, Curitiba 1941; **Ojciec osadnictwa polskiego w Brazylii** (The Father of the Polish Colonization in Brazil), in **Emigracja polska w Brazylii**, Warsaw 1971.

Nurzyński, Feliks: **Wskazówki sanitarne dla użytku wychodźców do Ameryki Południowej** (Sanitary Instructions for the Use of Emigrants to South America), Warsaw 1937.

Okołowicz, Józef: **Wychodźstwo i osadnictwo polskie przed wojną światową** (The Polish Emigration and Colonization before the World War), Warsaw 1920.

Olcha, Antoni: **Szumią dęby nad Iguassu** (Oaks Rustle over the Iguaçu), Warsaw 1959; **Wiosenna ziemia** (Spring Land), Warsaw 1960; **Profile brazylijskie** (Brazilian Profiles), Warsaw 1971.

Orłowski, Leon: **Maurycy August Beniowski** (Mauricius

August Beniowski), Warsaw 1961.

Ostrowski, Jerzy: **Brazylia** (Brazil), Warsaw 1933; **Ziemia Świętego Krzyża** (The Land of the Holy Cross), Warsaw 1929; **Pamiętniki emigrantów — Ameryka Południowa** (Memoirs of the Emigrants — South America), Warsaw 1939; **Polscy konkwistadorzy** (Polish Conquerors), Warsaw 1934.

Patka, Jan (Rev.): **Praca i działalność Księży Misjonarzy w Brazylii** (Work and Activity of the Lazarists in Brazil), in **Lud**, Curitiba 1963.

Pankiewicz, Michal: **Prawda o Paranie** (The Truth about Paraná), Warsaw 1911; **Z Parany i o Paranie** (From and about Paraná), Cracow 1916; **W sprawie wychodźstwa do São Paulo** (About the Emigration to São Paulo), Warsaw 1930; **Problem emigracji w Polsce** (The Problem of Emigration in Poland), Warsaw 1935.

Papiewska, Wanda: **Jan Hempel** (John Hempel), Warsaw 1958.

Pawłowicz, Bohdan: **Chlopiec z piniorowych lasów** (A Boy from the Pine Tree Forests), Lwów 1934; **W słońcu dalekiego południa** (Under the Sun of the Tropics), Warsaw 1937.

Piasecki, Stanisław (Rev.): **Prasa polska w Brazylii** (The Polish Press in Brazil), in **Kalendarz Ludu**, Curitiba 1948.

Piętka, Jan: **Z galicyjskiego bagna emigracyjnego** (From the Galician Emigratory Swamp), Cracow 1912.

Piotrowski, Wacław: **Polak w Brazylii** (A Pole in Brazil), 1914; **Opowiadania parańskie** (Tales from Paraná), Grodno 1928.

Piotrowski, Witalis: **Po szczęście do piekła** (To the Hell in Search of Fortune), Warsaw 1912.

Pitoń, Jan (Rev.): **Panorama emigracji polskiej** (Panorama of the Polish Emigration), Paris 1968; **Stulecie kolonizacji polskiej w Santa Catarina** (Centennial of the Polish Colonization in Santa Catarina), in **Kalendarz Ludu**, Curitiba 1969, also in **Emigracja polska w Brazylii**, Warsaw 1971; **Księża polscy w Brazylii** (Polish Priests in Brazil), in **Lud**, Curitiba 1969; **Najstarsze towarzystwa w**

Kurytybie (The Oldest Societies in Curitiba), in **Kalendarz Ludu**, Curitiba 1971, also in **Emigracja polska w Brazylii**, Warsaw 1971; **Prasa polska w Brazylii** (The Polish Press in Brazil), in **Kalendarz Ludu**, Curitiba 1971; **Saporski w ramach lat** (Saporski within the Framework of Dates), in **Kalendarz Ludu**, Curitiba 1971, also in **Emigracja polska w Brazylii**, Warsaw 1971; **Mapa ludności polskiej w Brazylii** (Map of the Polish Population in Brazil), in **Kalendarz Ludu**, Curitiba 1972; **U źródła emigracji polskiej w Brazylii** (Foundations of the Polish Emigration to Brazil), in **Kalendarz Ludu**, Curitiba 1973; **Jak stara jest emigracja polska w Brazylii** (How Old is the Polish Emigration in Brazil), in **Kalendarz Ludu**, Curitiba 1971; **Księża polscy w Brazylii 1848-1984** (Polish Priests in Brazil 1848-1984), in **Zmagania...** 4, Warsaw 1987.

Pomian, Bolesław: **Krzyż Południa** (The Southern Cross), Warsaw 1959.

Posadzy, Ignacy (Rev.): **Droga pielgrzymów** (The Pilgrim's Way), Poznan 1933.

Potocki, Antoni: **Listy z Brazylii przez wychodźców do rodzin pisane** (Letters from Emigrants in Brazil Written to Their Families), Warsaw 1891.

Potopowicz, Bolesław Żabko: **Osadnictwo polskie w Brazylii** (The Polish Colonization in Brazil), Warsaw 1936.

Radomski, Włodzimierz: **Wrzesien** (September), Curitiba 1947.

Robak, Zygmunt: **Dziwy brazylijskie** (Brazilian Wonders), Buenos Aires 19??.

Roguski, Bronisław Ostoja: **Pierwsi deputowani etnii polskiej** (The First Deputies of Polish Descent), in **Emigracja polska w Brazylii**, Warsaw 1971.

Romer, Tomasz: **"Śmiałym" do Rio** (On the Board the "Smialy" to Rio), Gdynia 1966.

Roski, Dzim: **Polacy w Brazylii** (The Poles in Brazil), in **Kalendarz Ludu**, Curitiba 1948.

Roszkowski, Wacław: **Na "Darze Pomorza" przez Atlantyk** (On the Board of "Dar Pomorza" across the Atlantic); **Sprawy**

morskie i kolonialne (Maritime and Colonial Questions), Warsaw 1934.

Rómmel, Waldemar; Sachs, Ignacy: **W kraju kawowych plantacji** (In the Country of the Coffee Plantations), Warsaw 1955.

Rusinek, Michał: **Wódz i wygnaniec** (Chief and Exile), Warsaw 1957; **Zielone złoto** (The Green Gold), Warsaw 1960; **Kolorowe podróże** (Colored Journeys), Warsaw 1964; **Dzika plaża** (The Wild Beach), Warsaw 1970.

Rzymetka, Jan (Rev.): **W cieniu parańskich piniorów** (In the Shadow of Pine Trees in Paraná), in **Wychodźca**, Warsaw 1929; **Botokudzi** (The Botocudos Indians), Curitiba 1928; **Krzysztof Arciszewski pierwszy Polak w Brazylii w walce z misjami katolickimi** (Christopher Arciszewski as the First Pole to Battle with the Catholic Missions in Brazil), 1925.

Samsel, Roman: **Brazylia — kochaj ją albo rzuć** (Brazil — Love it or Leave it), in **Kultura**, Warsaw 1970; **Róże dla Clelii** (Roses for Clélia), in **Kultura**, Warsaw 1970; **Komu postawić pomnik** (Whom to Raise a Monument), in **Emigracja polska w Brazylii**, Warsaw 1971

Saporski, Sebastian Edmund Wos: **Pamiętnik** (Memoirs),Warsaw 1938; **Międzynarodowe Towarzystwo Osadnicze** (International Colonizing Society), Warsaw 1927.

Sekuła, Michał: **Kolonie polskie w Paranie** (Polish Colonies in Paraná), Curitiba 1928; **Szkoły polskie w Brazylii** (Polish Schools in Brazil), Curitiba 1929; **Szlakiem polskich osiedli w Brazylii** (Following the Steps of the Polish Settlers in Brazil), Curitiba 1926.

Sęk, Jan: **Samotnik z Parany** (The Solitary from Paraná), in **Akcent** 1, Warsaw 1985; **Szkolnictwo polonijne w Brazylii w latach 1941-1980** (Polish schools in Brazil in the Years 1941-1980), in **Szkolnictwo polonijne w XX wieku**, Lublin 1986; **Literaci polonijni w Brazylii** (Polish Men of Letters in Brazil), in **50 lat Towarzystwa Polsko-Brazylijskiego - Seminarium Naukowe**, Warsaw 1987; **Polonijne programy radiowe w Ameryce Łacińskiej** (Polish Radio Programs in Latin America), **Lud**, 1988.

Siemiradzki, Józef: **Za morze** (Beyond the Sea), Lwów 1894; **Opis stanu Parana** (Description of the Paraná State), Lwów 1896; **Z Warszawy do równika** (From Warsaw to the Equator), Lwów 1895; **Szlakiem wychodźców** (Following the Steps of the Emmigrants), Warsaw 1900; **Mapa sytuacyjna kolonii polskich w Brazylii** (Situational Map of the Polish Colonies in Brazil), Lwów 1893; **Na kresach cywilizacji** (At the End of Civilization), Lwów 1896; **O Indianach Południowej Ameryki** (About the Indians of South America), Cracow 1924; Wolanski, Jan: **Sprawozdanie z podróży do Południowej Brazylii** (Report from a Voyage to Southern Brazil), Lwów 1902.

Sierecki, Sławomir: **Admiral Arciszewski** (The Admiral Arciszewski), Warsaw 1953.

Skarżyński, Stanisław: **Na RWD 5 przez Atlantyk** (On Board the RWD 5 across the Atlantyk), Warsaw 1934.

Skomorowski, Jan: **Od Patagonii do Japonii — dwadzieścia lat na obczyźnie 1900-1920** (From Patagonia to Japan — Twenty Years Abroad 1900-1920), Warsaw 1936.

Skowroński, Tadeu: **Páginas brasileiras sobre a Polónia** (Brazilian Pages About Poland), Rio de Janeiro 1942.

Słonimski, Antoni: **Pod zwrotnikiem** (In the Tropics), Warsaw 1925.

Sobieszczański, Franciszek Maksymilian: **O życiu i sprawach Krzysztofa Arciszewskiego** (About the Life and the Questions of Christopher Arciszewski), Warsaw 1850.

Sojka, Wojciech (Rev.): **Początki duszpasterstwa polskiego w Brazylii** (The Beginning of the Polish Apostleship in Brazil), in **Duszpasterz polski za granicą**, Rome 1967.

Sosnowski, Pawel: **Brazylia, jej przyroda i mieszkańcy** (Brazil, its Nature and Inhabitants), Warsaw 1892, 1909.

Sroka, Czesław: **Działalność polskiej grupy folklorystycznej União Juventus** (Activity of the União Juventus Polish Folkloric Group), in **Emigracja polska w Brazylii**, Warsaw 1971.

Stańczewski, Józef: **Polska w Brazylii** (Poland in Brazil), Cracow 1928; **Druki portugalskie i brazylijskie o Polsce** (Portugese and Brazilian Prints about Poland), Poznan 1929; **Polska bibliografia w Brazylii** (Polish Bibliography in Brazil), Cracow 1928; **Szlakiem wychodźców** (On the Trail of the Emigrants), Warsaw 1910; **Wpływ języka portugalskiego na język kolonistów polskich w Brazylii** (Influence of the Portugese Language on the Language of the Polish Settlers in Brazil), Curitiba 1925; **Narzecza polsko-brazylijskie w południowych stanach Brazylii** (Polish-Brazilian Dialects in the Southern States of Brazil), Curitiba.

Stotymwo, Kazimierz: **Sprawozdanie z podróży do Brazylii** (Report from a Voyage to Brazil), Warsaw 1931; **Wzrost, jego dziedziczność i zależność od nowego środowiska u emigrantów polskich w Paranie** (Growth, its Heredity and Dependence on the New Environment among the Polish Emigrants in Paraná), Warsaw 1932.

Sukiennicki, Hubert: **Problem osadnictwa w Południowej Ameryce w rozważaniach międzynarodowych** (The Problem of the Colonization in South America in International Resolutions), Warsaw 1939.

Szarecki, Jerzy: **Na pokładzie "Lwowa"** (On Board the "Lwów"), Warsaw 1929.

Szawleski, Mieczysław: **Kwestia emigracji w Polsce** (The Question of Emigration in Poland), Warsaw 1927.

Szukiewicz, Wojciech: **Sprawa wychodźstwa** (The Problem of Emigration), Warsaw 1910, 1928.

Szyszło, Witold: **Pod zwrotnikami** (In the Tropics), Warsaw 1911.

Śladkowski, Jerzy: **Chimarrão** (orig. title), Poznan 1948.

Taratczyński (Tarczynski?), Hipolit: **U nas a w Brazylii** (Here and in Brazil), Warsaw 1911.

Turbański, Stanisław (Rev.): **Kolegium im. Henryka Sienkiewicza w Kurytybie** (The Henry Sienkiewicz School in Curitiba), in **Zmagania...** 4, Warsaw 1987.

Turczynski, Juliusz: **Nasza Odyseja** (Our Odyssey), Lwów

1848.

Tuszyńska, Anna: **Brazylia** (Brazil), Warsaw 1955.

Uminski, Władysław: **Znojny chleb** (Toilsome Bread), Warsaw 1968.

Uniłowski, Zbigniew: **Żyto w dżungli** (Rye in the Jungle), Warsaw 1936; Pamietnik morski (Sea Diary), Warsaw 1937.

Wachowicz, Ruy C.: **Szkoły osadnictwa polskiego w Brazylii** (Schools of the Polish Emigrants in Brazil), in **Emigracja polska w Brazylii**, Warsaw 1971.

Wagner, Władysław: **Podług słońca i gwiazd** (In accordance with the Sun and the Stars), Warsaw 1934; **Pokusa horyzontu** (Temptation of the Horizon), 1937.

Warchałowski, Kazimierz: **Do Parany** (To Paraná), Cracow 1905; **Picada** (orig. title), Warsaw 1930; **Przewodnik dla podróżujących i wychodźców** (Guide for Travellers and Emigrants), Cracow 1905; **Na krokodylim szlaku** (On the Trail of the Crocodiles), Warsaw 1936; **Na wodach Amazonki** (On the Waters of the Amazon), Warsaw 1938; **Vade mecum** (orig. title), in **Zmagania...** 2, Warsaw 1987.

Wayma, Władysław: **Pod Krzyżem Południa** (Under the Southern Cross), Lwów 1921.

Wąsowski, Pawel (Rev.): **Wedrówki Lewinskich** (Journeys of the Lewinski) in **Lud**, Curitiba 1961, also in **Zmagania...** 2, Warsaw 1987.

Werpachowska, Helena: **Z prowincji Świętej Katarzyny** (From the Province of Santa Catarina), in **Zmagania...** 2, Warsaw 1987.

Wieloch, Stanisław: **Kolonia Cruz Machado w Paranie** (The Cruz Machado Colony in Paraná), Warsaw 1939.

Wieluniak, Józef: **Ciekawe wiadomości z Brazylii** (Interesting News from Brazil), Warsaw 1891.

Wierzbowski, Witold Teofil: **Ruch niepodległościowy od 1914-1920 w Brazylii** (The Independence Movement in Brazil from

1914-1920), Nowe Hajduki 1932.

Wiśliński, Jan (Rev.): **75-lecie istnienia kolonii Santa Candida** (Seventy-five Years of Existence of the Santa Candida Colony), in **Kalendarz Ludu**, Curitiba 1950.

Wiśniewska, Joanna: **Pamiętnik — Bałtyk, Atlantyk i ja** (Memoirs — The Baltic, the Atlantic and Me), in **Zmagania...** 2, Warsaw 1987.

Włodek, Ludwik: **Polskie kolonie rolnicze w Paranie** (Polish Agricultural Colonies in Paraná), Warsaw 1910; **Polacy w Paranie** (The Poles in Paraná), Warsaw 1910; **Ilustrowany przewodnik po Brazylii** (An Illustrated Guide to Brazil), Cracow 1909; **Kolonie polskie w Paranie** (Polish Colonies in Paraná), Cracow 1909.

Wojnar, Jan: **Polsko-brazylijskie stosunki handlowe** (Polish-Brazilian Commercial Relations), Warsaw 1933.

Wolniewicz, Janusz: **Ku wybrzeżom zielonej kawy** (To the Land of the Green Coffee), Warsaw 1960; **Porty, palmy i Polacy** (Ports, Palms and the Poles), Gdansk 1969.

Wójcik, Władysław: **Moje życie w Brazylii** (My Life in Brazil), Warsaw 1961; **Lubliniacy w Brazylii** (Lublinians in Brazil), Warsaw 1963; **Po obydwu stronach równika** (On Both Sides of the Equator), Warsaw 1966.

Wrzos, Konrad: **Yerba mate** (orig. title), Warsaw 1937.

Zaborski, Stefan: **Cukier, złoto i kawa — dzieje Brazylii** (Sugar, Gold and Coffee — The History of Brazil), Warsaw 1965.

Zając, Józef (Rev.): **Liczba Polaków w Brazylii** (The Number of the Poles in Brazil), in **Kalendarz Ludu**, Curitiba 1971, also in **Emigracja polska w Brazylii**, Warsaw 1971.

Załęcki, Gustaw: **Parana a Polska jako problem polskiej ekonomiki narodowej** (Paraná and Poland as a Problem of the Polish National Economy), Warsaw 1931.

Zapałowicz, Hugo: **Jedna z podróży naokoło ziemi** (One of the Voyages around the Earth), Lwów 1899.

Zarychta, Apoloniusz: **Wśród polskich konkwistadorów** (Among the Polish Conquerors), Warsaw 1927, 1958; **Emigracja**

polska 1918-1931 i jej znaczenie dla państwa (The Polish Emigration 1918-1931 and its Meaning to the Country), Warsaw 1933, 1939; **W szkole i dżungli** (At School and in the Jungle), Warsaw 1966.

Zdanowski, Feliks Bernard: **Kalendarz Polski** (The Polish Calendar), Porto Alegre 1901; **Przewodnik dla wyjeżdżających do Brazylii** (A Guide for Emigrants to Brazil), Cracow 1907.

Zieleniewski, K.: **Ludność polska na ziemi brazylijskiej** (The Polish Population in Brazil).

Zieliński, Czesław: **Pan Balcer na wesoło** (Mr. Balcer Cheerfully), in Zmagania... 2, Warsaw 1987.

Zieliński, Stanisław: **Dr. Józef Siemiradzki** (Dr. Joseph Siemiradzki), Warsaw 1935; **Wybitne czyny Polaków na obczyźnie** (Prominent Featsof Poles abroad), Wilno 1935.

2) Fiction

Polish writers have always felt an uncommon attraction for Brazil. And it is typical that all these writers feel for Brazil a special tenderness. The Polish settler is presentd not only as a single pioneer, a conqueror and adventurer in the new land, but as a character strictly attached to his adoptive land, to which he dedicates all his strength, all his feelings, linking with it his own destiny. Such feelings are not fictitious. They are real, as it can be easily testified in any region of Polish colonization in Southern Brazil.

Among these writers, one of the most prominent is **Eugeniusz Gruda**, who lived in Brazil for many years working as a teacher in the inland of Paraná, as well as an instructor of social life. This gave him the opportunity for a deep knowledge of the settlers and of the land too. he felt attached to the new environment, so much that he married a Brazilian woman of Polish descent in Marechal Malet. During the war he moved to England and afterwards to Poland. The product of his observtions and experiences was enclosed in the novel **Saudade**, the symbolic Brazilian title of his book. He recounts the history of the adaptation of the Poles to the Brazilian environment, their relations with the "caboclos" (Brazilian half-breeds of whites and Indians), the problems and difficulties the Polish emigrants had to face, but also their concern with the preservation of the cultural inheritance they brought from their native land.

The same impassioned theme is present in the novel **Pionierzy** (The Pioneers) of **Bohdan Pawłowicz**. In picturesque and romantic traits he presents the Mierzwa family. Hidden in the jungle of Ivaí, this family seeks its identification with the new land, so peculiar to the Polish peasant.

No less merits reveals **Bolesław Mrówczyński**. Although he never travelled to Brazil, he managed to write his trilogy **Bartochowie** based only on documents and researches he was able to do. The trilogy includes three novels: **Bitwa o Pilarzinho** (The Battle of Pilarzinho), **Osada nad srebrnym potokiem** (The Silver Brook Farm) and **Tętniący step** (Galloping through the Fields), in which he recounts in details all the adventures of the first Polish families who came to Paraná and settled in the neighborhood of Curitiba, as well as their headway to the inland of the state.

In the list below there are other names and other titles of Polish writers inspired by the Polish emigration to Brazil:

Choromański, Michał: **Macumba** (orig. title), in **Przekrój,** Cracow 1967.

Dygasinski, Adolf: **Na złamanie karku** (At a Breakneck Speed), Warsaw 1893.

Ficinski, Janusz: **Latarnia morska** (Sea Lighthouse), in **Lud**, Curitiba 1963; **Władcy przestrzeni** (Masters of the Vastness), Curitiba 1977).

Gruda, Eugeniusz: **Saudade** (orig. title), Warsaw 1955; **Zły bóg Mboi** (Mboi, the God of Evil), Warsaw 1968 (2nd eddition); **Trudny powrót** (Difficult Return), Warsaw 1968.

Hartman, Seweryn: **Miasto cieni** (The City of Shadows), Warsaw 1928, also in **Lud**, Curitiba 1965.

Krawczyk, Jan: **Ivagone** (orig. title), Warsaw 1959; **Pampa** (orgi. title), Lublin 1986; **Minuano**, Lublin 1988.

Kwiatkowski, Tadeusz: **Ucieczka z dżungli** (Flight from the

Jungle), Warsaw 1955; **Najlepsze skrzydlo Brazylii** (Brazil's Best Line), in **Opowieści z dalekich krajów**, Warsaw 1956.

Lepecki, Mieczysław: **Zew Ojczyzny** (The Fatherland's Appeal), Warsaw 1930.

Mrówczynski, Bolesław: **Bitwa o Pilarzinho** (The Battle of Pilarzinho), 1st part of the trilogy **Bartochowie**, Katowice 1968; **Osada nad srebrnym potokiem** (The Golden Brook Farm), 2nd part of the trilogy **Bartochowie**, Katowice 1968; **Tętniący step** (Galloping through the Fields), 3rd part of the trilogy **Bartochowie**, Katowice 1968.

Nostitz-Jackowski, Mieczysław: **Ojcze nasz** (Our Father), Poznan 1932; **Tumba** (orig. title), Poznań 1932; **Maria Antonina** (orig. title), Poznan 1923.

Ostrowski, Jerzy: **Cathangora, król Botokudów** (Cathangora, the King of the Botocudos), Warsaw 1931; **Kobuz** (orig. title), Warsaw 1931.

Ostrowski, Wiktor: **Życie wielkiej rzeki** (Life of the Big River), Warsaw 1967.

Pawłowicz, Bohdan: **Franek na szerokim swiecie** (Little Francis Roaming about the World), Warsaw 1930; **Córka latarnika** (The Daughter of the Lamplighter), Warsaw 1930; **Pionierzy** (The Pioneers), Warsaw 1930; **Załoga** (The Crew), Warsaw 1935; **Kolorowe serce** (Colored Heart), Warsaw 1936.

Piotrowski, Wacław: **Polak w Brazylii** (A Pole in Brazil), Cracow 1914.

Rusinek, Michał: **Wiosna admirała** (The Admiral's Spring), Warsaw 1950; **Muszkieter z Itamaryki** (The Musketeer from Itamarica), Warsaw 1950; **Królestwo pychy** (The Kingdom of Pride), Warsaw 1950.

Rychlinski, Jerzy Bohdan: **Przygody Krzysztofa Arciszewskiego** (The Adventures of Christopher Arciszewski), Lwów 1935, Gdynia 1957; **Słowo o admirale Arciszewskim** (A Word about Admiral Arciszewski), Warsaw 1947; **Madonna za złota** (The Golden Madonna), Warsaw 1963.

Wachowicz, Roman: **Maragatos** (orig. title), Curitiba 1965;

Szerszenie w raju (Locusts in Paradise), Curitiba 1962; published also as **Polskie korzenie** (Polish roots), Warsaw 1980.

Wójcik, Władysław: **Wojna domokrążców** (Hawkers in War), Curitiba 1930; **Zaglaimbaté — wódz niezwyciężony** (Zaglaimbaté — the Invincible Chief), Curitiba 1931; **Zemsta Indianina** (Indian Vengeance), Curitiba 1931.

Wydrzyński, Andrzej: **Umarli rzucają cień** (The Dead Cast a Shadow), Katowice 1966.

Zakrzewska, Helena: **Lulu** (orig. title), Curitiba 1926; **W obronie swego gniazda** (Defending One's Nest), Curitiba 1926.

Zaniewicki, Zbigniew: **Zielone piekło** (The Green Hell), Warsaw 1929; **Równik** (Equator), Warsaw 1936.

Zarychta, Apoloniusz: **Tambo** (orig. title), Warsaw 1929.

3) Poetry

The first appearance of Brazil in the Polish poetry may be found in Maria Konopnicka. Her work **Pan Balcer w Brazylii** (Mr. Balcer in Brazil), composed of six poems corresponding to six chapters, presents the tragic odyssey of a group of Polish emigrants who have to get through a series of misfortunes, tropical diseases, hunger and other sufferings and are decimated in their effort to return to their country. The survivor of this group, resembling a true human rag, returns to Europe and his dramatic adventures move all his listeners. The poetess intended to alert her fellow countrymen against the dangers they were exposed to in travelling to such a distant country, whose nature was wonderful but unfriendly to those not habituated to it. Although this work did no succeed in paralyzing the migratory wave, it certainly gave some contribution to its moderation.

Unlike the prose writers, the poets dedicated less attention to the social problems, and more to the luxuriant Brazilian nature. **Pan Balcer w Brazylii** was perhaps the only exception in this respect. As a rule the poets emphsize the territorial grandeur, the spell of the landscape or the captivating exotic features of the dizzy distances.

Among the many works published, the following should be

put in relief:

Breowicz, Wojciech: **Wybór utworów** (Selection of Works), Warsaw 1952.

Grzybicki, Tadeusz Milan: **Wianki parańskie** (Wreaths from Paraná), Curitiba 1921.

Konopnicka, Maria: **Pan Balcer w Brazylii** (Mr. Balcer in Brazil), Warsaw 1925.

Olcha, Antoni: **Różne strony czasu** (Several Sides of the Time), Warsaw 19??; **Oko delfina** (The Dolphin's Eye), Warsaw 1968.

Stańczewski, Józef: **Pod Krzyżem Południa** (Under the Southern Cross), Curitiba 1925.

Conclusion

The names and works presented show there is a vast material to make up what can be called the Polish-Brazilian literature. It is Polish because it was written in Polish. At the same time it is Brazilian because the subject of these writings concentrates on Brazil or on problems related to the Polish emigration to this country. Some prominent Poles linked with Brazil are also the subject of this literature, as for instance Arciszewski, a member of the Dutch government in Northeastern Brazil when the Dutch dominated this part of the country in the 17th century, or Saporski, dubbed the "father of the Polish colonization in Brazil". This survey includes books and major articles centered on the analysis of the Polish colonization in Brazil. In principle it does not include technical or religious works, as well as school handbooks, even those published in Brazil.

It is significant that this literature is in a constant growing. New works are being published. Among the most recent ones we could point out the interesting volumes (1,2 and 4) of memoirs entitled **Zmagania polonijne w Brazylii** (Struggles of the Emigrants in Brazil), organized by the Rev. Tadeusz Dworecki. The third volume is being prepared for publication.

Some of the aforementioned essays were published in Polish-Brazilian newspapers which of necessity also became publishing houses. They edited a good number of books in Polish-Brazilian topics. It was one of the most efficient means for fostering not only the Polish culture, but also describing the most important events in Brazil and within their own communities. The first Polish newspaper in Brazil appeared in Curitiba - the **Gazeta Polska w Brazylii** - founded by Karol Szulc in 1892. It was in circulation until 1941, when the foreign-language press in Brazil was suppressed. Many other publications had been in circulation in Paraná, some of them short-lived, others managed to survive for years. Among these the most prominent is **Lud**, founded in 1920, which now circulates as a weekly newspaper. Another rich source for the history of Polish colonization in Brazil is the **Kalendarz Ludu**, which started appearing in 1933 and which brings valuable information on our settlers in the states of Paraná, Rio Grande do Sul and São Paulo.

The history of the Polish ethnic group in Brazil has inerested scholars of both Polish and non-Polish descent. Some of their writings dating since the middle of the 20th century are particularly important for the variety of problems and because they were published in Portuguese. Thus, Tadeusz Skowronski's **Páginas brasileiras sobre a Pôlonia** (Brazilian Pages about Poland), Rio de Janeiro, 1942, describes Brazilian opinions on Polish culture, as well as on the laboriousness of the Polish-Brazilian population; Stanisław Fischlowitz's **General Christóforo Arciszewski** (Rio de Janeiro, 1959) relates the military activities of this Polish officer, who on behalf of Holland conquered northern Brazil in the XVIIth century. In 1981 Prof. Ruy C. Wachowicz published **O Camponês Polonês no Brasil** (The Polish Peasant in Brazil), presenting from a historic perspective the Polish farmer's work and adjustment to his new tropical environment. Dr. David da Silva Carneiro included in his **Galeria de ontem y de hoje** (Gallery of Yesterday and Today), Curitiba, 1963, biographies of Drs. Sz. Kossobudzki and J. Szymanski, co-founders of Paraná's Medical School. On the occasion of the centennial of Polish immigration to Brazil (1871), a group of intellectuals of Polish descent in Curitiba issued the **Annais da Comunidade Brasileiro-Polonesa** (Annals of the Brazilian-Polish Community). Its seven volumes of original research and translation of related documents were published between 1970 and 1977.

There are other Portuguese publications related to the Polish colonization as follows: **Centenârio no Brasil da Familia Filipak** (Centennial of the Filipak Family in Brazil) by Francisco Filipak (1980), presenting the expansion of this immigrant family in their new homeland; **A Seara do Semeador** (The Grainfield of the Sower) by Rev. Wendelin Swierczek (1980), and **75 Anos de Presença dos Padres Vicentinos** (75 Years of Presence of the Paulist Fathers) by the Rev. W. Swierczek and others (1978), analysing the activities of the Polish clergy in Brazil; **Murici - Terra Nossa** (Murici - Our Land) by Rev. Stanisław Turbanski (1978), a historic survey of the Polish colony on the outskirts of Curitiba.

Even the Polish language has aroused interest, especially at the Catholic University of Paraná, where two dissertations were presented about this subject: Mariano Kawka wrote **Os Brasileirismos do Dialeto Polono-Brazileiro** (Brazilian Idiom in the Polish-Brazilian Dialect), 1982, a study of the Polish language spoken in Brazil and how it was influenced by the Portuguese language; and Arlindo Milton Druszcz presented a study titled **O Bilinguismo em Araucaria** (Bilinguism in Araucaria), 1983, an analysis of the influence of the Polish language on the Portuguese, spoken by settlers of Polish descent in Araucaria, Paraná. In the field of linguistics two other works published by M. Kawka have to be mentioned: a **Polish-Portuguese Dictionary** (Curitiba, 1984) and a **Portuguese-Polish Dictionary** (Curitiba, 1996), both enriching the Polish-Brazilian culture.

On account of the ethno-cultural assimilation of our settlers in Brazil, more Polish-Brazilian authors publish their works in Portuguese. In addition to the before mentioned, there is a prolific fiction writer Ladislau Romanowski, whose story **Ciume da morte** (Jealousy of Death), 1945, won him a prize from the Academy of Literature of Paraná, and the poet Paulo Leminski who in one of his poetry

JAN KRAWCZYK

PAMPA

Wydawnictwo Lubelskie

Prof. E. Urbanski's
Polish-Latin-American
Book Collection

Lublin

1986

Jan Krawczyk, the Polish-Brazilian bi-lingual writer, occupies a distinguished place in the cultural community of Parana. Among his books on various topics, three novels are based on native Brazilian motifs: *Ivagone* (1960), **Pampa** (1986) and *Minuano* (1988). Also, most of **Ladislau Romanowski's** works in Portuguese such as *Ciume da morte* (1943), *E os trigais ondulavam* (1947) and *Chico Faisca* (1955), or **Dr. Ruy Wachowicz's** *Historia do Paraná* (1977) have a Brazilian background. All this confirms the existence of a perfect Polish-Brazilian ethnoc-cultural symbiosis and mutual tolerance.

collection **Polonaises** (1980) evokes his Polish ancestry and concern for the new peotic trend in Brazil. Another prolific novelist is Jan Krawczyk, who after publishing in Poland such works with Brazilian motives as **Ivagone** (1960), **Pampa** (1985), **Minuano** (1988) and **Ochotnicy z Rio** (Volunteers from Rio de Janeiro), 1988, is now engaged in translating them into Portuguese, which he also utilizes in his press articles. There are also bi-lingual authors such as Józef Stanczewski (Fredecensis), Roman Wachowicz and Thadeu Krul (Król), concerned with a variety of topics regarding Poland and the Polish-Brazilian matters, displaying thus their loyalty to both of them.

All this proves that Polonia in Brazil is alive and active, particularly in the state of Paraná which has the greatest concentration of Brazilian-Polish citizens. The increasing number of students and professors at Brazilian universities, who reinforce the Polish-Brazilian **intelligensia**, constitute good prospects for even greater enrichment of the Polish-Brazilian culture in the future.

The Poles in Argentina

Emil Ciawlowski
(Argentina)

Translated by: Edward Kaminski

Argentine history is marked by crucial periods which completely transform the economic and political structure of the country. When we go back to the time of discovery of South America, that is, the year 1516, we see that the Spanish monarchy considered the native Indians as free subjects. Slaves from Africa, on the other hand, were brought to do the work. The colonial administration was modeled on the metropolis; there were viceroys, "cabildos" (autonomous territorial governments), and some military garrisons for the maintenance of order. Life was tranquil and there was no need for immigrants. But the outbreak of the Napoleonic Wars brought the slogans of freedom to Argentina. Spain became completely absorbed in its own internal problems and consequently its colonies had to assume more self-responsibility.

The then-elite gathers, discusses Argentina's destiny, and subsequently concludes that this is the appropriate time to announce the country's independence. In order to have an independent, republican government, however, people were needed to settle the wide expanse of land. European immigration thus became a necessity.

Polish immigration begins in 1812, as evidenced by historical-military documents. These records show typically Polish names with their respective ranks. Information on Polish officers is more readily available than that dealing with enlisted personnel. Following the partitions, Polish émigrés went to France where they received grants-in-aid and schooling - general, military and special. During this period, they organized military units to serve with Napoleon's

Argentina: A native Indian girl from the jungle state of Misiones, Argentina, where many thousands of Polish immigrants settled, engaged in agriculture. The natural beauty of Missiones' virgin forests attracted also **Zygmunt Kowalski**, author of this painting.

forces or in Turkey. In 1808 Napoleon invaded Bourbon Spain and placed his brother Joseph on the throne. Polish legionnaires fought in such places as Zaragoza, Tudela, Somosierra, Guadarrama and Ocana. In 1810 and 1811 they are known as the "riders from hell", and carry into battle banners bearing the slogan, "For your freedom and ours". Consciously or not, they help to keep intact the military strength of the monarch, thus weakening the colonial government in Argentina. After the fall of Napoleon the Polish legionnaires did not wish to be subject to the rule of Grand Duke Constantine of Russia. Instead, as units or as individual volunteers, they took part in all wars of national liberation. Argentina suited the Polish fighters ideologically. Consequently, we see indisputably Polish names as participants in all the battles fought under the leadership of Gen. José San Martin, the national hero of Argentina. We see such names as Gen. Antoni Belina-Skupieski, Maj. Jan W. Bulewski, Lt. Antoni Mierz and others.

Following the 1831 Uprising, there is an increase in the ranks of military and civilian immigration from Poland. In 1854 Dr. Maksymilian Rymarkiewicz - together with others - arrives in Argentina. He helps to fight a yellow fever epidemic in Montevideo, Uruguay. Another immigrant - Feliks Żaba - becomes a professor at the University of Buenos Aires. At this time, too, Henryk Stpiczyński arrived in Argentina. His son, known in history as Gen. Henryk Spika, became a national hero in Argentina's war with Paraguay.

Another Pole, Gen. Teofil Iwanowski, took part in the battle against the Argentine dictator Rosas at Caseros on Feb. 3, 1852. He also participated in the war with Paraguay (1864-70) and served with distinction. He began as an enlisted man and received a field promotion to the rank of general. Iwanowski was loyal to the constitutional authorities. For his loyalty, he paid with his life at the hands of his rebellious troops. As a sign of appreciation, the Argentine regime erected a mausoleum to his memory in the province of San Juan, that is, in the place of his tragic death. Two other participants in the Battle of Caseros were Capt. Piotr Dubrocki and his brother, Lt. Roman D. Both had served in Garibaldi's Legion. The names Jackowski and Warszawa are found in the respective Marine and National Guards records.

The year 1863 brings a new wave of immigrants who enlisted in the war against Paraguay. This group was very numerous since the Argentine regime named Teofil Marecki as their chaplain with the rank of colonel.

Military and historical documents, and even various journals, make special mention of Col. Robert Chodasiewicz (Engineer) who served with Gen. Grant's forces in the U.S.A. He was held in particular high regard by Gen. Bartolomé Mitre, the President of Argentina, and the head of the allied armies. Col. Chodasiewicz's services as the sole military engineer are known from his work on fortifications. He was also the first to go up in a balloon in order to reconnoiter Paraguayan positions. Although he was not a line commander, this action undoubtedly contributed greatly to the allied victory. The Argentine Army Air Force has erected monuments to Chodasiewicz as a pioneer airman.

Chodasiewicz occupies a position in the annals of Argentine Polonia similar to that of Tadeusz Kosciuszko in the United States. His role in the war was principally directed at the strengthening defenses, particularly on the Uruguayan border. After the war, Chodasiewicz was named director of the Paraguayan railroad. He was given the task of reconstructing the shattered lines and equipment. He was given a similar assignment in Brazil. In 1900 Chodasiewicz was elected president of the first Polish society to be organized in Buenos Aires.

Col. Czeslaw Jordan-Wysocki - as an organizer and topographer - distinguished himself during a Patagonian expedition. He also established an ammunition plant and was employed as a planner of agricultural immigration. With the aid of some military detachments, he installed the most beautiful park in Buenos Aires (Palermo) on city marshes. In another area, Lt. Henryk Ozarowski - as a soldier and writer - took part in pacifying expeditions against the war-like Ranquelas Indians. A long-time resident of Catamarga, Karol Muntawski organized the first Institute of Weight and Measures, and the Dept. of Topography and Statistics. He also constructed the first

GŁOS POLSKI

LA VOZ DE POLONIA

KORZYSTAJ
Z WYGODNEGO KREDYTU
W KOOPERATYWIE SAN TELMO
c. Serrano 2076, Capital, Tel. 7747621

SEMANARIO DE LA UNION DE LOS POLACOS
EN LA REPUBLICA ARGENTINA

REVISTA PARA LAS FAMILIAS POLACAS
RESIDENTES EN LA AMERICA LATINA

KORZYSTAJ
Z WYGODNEGO KREDYTU
W KOOPERATYWIE SAN TELMO
c. Serrano 2076, Capital, Tel. 7747621

ROK LII — Nr 40 (3468) Buenos Aires, octubre 4 października 1974 Cena numeru $ Ley 2.50 (m$n. 250,—)

Mgr. WOJCIECH MOROZ

W Stulecie Śmierci

Generała Teofila Iwanowskiego

Osoba i historia życia generała Teofila Iwanowskiego, Polaka urodzonego w Poznaniu w 1827 roku, uczestnika powstania wielkopolskiego w 1848 r., jest dobrze znana czytelnikom "Głosu Polskiego".

Gen. T. Iwanowski rozpoczął służbę w wojsku argentyńskim w 1853 roku w stopniu szeregowca. W składzie 3 pułku piechoty liniowej brał udział w stopniu kapitana w bitwach pod Cepeda i Pavón. Następnie uczestniczy w wojnie z Paragwajem, oraz w walkach wewnętrznych Argentyny. Kilkakrotnie ranny, w 1873 roku zostaje awansowany na polu bitwy do stopnia generała brygady.

24 września 1874 w obronie praworządności i wierności żołnierskiej został zamordowany przez buntowane oddziały wojska w Villa Mercedes.

5 grudnia 1875 dekret podpisany przez ówczesnego Prezydenta Republiki Nicolas Avellaneda i Ministra Wojny Adolfo Alsina zarządził wybudowanie mauzoleum na grobie generała Iwanowskiego pochowanego na cmentarzu w Villa Mercedes, Prov. San Luis.

W uzasadnieniu tego zarządzenia dekret podaje: "para honrar la memoria del General Don Teofilo Iwanowski, victima del honor militar, presentandola como un ejemplo a la fidelidad del ejercito y a su disciplina".

Dla uczczenia stuletniej rocznicy tragicznego zgonu naszego rodaka, Gen. Teofila Iwanowskiego, odbyły się w dniach 21 i 22 września br. w Villa Mercedes następujące uroczystości:

• • •

Uroczystości w Villa Mercedes

Dnia 21 o godz. 16,30 liczna grupa Polaków przybyłych z Buenos Aires i Cordoby oraz Argentyńczyków zebrała się pod domem, gdzie zginął tragicznie gen. T. Iwanowski, celem odkrycia pamiątkowej tablicy ufundowanej przez miejscowe władze. Tablicę odsłonili p. Magdalena L. de De Giuseppe, Przewodnicząca Komitetu Obchodów w Villa Mercedes i p. Wojciech Moroz, Vicepreзes Zarządu Związku Polaków.

Po odsłonięciu tablicy przemówił członek lokalnego Komitetu Obchodów i Redaktor gazety "La Voz del Sur" p. Edmundo Tello Cornejo podkreślając specjalne cechy polskiego żołnierza jak również szlachetność i odwagę generała Teofila Iwanowskiego.

Następnie zebrani udali się na miejsce gdzie w ubiegłych latach stacjonował 3 Pułk Piechoty, którym dowodził gen. T. Iwanowski. W tym miejscu odsłonięto również tablicę pamiątkową przez p. Lorenzo M. Rowe, Viceprezesa Komitetu w Villa Mercedes i p. Stanisława Skowrońskiego, Prezesa Stowarzyszenia Polskich Kombatantów. Po odsłonięciu tablicy przemówił p. Clodomira Araujo.

Odsłonięcie trzeciej tablicy odbyło się na skrzyżowaniu ulic im. Iwanowskiego i Pedernera. Tablicę odsłonił reprezentant Rady Miejskiej oraz delegat Burmistrza Villa Mercedes. Przemówił p. Raul Merlo, Sekretarz Burmistrza wyrażając w imieniu miejscowych mieszkańców dumę złożenia hołdu tak dzielnemu żołnierzowi pochodzenia polskiego. W czasie tych uroczystości wzięła udział orkiestra wojskowa V Brygady z Villa Reynolds.

Wieczorem tego dnia odbyła się akademia w sali teatralnej Miejskiej Komisji Kultury. Na scenie wystąpiły Polskie Poczty Sztandarowe przybyłe z Buenos Aires i Cordoby. Po odegraniu hymnów narodowych Argentyny i Polski wręczono I i II nagrodę uczniom, którzy zostali wyróżnieni przez Miejską Komisję Kultury w Villa Mercedes za najlepsze prace w rozpisanym konkursie o życiu gen. Teofila Iwanowskiego. Z Komisją współpracowali p. Teresa Pikulska jako reprezentantka Zw. Polaków i "Głosu Polskiego" oraz p. Wojciech Moroz z ramienia Zarządu Związku Polaków. Wyróżnione prace zostałe odczytane przez uczni, którzy otrzymali nagrodę. W dalszym ciągu sławny historyk argentyński p. Clodomiro Araujo wygłosił odczyt na temat życia i działalności gen. Teofila Iwanowskiego.

Dnia 22 września br. w niedzielę o godz. 9,30 zebrały się w miejscowym Ratuszu delegacje polskie oraz reprezentanci władz argentyńskich. Przybył wraz z małżonką dowódca Garnizonu Artylerii Przeciwlotniczej z San Luis płk. Roberto Pedreira, reprezentant Dowódcy V Brygady Lotniczej z Villa Reynolds, Sekretarz Burmistrza Villa Mercedes p.

(Ciąg dalszy na str. 2-giej)

Title page of the Polish-Argentinian Weekly **Głos Polski** (Voz de Polonia), organ of the Federation of Poles in Argentina, published in Polish and Spanish in Buenos Aires since 1922. This article is dedicated to **Gen. Teofil Iwanowski**, who served as a private and finished as a general, being the commander of the 3rd Infantry Regiment. He was burried in a mausoleum in Villa Mercedes, where the Argentine Government placed a plaque with this inscription: "To Gen. Teófilo Iwanowski — Grateful Republic", which emphasizes his exemplary military service to his adopted country.

Argentina: A view from the state of Missiones with beauty of its rain forests and rich vegetation is gradually converted into farm land. As a "paradise" for artists, this view was painted by **Zygmunt Kowalski**, who has been living there for many years.

grain-cleaning machine, a prototype of the winnowing machine, adapted to local conditions.

Many Poles served in the Argentine army, but it is difficult to identify them due to the use of pseudonyms. These were used by the Poles in order to protect their relatives in Europe and also to avoid giving any clues to Polish political conspiracies. Apart form military specialties, many Poles devoted themselves to practicing their civilian occupations. Dr. Juliusz Jurkowski established the first sanatorium for lung diseases; Dr. Ryszard Sudnik was a recognized pathologist and specialist in electric therapy; Engineer Karol Loewenherd served as a lecturer on spatial geometry, cosmography, and topography; Engr. Zdzislaw Celinski was a cartographer with the Army Geographical Institute; Gustaw Kujawa lectured on mathematics; Fryderyk Muntawski lectured on foreign languages; Karol Nowakowski was an instructor in the English College; and Michael Górski was the head of the Fryburg Institute for the Argentine aristocracy. He is, perhaps, the only insurgent who returned to an independent Poland.

Numerous Polish scientists and engineers were employed in the petroleum industry, particularly in the Mendoza region. Others helped to construct irrigation canals and railroads. For example, Engr. Wladyslaw Dobrowolski was the director of a railroad in the Province of Buenos Aires and, at the same time, a university professor. From the above list, it can be seen that this group represented a pioneering vanguard which tried to bring Argentina up to the level of European countries. Polish prestige was duly esteemed.

In 1897 a group of about one hundred Galician families sailed for the U.S.A., but were turned back on health grounds. So the would-be immigrants headed for Argentina and landed in the Misiones. This was the beginning of the agricultural immigration. Their working conditions were difficult, different farming methods were used, different crops wre raised, and they had a permanent battle with various insects. The Polish and Ukrainian farmers withstood the test, transforming the entire landscape. Little white homes, roadside chapels churches and schools were built. It resembled Podole or the

Ukraine. It was apparent that a distinct, distant civilization had reached this province, later reinforced by new immigrants, principally relations or friends. Several thousand arrived by 1905.

In the inter-war period about 200,000 small farmers emigrated from the Polish-Eastern Borderlands. This was an economic migration. More emigrees went to Paraguay than to Argentina, since the Paraguayan Syndicate had estblished recruiting centers in Poland. Conditions in Paraguay were worse, and consequently, there was a gradual move to Argentina. Their aim was to earn money and return home. Then, too, not many settled on the land. They worked seasonally at harvest time, in refrigeration plants, on the railroad and in the oil industry - in a work, where work was available! At the time; manufacturing was negligible, and in any event, could not compete with English products. The economic crisis of the thirties deeply affected Argentina, too. The immigrants congregated close to cities like Buenos Aires, Cordoba, Rosario and Santa Fe. It was during this period that the ties of nationality were deeply felt. The Poles strenghtend their organizations or created new ones.

When the Germans invaded Poland in 1939, patriotic feelings were aroused among the immigrants. About 3000 immigrants - Poles and others - volunteered for service in the Polish Armed Forces. The recruiting commission accepted 1,140 volunteers for service in Polish units stationed in England.

After the war, more than 25,000 Poles applies for entry permits into Argentina. The post-war immigrants were specialists. And nearly every one had at least some money and free transportation. The majority, having been in mechanized divisions, came with a good knowledge of general and automobile mechanics. Just in the Polish Organization of Engineers and Technicians there were 441 members. More than 300 scientists and engineers were employed in responsible and managerial positions. Some engineers signed contracts to work for the government. Others signed contracts with multi-national companies. One can only give a superficial idea of their high qualifications. The first group of seventeen engineers - led by Witold Wierzejski - was contracted by an arms factory. The next group of

Argentina: A natural size sculpture of an Argentine creole lady, made by **Jerzy Jur-Jurewicz**, a Polish artist who spent many years in Argentina. Most of his artistic motifs were Argentine people.

Argentina: Sculpture of an Aregntine cowboy called "gaucho tropero", made by **Jerzy Jur-Jurewicz**, a Polish artist who spent many years in Argentina. Most of his artistic works were based on Argentine motifs.

Argentina: Color painting "Country wedding in eastern Poland", executed by Piotr Pawluczuk, Polish artist living now in Argentina.

petroleum geologists and mining engineers was employed, respectively, in the oil industry and in coal and ore mines. About twenty meteorologists were hired to work at airports and on scientific expeditions to the Antarctica. Others - both engineers and technicians - found employment fairly rapidly upon their arrival in Argentina. Some engineers organized their own firms. Poles were also engaged in the production of farm machinery and as representatives of U.S. machine products.

The post-war arrival of immigrants of various nationalities caused a housing shortage and a consequent urgent need for same. Some of necessity - with the aid of their colleagues - built their own homes, and subsequently opted for this remunerative trade. After some time, they ran their own profitable businesses. In the suburban region of Merlo, a lovely Polish colony was built. It was called "Aguila Blanca" (White Eagle).

Only sometime towards the end of the 1950's did mechanization start in Argentina. A score of automobile and tractor plants were built. Since Poles much prefer inedependent work, they often leave their factory jobs and set up their own shops.

About a hundred Poles practiced the liberal professions (lawyers, doctors, pharmacists, artists, etc.). Some had to change their original professions, either working in an allied field or going into something new, such as business. Insofar as performers are concerned, some were permanently engaged by Argentine theatres. These included singers, musicians, and ballet masters.

There is no exact figure on the number of Poles in Argentina or those of Polish descent. This is due to the fact that Argentine statistics list as Argentine citizens those naturalized or born here. In the 1950's community leaders calculated that there were about 200,000 Poles. Now - in 1984 - there are much less, about 130,000. About 10% of this latter figure take part in Polonia's community life. A number of factors are responsible for the population decline. Many immigrants were single and eventually died; others left to join their families in the U.S.A., Canada or Poland; and finally, mixed marriages have resulted in the gradual "de-Polonization" of two young generations.

In the past several years some immigrats have arrived from Poland, but the numbers are insignificant. To begin with, Argentina does not receive immigrants from "Iron Curtain" countries. The president of the SPK or the Związek Polaków must personally vouch for any immigrant from Poland in the Dept. of Immigration.

With the arrival of the post-war immigrants in 1947-52, Polonia's profile completely changed. These were politically and socially-accomplished people. There was a complete reorganization and the Związek Polaków (Polish Alliance) was created. In 1950 a large building was bought to serve as central headquarters. In 1952 the statue of the Związek was changed in order to unite all the Polonia organizations in Argentina. In 1961 the Polonia Council approved a basic resolution calling for independent, non-communist Poland. Thirty four country-wide organizations belong to the Związek. These groups have their own buildings which house schools, libraries, meeting rooms, etc. To this must be added those central organizations which have their headquarters in the Dom Polski in Buenos Aires.

The young people who were born here are college-educated, or at least have a secondary vocational education, and have already entered the market place. National schools are free and private education is not expensive, so young Polonia took advantage of the available opportunities. It is necessary to stress that Catholicism has a great influence here, and consequently there are no "hippy" or drug-addiction problems. Insofar as choice of profession is concerned, young men have chosen well-paying studies, such as engineering, medicine, economics and science. Girls have selected teaching, medicine, pharmacy and dentistry. Basically, all are working in their chosen professions. There are no unemployed.

Social integration with other Argentinians has proceeded well. Naturalization is not required. Foreigners are treated better than Argentina's own "Creoles". This benevolent attitude is duly appreciated by Poles. Besides, Poles have a moral right to feel here "as if in their own home", for their ancestors participated in both wars of liberation, as well as in the pioneering development of the industry and culture.

The Polish-Argentine Press Before and After World War II

Michał Więckowski,
(Argentina)

Whenever a sizable number of Polish immigrants settles in a foreign land, usually a Polish periodical sprouts there. This explains the existence of the Polish-language press in Argentina, where the Polish immigration was always incomparably smaller than in the United States and even in Brazil. Before World War II the Polish community in Argentina possessed only one daily, the **Codzienny Niezależny Kurier Polski w Argentynie** (The Daily Independent Polish Courier in Argentina), established in 1928 by Messrs. Kondratowicz and Lasecki, and one weekly founded in 1922 **Głos Polski** (The Voice of Poland), the official organ of the Związek Polaków w Argentynie (Union of Poles in Argentina). Both papers appeared in Buenos Aires, where the **C.N. Kurier Polski** in 1932 also started publishing a bilingual Polish-Spanish monthly **Argentyna.** During the Easter Holidays of 1939, another paper appeared, **Bóg i Ojczyzna** (God and the Homeland), edited by the Rev. Aleksander Michalik, the pastor of the local parish, also the Rector of the Polish Catholic Mission in Argentina. Two biweeklies appeared in the province of Misiones: since 1924 the **Orędownik** and since 1933 **Osadnik**, the latter being the organ of the Union of Polish Associations in Misiones.

The Buenos Aires-based **C. N. Kurier Polski** played an especially important function since the German-Soviet aggression of Poland in 1939, for it extensively informed the Polish-Argentine community about the war events. Thanks to its publicity, about two thousand Polish volunteers mostly from Argentina, also some from Brazil, Paraguay and Uruguay were recruited to the Polish Armed Forces, these being organized first in France and later in England. In spite of its noble function, the publishers ran into financial difficulties, which in 1947 caused the sale of their printing shop and the closing of both the **C.N. Kurier Polski** and **Argentyna.** It was an irreversible loss for the Polish-Argentine community, especially since soon after about 20,000 Polish ex-combatants arrived in Argentina from England, and possibly could have supported those papers. A similar crisis also touched the Polish-language paper in Misiones, where the demise of the older immigrants caused a shrinking readership of the **Orędownik** and **Osadnik**; eventually they ceased publication.

The new wave of Polish military migration reinforced, however, the membership of the existing Polish organizations in Argentina, also giving an impulse to reestablishing there a Polish-language press. Thus, in 1947 Stanisaw A. Smyczynski started publishing a new independent paper called **Nowy Kurier**, which unfortunately folded in 1948. Almost simultaneously a paper of leftist tendency **Polska Wyzwolona** (Liberated Poland) appeared in Buenos Aires under the editorship of an unknown individual Marcin Raduj, who in 1949 was substituted by similarly unknown Zygmunt Łukasiewicz. Due to insufficient readership this leftist paper lasted only three years (1947-1950). A similar fate also met a short-lived paper of confused ideology **Nowa Polska** (New Poland), edited by an activist and a former President of the Związek Polaków w Argentynie, Stanisław Kowaleski. Significantly, after the failure of his editorial venture, Kowaleski left for Poland. In 1949 the Legation of the Polish People's Republic in Buenos Aires started editing an illustrated magazine in Spanish called **Polonia**. Its contents were, of course, presented for the Marxist perspective. The last issue (No. 105) of that magazine appeared in 1958.

New editorial ventures of an ideologically undefined purpose were undertaken by Wienczysław Stasiejko, unknown to the Polish community in Argentina. He launched in 1951 a short-lived weekly **Tygodnik Polski** (The Polish Weekly). In 1952 another weekly

Ogniwo (Link) appeared under his editorship, the seeming purpose of which was to unify the Slavic ethnic groups in Argentina and establish a common political front. For various reasons, one of them being the antitotalitarian attitude of Argentine authorities, after seven years **Ogniwo** ceased to exist in 1959. Although this weekly was edited in Polish, it did not find enough support among the "old" Polish immigrants and none among the Polish "military" migration of the 1940s, which staunchly stood on the ground of a politically independent Poland.

Owing to these circumstances, members of the Polish migration in Argentina made various attempts to establish their own press. Thus, Zdzisław Bau and Jerzy Chołodziński launched in 1948 a periodical **Kombatant Polski w Argentynie** (Polish Combatant in Argentina), but were able to publish only two issues. Another periodical **List z Europy i Polski** (A Letter from Europe and Poland), edited by Zdzislaw Bau and Roman Dąbrowski, both professional newsmen, was more successful. Thirty issues of that vivaciously edited **List** were published in 1949. Unfortunately, its sensational approach to certain problems of the local Polonia, caused protests of various Polish Argentine organizations, which along with financial difficulties, contributed to the end of this editorial venture.

The Polish Association of Engineers and Technicians in Argentina (SITP) published in 1950 its only issue of a professional review called **Technika.** Also the Polish Boy Scout movement started publishing in 1950 its magazine **Nasz Znicz**, which prospered for three years, i.e. the period of its greatest activities in Argentina. A pleasant surprise caused the initiative of Władysław Lerski, who in 1952 published three issues of a humor magazine, **Mucha-La Mosca** (Fly) in Buenos Aires, however, without prospects of continuing this intellectual adventure, Sharp political and social jokes cheered up, nevertheless, the Polish community for a few months, helping it to forget partly the tragic post-war fate of their motherland betrayed politically by England and the United States, on the side of which the Polish Armed Forces fought until Germany's defeat.

In the meantime the Polish Combatants Association in Argentina (Stowarzyazenie Polskich Kombatantów" decided to have its own organ, which as **Nasza Sprawa** (Our Cause) was published as an information bulletin between 1952 and 1956, to be continued as a printed weekly until 1957. And the Polish Educational Association (Polska Macierz Szkolna) issued for its youth a little magazine called Macierzanka. Its twelve issues were published in 1957 and eight issues in 1958.

The year 1957 was a milestone in the post-World War II history of the Polish Argentine press, marked by the establishment of a weekly **Kurier Polski**, with a subtitle "Tygodnik Niezależny na Amerykę Południową". Its ambition was to capture the readers who were dissatisfied with the uneven level and certain attitudes of the **Głos Polski**, organ of the Union of Poles in Argentina. This competition proved profitable for both papers as it raised their cultural standards. **Kurier Polski** was professionally managed by an experienced journalist, Feliks Zahora-Ibianski for fifteen years. It strongly patronized culture and the arts, publishing until 1971, 747 issues. The paper's good reputation could not overcome the death of its editor and financial difficulties, nor could the competitiveness with the **Głos Polski**, which as an organ of Związek Polaków w Argentynie, had a sounder financial status.

Polish-Argentine scouting benefited greatly from a magazine **Młody Las** (Young Forest), professionally edited by Waclaw Blicharski from 1959 till 1971, who during those thirteen years published 67 issues. From among other mass media utilized by the Poles in Argentina were xeroxed bulletins, periodically published by various organizations such as the culturally prestigious Klub Polski and Biblioteka Polska im. Ignacego Domeyki, as well as by the Union of Concentration Camp Victims and the Explorers Andenist Club of the Boy Scouts.

Characteristically, also a private bulletin called **Komunikat** was issued by Czeslaw Ciechoński in 1969. In its seventeen issues it contained the individual viewpoint of the author on various social problems of the Argentine Polonia. Various organizations were also issuing occasional printed publications. Thus, the Singing Association Frederick Chopin in Buenos Aires issued such publications commemorating its fifth, tenth, twentieth, and twenty-fifth anniversaries. The Assnociation of Polish Engineers and Technicians in Argentina issued such a publication on its thirtieth anniversary (1947-1977). Which contains valuable data on the activities of its almost 400 members (110 p). Similarly impressive, published in Polish and Spanish was the **Informator Społeczno-Gospodarczy Polonii w Argentynie** (Socio-Economic Guide of the Argentine Polonia), which was issued by the Polish Combatant Association, commemorating the 50th anniversary of the Związek Polaków w Argentynie in 1977 (304 p). It is a rich informative source for future historians.

Less fortunate was the fate of the monthly **Bóg i Ojczyzna**, organ of the Polish Catholics in Argentina, which passed through various vicissitudes. After the death of Rev. Aleksander Michalik in 1960, who edited it since 1939, it was temporarily managed by the Verbist Friars and since 1962 taken over by Rev. Lucjan Łuszczki, the new Rector of the Polish Catholic Mission, which became it co-publisher. This arbitrary step was counteracted by the president of the Catholic Circle, Aleksander Rawa-Jasiński, who secured from the Argentine authorities confirmation of its ownership by that circle. This led to the interruption of the editorial cooperation, after which this patriotic-religious magazine was again managed by the Verbist Frairs, who in 1973 were replaced by Rawa-Jasinski as editor. These frequent changes and the ambition of the new editor, unfortunately contributed to the gradual downfall of that valuable paper, which on an irregular basis was published until 1976. During the span of thirty-eight years 419 issues were published.

Thus, **Głos Polski** has been since 1971 the only Polish-language weekly and since 1976 the only Polish paper in Argentina. It is not only the organ of the Union of Poles in Argentina, but also the press tribune for all the Polish-Argentine organizations in that country. To these belong: Social Welfare Section (Sekcja Opieki Społecznej, SOS), Polish Educational Society (Polska Macierz Szkolna, PMS), Polish Youth Center (Polski Ośrodek Młodzieżowy, POM), Circle of Polish Artists (Koło Polskich Artystów Plastyków w Argentynie,

KPAPA), Polish Combatant Association (Stowarzyszenie Polskich Kombatantów, SPK), Assn. of War Invalids (Związek Invalidów Wojennych), Assn. of Fr. Chopin (Tow. Śpiewacze im. Fr. Chopina), Polish Club (Klub Polski), Union of Polish Boy Scouts (Związek Harcerstwa Polskiego, ZHP), Our Ballet (Nasz Balet), Our Small Ballet (Nasz Balecik), Chessplayers Club (Klub Szachistów), etc. Also, the performances of the Cabaret "Rewia", more active before than now, were duly recorded.

According to Argentina's press regulations, **Głos Polski** always carries an editorial in Spanish, whether it is a reprint form Argentine press on a Polish subject or an original on a worthy topic. It contains a news section on Polish affairs, as well as news from the whole world. Polish cultural, women's affairs and youth matters receive considerable attention. For several years, this weekly also featured a Spanish section on the activities of the Polish graduates of Argentine universities, and since 1984 another Spanish supplement called "La Joven Polonia" (Young Poland), which is destined for readers who understand little of the Polish language. A separate section called **"Głos Wiary"** (The Voice of Faith) has been edited by the Polish Catholic Mission in Argentina since 1973. Thus, the **Głos Polski** mirrors practically all the aspects of Polish-Argentine political, cultural, and social activities, including Buenos Aires, Gordoba, Misiones, Rosario, and Santa Fe. In spite of progressive social integration into Argentina's society, the Polish ethnic group there is still alive.

Arkady Fiedler and his travels in tropical South America (1928-1979)

Krzysztof Szymonik

This short essay is devoted to an outstanding Polish writer and wayfarer whose peregrinations bring to mind the exploits of Alexander von Humboldt. Although Arkady Fiedler did not share von Humboldt's strictly scientific preoccupations, he did possess, like the famous German, acute powers of observation that enabled him to note the fine points of an exotic landscape. Fiedler not only had the well developed perceptions of a first class reporter, but he also was blessed with a considerable literary talent. That is why Sisyphean exertion is not required when a reader decides to page through one of the Polish author's fascinating accounts of life in South America.

But before the focus is turned towards some of Fiedler's South American travels, mention must be made of pertinent biographical information that can give an accurate picture of this dynamic personality.

According to Professor Edmund S. Urbanski's article, in the Polish-Brazilian weekly **Lud** (No.730) of 1981, entitled **Arkady Fiedler w Ameryce Południowej (1928-1979) (Arkady Fiedler in South America 1928-1979)**, Arkady Fiedler was born in 1894 in Poznan. His academic background included the study of the natural sciences and philosophy at the universities of Poznań, Kraków, and Berlin. Among the factors that pushed Fiedler in the direction of exploration included his work in the natural sciences at the university level and a predisposition to travel. The second factor is best corroborated by the fact that he visited Latin America on eight occasions at different points in time between 1928 and 1979. His first expedition to southern Brazil which took place in 1928-1929 netted 8,000 specimens of Brazilian fauna. Not only was Fiedler's professional interest satiated at this juncture. He also had the opportunity to meet his fellow Poles in the southern Brazilian state of Paraná. This is but one example of how this indefatigable Pole combined hard work in his specialty with broader humanistic and patriotic concerns.

In order to better understand Fiedler, it is necessary to take into account his own preoccupation with émigré Poles who happened to be living in the countries that he visited. Maciej M. Kozlowski's article **Barwny świat Arkadego Fiedlera (The Colorful Wold of Arkady Fiedler)**, 1957, makes note of the Polish element in Fiedler's journeys. Although at the outset the Poles that Fiedler met along the way were chance acquaintances, with time he made it a point to search them out and to investigate their plight. Kozlowski contends that it was because Fiedler wrote about the predicament of Polish settlers in the Brazilian jungle that the public in Poland came to realize the social causes of the Polish emigration that wanted to better its economic position. Fiedler's contribution in this instance was apparent. In Kozlowski's estimation, the Polish traveler informed "thousands of readers" that there was a reason why Poles left their country. It was poverty among the small landholders with very large families.

It should also be mentioned that South America played a special role in Arkady Fiedler's life. Kozlowski is of the opinion that this continent was very close to the Polish explorer. Interestingly, almost half of his books are devoted to this strange and beautiful area. Perhaps this is not unusual given the rich history and the sharp contrasts that characterize it. South America not only produced the culture of the Incas in Peru and the Promethean Simon Bolívar of Venezuela, but also the sophistication of Rio de Janeiro and the surrealistic otherworldliness of Brasília, the architectural marvel of South America.

At this point a digression must be made in order to present the complexity of the continent that occupied such a prominent place in

Arkady Fiedler's life. The realization must be made that South America has the intricacy of a Byzantine mosaic. Neat definitions can in no way do justice to its varied customs and ethnic diversity.

Professor Edmund S. Urbanski's scholarly synthesis entitled **Hispanic America and Its Civilizations. Spanish Americans and Anglo-Americans (1981)** paints a splendid portrait which makes Fiedler's South American odyssey more understandable to those individuals who are not specialists.

Urbanski argues that Hispanic America does in no way resemble a cultural monolith. It does not possess one civilization, but rather many civilizations which are a function of ethnic and biological variables. In those countries where Spanish is spoken and the Catholic Church is highly visible it is a mistake to make the assumption that ethnic and religious uniformity is the norm. On the contrary, there exist many groups and sub-groups which bring their own ethnicity and value systems into the Hispanic context. Hispanic America is not purely Spanish, Indian, Black, and Mestizo civilizations interact with the Creole civilization to create a kaleidoscope whose colors swirl to the lively beat of the emotional Iberian heart.

Urbanski's analysis can easily be carried over to non-Hispanic South American countries such as Brazil and British Guyana. (When Fiedler was making his South American tours Guyana did not have its present republican status). On the one hand there is the Portuguese heritage of the Brazilian giant with its fusion of Indian, Negro, and various white strains, while on the other hand there can be found the small state of British Guyana with its polyglot population of East Indians, Indians, and Blacks. Certainly, neither of these countries can be seen through a simplistic intellectual apparatus which attempts to reduce cultural richness to a few dominant influences, such as the English, the Portuguese or the Indian.

It is with Professor Urbanski's thesis in mind that a trip can now be made with Arkady Fiedler through Brazil and British Guyana. The guide for this adventure is Fiedler's **Spotkałem szczęśliwych Indian (I met Happy Indians)**, 1968. The narrative is colorful and the description of nature quite engaging. It would not be an exaggeration to compare Fiedler's observational powers with those of other writers: Aguilera Malta of Ecuador and Horacio Quiroga of Uruguay, even though all of them somewhat "humanized" the jungle, usually called the "green hell"...

While on route to the new Brazilian capital city of Brasília Fiedler noticed that the white natives of this largest of South American countries who were on the plane with him demonstrated charm and cheerfulness (p.8). Although these were young people (p.8), their emotional buoyancy no doubt revealed something of the Brazilian national ethos.

Fiedler may have consciously preceded his very short segment devoted to Brasília by a reference to the Brazilian youths that he confronted because Brazil's new capital seems to be the very personification of youthful optimism. Fiedler felt that this metropolis was a "creative folly" (p.10). Why? Because of the force of will that had to be exercised in order to build it. Nothing tangible existed (p.10) where Brasília now stands. Absolutely everything, from iron and cement, to food and human beings, had to be transported by air to the wilderness that would serve as (p.10) the foundation for a futuristic city. Fiedler wryly commented that the fantastic architecture of this city could not obfuscate such mundane occurrences as the exchange of gun fire between two senators during the deliberations of the senate in December, 1963 (p.11). The point of contention was a source of illegal funds, which both senators claimed as their own (p.11). The result of the feud was that the warring parties missed each other, but shot a third senator in the process (p.11). It was Napoleon who remarked that it is a short step from the sublime to the ridiculous.

From Brasília Fiedler made his way by air in a northwesterly direction over an almost 2,000 km space of territory to Manaus (p.12). Here he could appreciate the pronounced contrasts in Brazil. Whereas Brasília was a showpiece whose symmetrical buildings seemed to reach for the future, Manaus was something of a backwater. With a population of 150,000 (p. 16), it could hardly be called a well planned town. In fact, one of its most salient features was the lack of maintenance (p. 16). Cracks in the sidewalks, deep holes in the road, and the lack of lighting at night, combined with unbearable heat and humidity, (p. 16) did not give it the appearance of a tropical paradise. The Brazilians called Manaus "the city of the smile" and the "gateway to the green hell" (the second designation being an obvious reference to the surrounding tropical forest). (p.16). In spite of the hellish conditions which seemed to make Manaus' second sobriquet more fitting than the first, Fiedler did not abandon hope and moved on to his next destination in British Guyana.

From Manaus Fiedler flew to Georgetown, the capital and largest city of British Guyana. Although he was quite captivated by the city's atmosphere with its profusion of neglected gardens behind every house and its moving sunsets (p.24), he came on the scene at a time when local political passions were aimed at the British overlords. Anti-British sentiment could be seen, for example on a painted sign which read "White dogs, get out!".

One of the most intriguing aspects of British Guyana was the influx of many ethnic groups during the colony's period of formative development. According to Fiedler, when British planters were forced to free their black slaves in 1833 and the freed men did not agree to remain, new workers were brought to the colony under a contract system, whose conditions were not that much different from slavery (p.21). Indians from India, Chinese laborers, and Portuguese workers from Madeira (p. 21) supplemented the needs of the British growers. However, the Chinese and the Portuguese did not pass the endurance test in the field and freed themselves in order to move into commerce, ultimately forming the wealthy middle class (p.21) in British Guyana. Unfortunately, the Indians from India, for the most part, remained on the land (p.21). Thus, social and monetary inequities among various ethnic groups against the backdrop of British colonial policy contributed to a volatile internal situation.

While in British Guyana Fiedler had the opportunity to see the Arawak Indians. Historically, the Arawaks lived in the vicinity of the Atlantic seacoast and maintained themselves from the river, the forest, and the land (p. 33). They attained a certain measure of affluence, became more refined with time, and soon were considered to be an elite tribe among other Indian tribes (p. 33). Their qualities were appreciated by the white colonizers, and the Arawaks at one point looked after the forests of Dutch expansionists (pp.33-34). They also constituted the first tribe in British Guyana to be converted to Western Christianity (p. 35).

Fiedler's impressions of the Arawak Indians were quite favorable. Because of the zealousness of Anglican missionaries, this tribe exhibited an almost Puritan quality (pp.45-46). For it, religious concerns became the dominant preoccupation (p.46). The ability to have many children was proof of God's grace (p. 46). To raise children in a strict environment was interpreted as being highly pleasing to the Creator (p.46). What a transformation had taken place since the time when these Indians could participate in a mad dance, after the death of a loved one, in which all the revelers beat each other with whips so that an evil demon would not harm the departed (p. 34).

In his book **Zwierzęta z lasu dziewiczego (Animals from the Virgin Forest)**, 1969, Fiedler describes the Coroado Indians in the Ivai region of the state of Parana. They were friendly and helpful in his zoological expedition. In a jungle hamlet Fiedler noticed a little Brazilian ape of the "macao" family, perched on a shoulder of a young Indian girl. He wanted to buy that rare ape, but was refused. Instead, Zinio, the village chieftain, offered the Polish explorer the girl together with the ape, provided that he settle at their "toldo" (settlement)... Very perceptive and of "macho" mentality, the Coroados were superstitious and animistic, and displayed all the virtues and defects of jungle people. More westernized were the "caboclos" (mestizos), the cross breed between the Portuguese and Indians, who are, however, more tricky and less trustful. Fiedler noticed also the same human traits in the Spanish American mestizo in the tropical Ucayali River area in the Peruvian Amazonia. There, a mestizo sold him a wounded sloth for a healthy animal, which shortly died. An infuriated local Indian girl, not sharing his dishonesty did beat him up for this, displaying thus her natural reverence for the jungle's animal world, and compassion for the sloth!

A different impression is gained from Fiedler's another book

Rio de Oro (1978), when he again came in contact with Coroado natives inhabiting the Rio de Oro region. They were unfriendly and suspicious of strangers, remembering the massacre of which they were victims of white Brazilians in the 1920s, who disposed them of their lands. Though unreliable and understandably cautious, they were excellent hunters. After learning of the Pole's peaceful intention, they changed, however, their attitude an became more friendly and even helpful. A useful conclusion can be drawn from these facts. Whereas, the Coroado Indians from the Rio de Oro were still nomadic, these from the Ivai River region were already settled and lived from agriculture, although all of them belonged to the same tribe. The latter were already acculturated, which played a visible role in their behavior. This useful comparison underlines, thus, the values of civilization, although both groups lived in similar ecological and climatic environments.

In similar vain are Fiedler's other novels, especially **Piękna, straszna Amazonia (Beautiful, Frightening Amazonia)**, 1971, which describes the unusual beauty and charm of the rain forest's botanical richness, contrasted with the danger of living there being exposed to millions of insects and hundreds of wild animals. It constitutes a rare combination of impressionistic feelings and the sobriety of an alert explorer. Fiedler's another fascinating novel bears an unusual title **Ryby śpiewają w Ukajali (Fishes Sing in Ucayali)**, 1935, which is the name of a river in the vicinity of which the Polish naturalist conducted his explorations. He relates in it his adventurous experiences, both on that Peruvian waterway and while living among the Peruvian jungle Indians, whose peculiar customs he observed. Of similar travel attraction are his other books: **Wyspa Robinsona (Robinson's Island)**, 1954, **Orinoko (Orinoco)**, 1957, and **Biały jaguar (The White Jaguar)**, 1980, which constitute a true "jungle trilogy". They describe his scholarly adventures in the northern regions of South America and are full of curious events. Not less fascinating is Fiedler's early novel **Zdobywamy Amazonkę (Conquering the Amazon)**, 1937, relating on that region's tropical people and their customs. Due to unusual topics, Fiedler's books were translated into various languages and attained altogether about ten million copies! This great editorial success and public lectures permitted Fiedler to establish a private museum with Indian artifacts and specimens of South American fauna and flora in Puszczykowo. Unfortunately, it was partly destroyed during the German invasion of Poland in 1939.

Professor Ignacy Domeyko in Chile (1838-1889)

Marceli Charaszkiewicz

A famous geologist, explorer and the author of many scientific works dealing with mining, chemistry and physics worked in Chile for about 50 years. Born in Lithuania in 1802, he received his higher education at the University of Wilno, where he secured an MA degree in 1822. This institution was then at the pinnacle of its excellence. It was due mainly to the fact that professors there turned out to be of the highest caliber, such as brothers Jan and Andrzej Śniadecki, Joachim Lelevel, Horodowski and Niemcewicz. Domeyko himself was majoring in geology and mining under strong influence of his uncle Joseph. During the course of his studies, he became very friendly with the future great Polish poet and patriot Adam Mickiewicz. He joined the secret student patriotic organizations dominated by our poet and his close associates such as Jan Czeczot and Korsak. For their patriotic work Domeyko and Mickiewicz were jailed by the Russians, and remained a few years under the Tsarist surveillance.

When the greatest Polish uprising broke out in November 1830, he joined as a volunteer the forces of Gen. Chłapowski fighting the Russian enemy. After its defeat, Domeyko left for Prussia where he was temporarily interned. Later he went to Dresden where he met Mickiewicz. Together they travelled to France which, at the time of Partitions, was the focal point for many Polish intellectuals and patriots. Domeyko lived in Paris from 1832 until 1838 where he was continuing studies in mathematics and physics. In 1837, he graduated from the Parisian School of Mining receiving a diploma of Mining

Engineer. Thus, mining became his specialty.

While in Paris, Domeyko was the first person allowed by Mickiewicz to read the first rough draft of his famous immortal poem, "Pan Tadeusz." Our poet respected Domeyko's opinion very highly.

At this period of his life, Domeyko prepared a physiographic map of Poland and wrote scientific tract in French titled: "Essay on Hydrography, Geology and the Natural Resources of Poland." Hard to believe, but it was the first authentic physiographic synthesis of the Polish country. Amazingly enough, this work was translated into Polish and published only in 1929.

In the first half of the 19th century, the Spanish colonies in South America managed to gain independence through a series of revolutions and armed struggle against the Spanish overlords. Independence in turn created a burning necessity to build up their own educational institutions. Of course, to achieve this goal, they looked to Europe which was then the fountainhead of modern learning for the world. That's why our Domeyko was offered an opportunity to teach chemistry and mineralogy at the College of Coquimbo, which he accepted and signed a contract for six years. While teaching, at the same time he also conducted practical exploration for natural resources in the Chilean mountains.

But, like many other Polish patriots, he was deeply afflicted with the nostalgia for his native Poland. He never gave up the idea to return and planned to do so after his contract with the government expired. Thus, with this thought firmly in mind, he was thoroughly educating a cadre of the young Chilean geologists who should be able to continue his scientific work after Domeyko's departure.

But fate, as it often happens in the human life, interfered and due to some unexpected events, changed completely his plans. One was an explosion of a nearby volcano. The other one was a fire that destroyed totally his lab in Coquimbo. It had to be rebuilt, but this time on grounds of the newly created University of Santiago in 1843. Also, he was given a task of activating the educational reform that he proposed previously to the government of Chile.

Getting deeply involved in such important projects firmly

IGNACIO DOMEYKO

MEMORIAS

RECUERDOS DE UN EMIGRADO

Traducción al castellano de
la versión francesa por
MANUEL DE FERRARI
(Juan Carrera)

VOLUMEN PRIMERO

PRENSAS DE LA UNIVERSIDAD DE CHILE
1946

Chile: The scientific impact of the Polish mineralogist-chemist Ign. Domeyko on Chile where he spent ca. 50 years (1838-1889), also his influence on the Chilean cultural development, are still deeply felt in that country. An example of many publications dedicated to him is a book **Memorias, recuerdos de un emigrado** (1964) i. e. *Memoirs, Reflections of an Emiegré,* translated from French into Spanish by the Rector of the National University in Santiago, and published by the University Press.

cemented his ties to the adopted country of Chile which eventually became his second motherland. While in Santiago, his time was split between lecturing in chemistry, physics and geology. Also he worked hard preparing his program for proposed modernization of the higher education. Then he undertook many scientific exploration trips into the surrounding mountains and accepted a quite important role of the mediator in disputes between miners and the management.

Contrary to nearby Peru where San Marcos University was established back in the 16th century, Chile lacked a university. Newly created University of Santiago wasn't so much an institution of higher learning as it was administrative center for the Chilean network of schools. Thus, transforming this bureaucratic center into a modern institution of higher learning patterned on the contemporary European models, like the French Sorbonne or his Alma Mater University of Wilno, wasn't easy at all. But Domeyko put all his heart into this effort taking advantage of his European experience and succeeded to his greatest satisfaction that comes from a job well done.

It was greatly appreciated by the Chilean government which, in recognition of his achievements for that country, bestowed upon him Chilean citizenship in 1848. In 1850 professor Domeyko married señorita Enriqueta Sotomayor Guzman. Consequently they became parents of several children: first was a daughter Anna, then son Leon who later became a member of the Chilean Congress. Another son, Hernando, went into the priesthood. A third son, Casimiro, became afterwards the founder of a Mining School. Still later he was holding the position of a Chilean consul abroad. Then, as a result of Casimiro's marriage with señorita Dominga Alamos de la Cuadra in 1889, the Chilean branch of the Domeyko clan grew quite a lot in numbers. One of Casimiro's sons, Juan Domeyko, held a position of the Chilean consul in San Francisco, California and later as an ambassador to Australia.

While residing in California in the 1950's, he met Professor Edmund Urbanski who taught at the University of San Francisco and who thus learned the colorful story of the Domeyko's clan in Chile.

Another great honor for Professor Domeyko came in 1867

when he was elected President of the Santiago University. He accepted it and consequently was holding this position for sixteen years until 1883, considerably improving the Chilean learning system.

Domeyko's scientific creativity was quite extensive and covers about 130 bibliographic positions in several fields. They were written in Spanish, French, Polish and German. These works were published in the scientific journals of several American and European countries, in addition to a few books.

The majority of his work covers his specialty which is geology. But he was also involved in the chemistry, meteorology, ethnic problems and in studies over the volcanic activity. All of that emphasizes his extensive mental horizons. In addition, he was the author of many textbooks on physics, geology, and hydrotherapy used for the learning purposes in Latin America and Spain.

In 1840, Professor Domeyko discovered in Chile another variety of the silver ore that yielded a very large percentage of this precious metal. It was called "arequita" in Spanish. Another mineral discovered by him was in turn named "domeykit" by an Austrian scientist, W. Haidinger. This mineral was a mixture of the copper ore and arsen.

In 1846, Professor Domeyko created the first geological map of Chile. Then, against convictions of Darwin and Humboldt, he proved appearance of the juraic formation in the Andes. He also noticed a rise of the western South American coast in the geological past and as the first European conducted studies of the volcanic areas in Chile, often under highly dangerous conditions. But it should be pointed out that the most important scientific discovery of his life from the practical viewpoint was finding rich deposits of silver ore and coal. This, in turn, served as a base for development of the mining industry and iron melting.

As his notes show, Professor Domeyko also investigated chemical contents of the local mineral springs. He even wrote a thesis on this subject. That was his contribution to the therapeutic medicine.

In 1845, Domeyko organized an ethnographic expedition to the area in Chile inhabited by the warlike Araucanian Indians. This tough tribe was only partly conquered by Spaniards. A very large segment of Araucanians stubbornly refused to recognize the Chilean authority over the land until the middle of the 19th century. Their stubborness caused authorities to get involved in the genocide action while attempting to subdue the proud Indians. Domeyko opposed this in his book, **Araucania y sus habitantes** (1845), published later in Polish (Wilno, 1860), in which he described these Indians' customs and traditions. Professor Domeyko strongly influenced the Chilean opinion towards adopting a more positive attitude regarding the Indian tribes. Acts of genocide were halted and the Indian population began to increase. Also, their economic conditions improved without the constant warfare.

After retiring from his position as the University Rector, the Chilean government rewarded him with a quite large pension and paid a tribute emphasizing that "Señor Domeyko was much more than a professor. He became an apostle of science in Chile." Also a gold medal was struck with his bust and inscription „Knowledge-Work-Unselfishness." About twenty years later, in 1903, his scientific works were published by the Santiago University in five volumes.

Domeyko left for Poland in 1884. After arrival in his native country, he was welcomed heartily and with a great pride. Some better educated people already were informed about his scientific achievements in South America. For his countrymen, he was a symbol of a great scientist covered with glory in South America.

Professor Domeyko settled in the country home of his daughter and started writing his memoirs. But that didn't prevent him from making a trip to France, Italy and the Holy Land.

The Polish Academy of Science in Kraków made him an honorary member. Professor Domeyko symbolized the Polish pride. Consequently, the old Jagiellonian University presented him with the honorary degree of "Doctor of Medicine," which added to the cluster of honors received from other respected institutions abroad.

In 1888, Professor Domeyko made a trip to Chile, his adoptive country, taking with him his sons who, by then, finished their studies in Europe. He died in Santiago on January 23 at the age of 87. He was buried there at the expense of the Chilean government. In 1902, grateful Chilean citizens funded a marble monument with Domeyko's bust, which was placed on his grave. His memory is immortalized through naming one of the mountain ranges as "Cordillera Domeyko," then a mountain peak acquired the name of "Cerro Domeyko" and one of the seaports became "Puerto Domeyko."

Between 1946 and 1950 the University of Santiago published two volumes of Domeyko's memoirs under the title, "Memoirs of an Exile." During the 150th anniversary of his birth, Chile printed a special commemorative stamp with Domeyko's bust.

In spite of almost 50 years spent in Chile, Domeyko never lost contact with the country of his birth and Polish friends like Adam Mickiewicz. Between the years of 1857 and 1889, he was sending regularly interesting observations and essays to periodicals published in Poland. As far as they didn't contain political material, the Russian censorship left them without interference.

Materials and notes covering his experiences in Poland and abroad are collected in nine volumes that are presently in the archives of the Polish Academy of Science in Krakow. Thanks to this collection, it was possible to publish five volumes under the title: "Ignacy Domeyko: My Trips, Memoires of an Exile." It was published in Wroclaw by the Ossolineum Publishing house in Warsaw in 1976.

The other bibliographic position is "Letters to Wladyslaw Laskowicz" published by the Catholic publishing house Pax in Warsaw in 1976.

In addition to his scientific talents, Domeyko was also a sharp observer of individuals and nations with which he was personally acquainted. They are observations of the sociological nature testifying to the broadness of his keen mind.

Relatively speaking, Domeyko wasn't too well known in Poland itself. Only in the last quarter of the 19th Century he became much better known when he visited his beloved Lithuania plus Krakow and Warsaw in the 1880s.

Scientific and human activities of Professor Domeyko puts him in the vanguard of the South American scientists, position that he richly deserved. As such, he is noted in the Latin American scientific journals, which usually consider him a Pole but sometimes also as a Chilean that he was through acquired citizenship and total dedication to his work. The Spanish edition of the "Encyclopedia Larousse" considers him a chemist. On account of his work about the Araucanian Indians he is also noted in the scientific ethnographic literature. This work and observations are now and then quoted by various anthropologists, thanks to the fact that it appeared in several languages.

This essay should end with the words of a Hispanic writer, Rubén Darío, who wrote about Domeyko: "His scientific works introduced the country of Chile to Europe. Also he was the tutor to three generations and left a monument to the general knowledge."

The Father of White Gold: Activities of Dr. Waclaw Szumkowski in Venezuela (1948-1967)

Krystyna Mickiewicz-Unkiewicz
(Venezuela)

When you look back, there is always one person in your life that has helped shape your future interests and maybe even your entire career. For me that person was my grandfather, Dr. Waclaw Szumkowski, of who I will speak to you today.

Back as a child I remember visiting his laboratory and observing for the first time tiny unicellular life forms found in pond water. I remember the thrill of seeing these tiny creatures - a thrill of biological observation which has stayed with me thanks to him.

My grandfather was a biologist. He had a rather unusual career in that he really started practicing his scientific vocation in full after his 50th birthday - a true mid-life career move. This was quite a serendipidous occurrence, as a result of World War II.

But let me now give you some background. My grandfather was born in 1889 in Prepunty, Poland. His biological interests led him to the Sorbonne University where he obtained his doctorate degree in Biology in 1914, specializing in entomology.

In 1919 he returned home to manage his family's estate which after World War I was in Lithuanian hands. There in the early 1920's he was a member of the commission for the quality control of seed production.

By the end of 1944 he was forced to flee his native home when the Russian troops took over the estate. Through Austria he found himself with his family in Germany at the end of the war. There he was appointed by the Polish government in exile in London in 1945 to head up a team whose function was to locate Polish youth in the English and American zones of occupied sectors of Germany and to place them in universities so they could finish their studies which were interrupted by the war. This function he fulfilled for four years.

Then, upon the recommendation of friends who had made the trek earlier, at the age of 57 he went to seek a new life in Venezuela.

Once in Venezuela he joined the Entomology Department of the National Agricultural Institute. Later he was named head of the section dealing with the cotton crop.

His efforts soon began to be centered on two main issues: how to produce a better quality crop and how to prevent its destruction by various pests. It is because of this second goal that he started to investigate biological and non-chemical way to eradicate these pests.

During this process he conducted various field trails. To do so he first had to find suitable locations, which led him to travel all around the country from the snow-covered Andes Mountains to the plains with temperatures in the 100's. These travels led him to start his field trials in more traditional places such as in the states of Turen, Acarigua and Portegera. Later he decided to try more remote territories along the Orinoco River, places so remote that they had neither roads nor airports. These long, hard journeys to the heart of the country led him to places where few others had entered before. His mode of transportation on these journeys varied: jeeps, donkeys, helicopters, dug-out wooden boats with attached motors.

Still rigorous for his age, he would make these treks to the countryside even when he was in his 60's and 70's. On these journeys there was also the constant threat of tropical diseases and unfriendly fauna. On one of these trips he developed an attack of Dengue fever which is a tropical disease carried by mosquitoes and which causes severe joint pain and fever. It was so severe that he had to be air-lifted to a hospital. Another time he required treatment for rabies after being bitten by a bat.

In between these field trips he was able to formulate an

artificial diet for the laboratory development of the lady bug, which he found was the best natural enemy of the cotton crop pests.

He was also able to publish a grand total of 39 articles. These publications dealt mostly with pests endemic to Venezuela and especially those infesting the cotton crop. He also devoted several articles to the concept of biological control.

He represented Venezuela in many international meetings like the 9th and 10th International Congress of Entymology which was held in 1951 and 1960 in Amsterdam. In 1955 he was elected member of the Royal Society of Entymologists in London and then in 1965 he became a co-founder of the Venezuelan Society of Entymology.

His efforts at finding a biological way of combating the cotton crop problem were successful. The quality of the resultant cotton, was second only to the the Egyptian cotton. This later translated to a net income from exports of 30 million bolivars a year.

The Venezuelan government awarded him an honorary diploma and the celebrated Great Cross of Ceres for all his contributions over the 20 years that he was employed. A village in the Orinoco was named after him. For their part, the villagers used to warmly call him the "Father of White Gold" after the variety of long fiber cotton that was finally able to be cultivated.

At the age of 75, still in the fullness of health and active research he died in a tragic car accident. He was coming back from Caracas where he was preparing his last article on biological methods to combat pests. His memory still lives on in our family and in the Venezuelan Department of Agronomy which still displays a bronze plague in his honor.

The Polish-Mexican Writer Elena Poniatowska And Her Literary Achievements

Janina Kusielewicz

Who is Elena Poniatowska Haro? Is she French, Mexican, American, Polish, all, or none of the above? A journalist, a poet? I would like to present to you a short discussion of Elena Poniatowska's life, works and the multicultural influences that shaped her personal, spiritual and literary development. Who is she? Let's find out.

Elena Poniatowska was born on May 19, 1933 in Paris to Paula Amor and Jan Poniatowski. Her father's family came to France from Poland during the 18th century. She is a descendant of Prince Jan Poniatowski, Marshall of France under Napoleon and of course Poland's last king: Stanisław August. Her grandfather Andrzej Poniatowski, himself a well known writer, left France to found the Pacific Sierra Railway in San Francisco, only to return to raise his children in Europe. Her mother is a French-born Mexican descendant of Russian aristocracy. Elena Idaroll, a Russian Countess and Mexican landowner Felipe Iturbe, were her great-grandparents. Her maternal grandmother was known in European aristocratic circles as "la madonna de los sleeping", because she travelled by train throughout France, Great Britain and Spain, raising her children in hotels.

In an interview Elena Poniatowska stated that "all this rootlessness (in my background) affected me as a child and I wanted to belong to (one) country" (Gazarian, 204).

This eclectic heritage caused her to feel culturally unrelated to any one place. She wanted desperately to give herself a tangible nationality. When she was eight years old she moved to Mexico with her mother and sister. Once her family had settled in Mexico she took advantage of the chance to identify herself with one country and proceeded to make herself fully Mexican. In adopting a Mexican identity, she adopted Mexico's troubles. She became Mexican in spirit, and as such, dedicated herself to voicing injustices within her adoptive homeland in both her journalistic writings and novels.

Although she considers herself Mexican, she is very proud of her Polish heritage. She uses her Polish surname in all of her writings, albeit married to Mexican astrophysicist Guillermo Haro. She went to a French school in Mexico and later a Convent school in Philadelphia. Growing up her languages were French and English. She learned colloquial Mexican Spanish from the servants, not through formal study. Her education was multilingual, yet Polish was not included. When I asked why she never learned Polish, she responded: "Polish is my heritage. I learned individual words "jabłko" "sufit" and "widelec", but Polish was never my everyday life. I set out to be Mexican and focused on that which surrounded me. Perhaps I will learn Polish, but it seems difficult. I have been to Poland and was very impressed with the spirit of the people ... making, me proud of my (Polish) forefathers".

Her respect for Poland and her Polish heritage, provides us with a glimpse of the passion with which she approaches her adopted homeland. In adopting Mexico, she adopted the pain of the oppressed, the silenced and the marginals. She has dedicated herself to the defense of human rights and has been called "la voz del pueblo" (the voice of the people) for her impassioned journalistic writings. In 1954, against her father's wishes (he wanted her to use her linguistic talents as a secretary), she entered the field of journalism. Her first position was as a reporter for **Excelsior,** one of Mexico's foremost newspapers. By, 1957 she not only had a reputation as an effective interviewer, but also graduated from the "Centro Mexicano de Escritores", eventually receiving a Master's Degree in Literature and Journalism. In 1978 she received the "Premio Nacional de Periodismo", a much coveted Mexican Journalism award, for her unique interviewing style. Her articles and interviews have appeared in many newspapers and magazines such as **Novedades, El Día, Siempre!, Mañana, Artes de México** (Camacho-Gingerich, 534) among others. As a journalist she has had the opportunity to interact with a wide variety of literary, cultural and political figures. In 1961 she published **Palabras Cruzadas** a series of essays based on interviews and conversations with Juan Rulfo, Diego de Rivera, Alfonso Reyes and Lázaro Cardenas. The work **Domingo 7** is a collection of her interviews with the presidential candidates for the 1982 elections in Mexico and is representative of her singular interrogative style. Her journalistic endeavors continue today, most recently with a series of interviews entitled **Todo México** published in 1990. Her journalistic prowess is exemplified in her biographies. Her 1963 biography **Todo empezó el domingo** was the result of one year spent watching the artist Alberto Beltrán draw and paint. She was asked to write a screenplay about Tina Modotti, the lover of the photographer Edward Weston, this developed into a decade long project. Finally, in 1992, the six hundred and sixty three page biography **Tinisima** was published. She jokingly told me that "this heavy book is a brick to throw at someone , if for nothing else my years of research are a good (self-defense) weapon".

Elena Poniatowska is not just a journalist but an author as well.

Both her literary and journalistic careers began in 1954, have shared a parallel evolution. Her first literary work **Lilus Kikus,** was published in the collection **Los Presentes** which featured pieces by such authors as Octavio Paz and Carlos Fuentes. This publication coincided with the beginning of her journalistic career at **Excelsior.** The apparent dichotomy between these two opposing careers, between the presentation of fact and the creation of fiction, has influenced her work throughout her career. Even fictional books such as **La "Flor de Lis"** show evidence of strong realistic and journalistic influences. Her compassion for the oppressed and the persecuted also influences. Among other books, she rails against social personal tragedy in her chronicles: **La noche de Tlatelolco, testimonios de historia oral** deals with media suppression of the 1968 student massacre where over two hundred protesting students were slaughtered while the world sat idly, watching the Olympics (this volume has had more than forty-two editions in several languages since its first release in 1971); **Fuerte es el Silencio** (1980) describes Mexico's social and political climate in a series of essays reflecting events such as hunger strikes by mothers of the "desaparecidos" and the 1968 student movement; **Nada, Nadie,** published in 1988, deals with the September 1985 earthquake and its aftermath; **Angeles de la ciudad** and **La colonia Rubén Jamarillo** bring to light the intolerable situation of the poorest Mexicans in the streets. In **Gabby Brimmer** published in 1979, she speaks about her experiences working with a high spirited paraplegic woman whose only method of communication is to spell words using her toe to point out the letters (impressively, Gabby Brimmer happened to co-author this work).

In an interview with our mutual friend, Dr. Gazarian-Gautier, Elena explained the political philosophy behind the vocal defense of the oppressed that is so often her inspiration to write:

> Poniatowska: The only posture that I have maintained through the years is my defense of the weak and oppressed of the earth. I believe that everything is political, and as such should concern all of us. Authors who claim they don't deal with politics in their work are being naive because even that is a political stance.
>
> (Gazarian-Gautiert, 207)

Elena Poniatowska represents her country through her literary chronicles, or better yet "political works", since, according to her, everything is political.

Even her narratives reflect reality and demonstrate journalistic influences. **Hasta no verte Jesús mio** (1969) (for which she received the "Premio Mazatlan"), documents the life of an uneducated woman, Jesusa Palancares, who played an important role in the Mexican Revolution. This fictional story is based directly on a real "Jesusa" who insisted upon remaining anonymous after Poniatowska interviewed her. **Querido Diego, te abraza Quiela,** a 1978 romantic epistolary story, is based on Diego Rivera's lover Angelina Beloff. **De noche vienes** (1979), a volume of romantic stories narrated by women, hones her skill of intertwining romance with realism. She has said of her book **¡Ay vida, no me merèces!** (1985) that her writing was "Fuentesized" like that of the rest of her generation. Although the influences of Carlos Fuentes are evident, Elena Poniatowska's unique perspective dominates. And, of course, the 1988 novel **La "Flor de Lis"** is based on her own life.

In addition to her endeavors as novelist and biographer, Elena Poniatowska has expressed herself in other genres as well. In 1955 she wrote a dramatic stage comedy entitled **Melés y Teleo,** a play on words translated as "You read me and I read you" She also penned book of poetry, **Rojo de vida y negro de muerte,** from which three poems were chosen to appear in Carlos Ciccioli's anthology. Her artistic creativity and vivid imagination are combined with journalistic flair in her photo-journalistic productions. Among her photo-journalistic books are: **Juchitán de las Mujeres,** published in 1991; **Compañeras de México: women photograph women,** written in collaboration with Amy Conger; and **La casa en la tierra,** a purely visual collection put together with Mariana Yamplonsky (Elena's cousin on the Poniatowski side, who married a Polish Frenchman).

Her works are genre spanning, always reflecting her personal journalistic/literary style. Each piece carries the unique stamp that only someone with her multicultural background and experiences could have. She is simultaneously involved in pure journalism, "new journalism" (also known as testimonial literature) and literary creativity. One cannot categorize her works, or the evolution of her individual style, sequentially. Rather, this all must be taken into account like a collage growing outward from one central point: her soul.

When asked why she writes, she claims that she herself does not know. But the answer to this can be found in her opinion of writing itself. In response to the question:

> Interviewer: Do you view writing as a social weapon or a form of pleasure?

Poniatowska: I think writing is like an instrument of love. Writing is a link established with other beings, over time and oceans, who identify with what you write.

(Gazarian-Gautier, 214)

To write is to communicate and communication is the only way to inform, to influence and to change the status quo.

Literature is the mirror of our time and journalism its reportage. The collage of Elena Poniatowska's talents presents to the world the contemporary history of Mexico and its population. Although she considers herself a Mexican, the Polish blood in Elena Poniatowska's veins is evident in her fiercely nationalistic and idealistic attittudes toward her volatile adoptive country. Her nationalistic yet multicultural attitudes are respected worldwide. Most of her books have been translated into French, some into English and even one **Hasta no verte Jesús mio** into Polish. Only Poniatowska herself could fill the shoes of "voice of the people" so well.

Elena feels that all literature has autobiographical elements. **Lilus Kikus,** her first published fiction, was influenced by her experiences and is based on a childhood friend. Her 1988 novel **La "Flor de Lis"** however, is considered by many to be her autobiography. This narrative begins with a prose portrait of an aristocratic vicissitudes of WWII. When the plot places the family into the "expatriate French community in Mexico, the contrast between the European mantle of 'civilization' and the grubby Mexican sarape of barbarism brings about a cultural and political crisis in the family that war did not precipitate" (WLT, 14). Repeatedly, the young protagonist Mariana (Elena herself) defends her Mexican identity. One such interlude is as follows:

—Pero ta no eres de Mexico ¿verdad?
(You are not Mexican are you?)
—Si soy.
(Yes I am.)
— Es que no pareces mexicana.

(It's just that you don't look Mexican.)
—Ah si entonces ¿que parezco?
(Oh, then what do I look like?)
—Gringa.
(A Gringo.)
—Pues no soy gringa, soy mexicana.
(Well,I'm not a Gringo. I am a Mexican!)
—No se te ve.
(You don't look it.)
—Soy mexicana porque mi madre es mexicana; si la nacionalidad de la madre se heredera como la del padre, sería mexicana.
(I am Mexican because my mother is Mexican; if nationality were inherited from the mother as it is from the father than I would be Mexican.)
—De todos modos, no eres de México.
(Anyway, you're not from Mexico)
—Soy de México porque quiero serlo, es mi país.
(I am from Mexico because I want to be, it is my country.)

(Flor,75)

Even this fictional counterpart, expresses Elena's fierce attachment to her adoptive homeland. Such burning nationalistic passion again reflects the fiery and spirited Polish blood in her veins.

This "novelized" biography of her family, hints at her Polish heritage. She mentions a Polish cousin Vladimir (Flor, 26) thought to be based on one of the Poniatowski family who remained in France. In a section defending her upbringing, Mariana states that she descended from "una buena familia aristocrética y regal" (a good royal aristocratic family), implying her relationship to Poland's last King. Mariana's education, as recounted in the book, parallels that of Elena. She lists her favorite authors and among them we find the Polish writer Brandys. In an interview, Elena had stated that she was most influenced by French Catholics like Leon Bloy and Daniel Rops. But Brandys, too, had a strong affect on her. She says of Polish literature that "it is very intense literature of heroic zeal, such as that of Brandys which has have an overwhelming desire to have heroes who carry out exploits." (Gazarian-Gautier, 213). Her interest in intensely heroic literature is mentioned in this autobiographical fiction but is also reflected in Elena's own writing style.

Within **La "Flor de Lis",** is a religious subtext referring to "el culto de la virgen". During a discussion I had with the author about Mexico's rich folk heritage, parallels were drawn between these references to "La Madona mexicana" and the Polish virgin cult surrounding "Matka Boska Czestochowska" (the Black Madonna of Czestochowa). Interestingly, in 1991, in Warsaw, a sensational collection of Polish and Mexican folk art representing these two cults of the Madonna was put on exhibit.

The autobiographical influences in this novel are subtle. But the parallels in the life of the protagonist Mariana and Elena herself are quite obvious. References to her Polish heritage are implied rather than explicitly stated.

But pride in these roots is nonetheless apparent. Elena Poniatowska may consider herself Mexican, but her multicultural upbringing allows her to respect her Polish heritage. It is said that art imitates life. In the case of Elena Poniatowska, the reverse also holds true. The many cultural influences provided by her eclectic family and the multilingual atmosphere in which she was raised, gave Elena a perspective of the world few other have had. She was effectively able to choose her homeland, yet the multiethnic tapestry of her life remains apparent in her attitudes and her style of writing. She was asked:

> Interviewer: Both your narrative and journalistic work blend the genres of letter writing, the interview, the chronicle, the diary, the picturesque story, and poetry into a highly original collage. How did you find your style?
>
> Her response was:
>
> Poniatowska: "My style derives from my daily life. In the first place, I was not born in Mexico but in France, and this accounted for my great interest and curiosity in everything that surrounded me, particularly the language of the people, which was a very new one for me. Before learning Spanish, I spoke French and a little English. I was born into a French family of Polish origin. (And after all) among my ancestors was the last King of Poland."
>
> (Gazarian-Gautier, 204)

Our much esteemed Dr. Urbanski included Elena Poniatowska Haro in his two volume work **Sylwetki Polskie w Ameryce Łacińskiej w XIX i XX Wieku.** He calls her a Polish-Mexican writer. Based on the influence her heritage has had on her life, work and literary style, she deserves this distinction. Earlier I posed the question "Who is Elena Poniatowska?" She is a talented, captivating, righteous journalist and author. A wife, mother and a socio-cultural representative. Elena Poniatowska is not simply some Mexican writer of Polish descent, she is the respected, passionate Polish-Mexican voice of her people.

Works Consulted

Gazarian-Gautier, Marie-Lise. **Interviews with Latin American Writers.** Dalkey Archive: Illinois, 1989.

Kusielewicz, Janina. Interview with Elena Poniatowska. New York, April 1991, May .1993.

Poniatowska Haro, Elena.**¡Ay vida, no me mereces!.** Mortiz: México, 1985.

De noche vienes. Grijalbo: México, 1979.

Domingo 7. Oceano: México, 1982.

Gaby Brimmer. Grijalbo: México, 1970

La "Flor de Lis" Era: México. 1988.

Hasta no verte Jesús mio. Era: México 1969.

Nada, Nadie. Era: México, 1988.

La noche de Tlatelolco, testimonios de historia oral. Era: México, 1971.

Palabras Cruzadas. Era: México, 1961.

Quierido Diego, te abraza Quiela. Era: México, 1978.

Tinisima. Era: Mexico, 1992.

Todo empezó el domingo. FCE: México, 1963.

Urbanski, Edmund S. **Sylwetki polskie w Ameryce Łacińskiej XIX i XX wieku.** Artex: Wisconsin, 1991.

Writer Andrzej Bobkowski in Guatemala: 1947-1961

Edward Kaminski

Andrzej Bobkowski was a Polish émigré writer whose post-war activities are perhaps better known among Polish exile circles in Europe than in America. The fortunate fact that his Guatemalan papers were recently bequeathed to PIASA, enables us now to present his literary profile with more clarity and in a comprehensive way, especially since his writings are scattered in various European publications.

Andrzej, son of Henryk Bobkowski and Stanisława Malinowska, was born on October 27, 1913, in Wiener Neustadt, Austria. His father was an instructor in the Theresianische Military Academy in Vienna, and later served with Pilsudski's Legions during the First World War. Following the conclusion of hostilities, he joined the regular Polish Army and participated in the struggle for Polish independence. During the inter-war period, he rose to the rank of general. The family eventually settled in Cracow where Andrzej graduated from St. Anne's Gimnazjum. Later he completed his studies at the Wyższa Szkoła Handlowa in Warsaw.

In 1939 Andrzej married Barbara Birtus. Shortly afterwards - thanks to the assistance of Viceminister Alexander Bobkowski - the couple left for Paris where Andrzej planned to continue his studies. When the war broke out, Bobkowski reported for military service but was not called up due to the flood of Polish refugees. He began work in the Atelier de Construction de Chatillon as a social worker. He was in charge of taking care of the needs of the many Polish workers employed at the plant. When Paris fell, he went with the Chatillon group to southern France. In the meantime, his wife remained in the capital. Two months later, convinced that his chance of an escape to Spain were quite meager, he decided to return to Paris to continue his work among the Polish workers. He took a job with the commercial liquidation office of the Atelier de Construction de Chatillon.

Col. Chapelle, the head of the office, together with Dr. Kozianski and Bobkowski, established an organization to provide secret help to Polish workers in Paris and its vicinity. Bobkowski's work mainly consisted of preparing papers and work permits, finding employment and obtaining funds. This was done with the express purpose of preventing the deportation of Poles to Germany for forced labor. Considerable risk was entailed, for Bobkowski had to make many visits to German military and Gestapo headquarters. In a biographical sketch, Barbara Bobkowska declared that it was difficult to understand how the Germans never learned of his activities, nor of those of the Chatillon underground cell.

When the war ended, Bobkowski found employment as a warehouseman for the Y.M.C.A. in Paris and later worked as a bicycle repairman. At the same time, he participated in the activities of "Niepodległość i Demokracja", as well as in those of the Paris branch of Gen. Anders' Polish Second Corps. He also edited the weekly **Biuletyn Informacyjny** and collaborated with **Kultura** under the direction of Jerzy Giedroyc. And it is in this newly-born émigré publication that Bobkowski's first literary essays appeared.

During the German occupation of France, Bobkowski kept a diary in which he described the more important events taking place in France and those directly concerned with his own life. This diary was published by **Kultura** (Paris, 1957) under the title **Szkice Piórkiem** (Sketches with a Quill). Prior to publication, however, he had eliminated certain pages dealing with his conspirational work, stating that he did not wish to praise himself. Bobkowski had recorded his wartime journal in several notebooks and these, fortunately, were preserved by his wife. Following her death, Bobkowski's diary and other personal papers were turned over to PIASA where they were placed in the Polish-Latin American Collections. This valuable contribution was made possible through the good offices of attorney Sierpinski.

As a Pole who was dedicated to the ideal of Polish independence, Bobkowski was deeply affected by the Allied betrayal of Poland into the hands of the Soviets. His war-time journal shows that he was also disheartened with Vichy France. As a result of this disenchantment with Europe, he and his wife decided to leave for Guatemala in June of 1947. According to Kazimierz Wierzynski, Bobkowski chose this Central American country because he didn't know anything about it, and because he felt that it would be most unlike Europe. He wished to start a new life, change his environment and seek new cultural horizons. These horizons were undoubtedly expanded, for as a European he came in contact with the Latin American mentality and the influence exerted on this frame of mind by the United States.

Consequently, Bobkowski extended the range of his literary topics. He now began to write novelettes and short stories with a Central American background. The majority of these stories deal with Guatemala and its Indian-mestizo population, culture and exotic customs. He also thoroughly familiarized himself with the politico-social system of the country. As a result, he concluded that Guatemala - aside from exotica - had a Spanish cultural heritage, as was true of the other Central American countries. It should be noted here that Bobkowski did not know Spanish when he arrived in Guatemala. In a comparatively short time, however, he mastered the language, being aided in this endeavor by his reading of Salvador de Madariaga's historical works.

This is how Barbara Bobkowska described the initial period of their stay in Guatemala: "We arrived in Guatemala with only one hundred dollars in our pockets. The beginnings were very difficult. Andrzej fell on the idea of constructing airplane models. After a number of years, he succeeded in opening his own shop. Almost from the start, he was surrounded by a group of young enthusiasts of airplane modeling. Soon the first Club Aeromodelista Guatemalteco was founded in Guatemala City. These youngsters were very fond of their 'querido Bob' (dear Bob) and respected him like a father and best friend. He not only taught them a beautiful sport, but was also a teacher of moral principles. He developed their minds, and demanded of them hard work and a spirit of fellowship."

The Bobkowskis grew very fond of Guatemala and it quickly became their second homeland. They became Guatemalan citizens and made many friends. They were particularly close to the family of Dr. Julio Quevedo whose four sons had taken up airplane modeling. The Quevedos referred to Andrzej as "Bob" and held him in the highest esteem.

The Bobkowskis also came in contact the small Polish colony in the capital. Of the Poles with whom they socialized, the writer mentioned Jozef Flach, identifying others only by their initials. One of the most interesting of the latter group was Leszek M., a former Lieutenant in the Polish People's Army. He had witnessed the terror unleashed by the Communist regime of Boleslaw Bierut and had decided to escape. In 1948 he successfully crossed the border and eventually made his way to Guatemala. There he married a local teacher and bought a piece of land. A few years later his only tractor was confiscated by the leftist junta of Col. Jacobo Arbenz. As an ardent foe of communism, he joined the guerrilla forces of Col. Castillo Armas as an arms instructor. In 1954, Leszek M. entered the capital with the victorious guerrillas.

Andrzej Bobkowski's stay in Guatemala was marked by a period of intense literary activity. His creativity was uncommonly fruitful, particularly in light of his material circumstances. It was there that he prepared for publication of his **Dziennik Podróży** (Diary of a Voyage). Bobkowski had recorded his impressions aboard the Polish liner "Jagiełło" as it sailed from France to Guatemala. The journal has the following chapters: 1. Departure, 2. On the Mediterranean, 3. Atlantis, 4. In the Tropics, 5. La Guaira, 6. The Atlantic - On the Caribbean, 7. Panama - Guatemala. The accounts of this trip appeared in a series of articles in the **Tygodnik Powszechny** (Cracow) in 1949-1950.

Between 1951 and 1957 Bobkowski wrote a series of stories with a Guatemalan or Mexican background. These first appeared in Polish literary journals in Paris and London. The stories were subsequently collected and published under the heading **Coco de Oro** (The Golden Coconut) by the Instytut Literacki (Vol. 194, Biblioteka "Kultury", Paris, 1970). The book contains a preface written by Jozef Czapski shortly after Bobkowski's death in 1961. It is entitled "Querido Bob" and is a moving tribute to Bobkowski, the man and the writer.

Coco de Oro is a novelette set in the Caribbean area. The story takes its title from the name of a merchant ship owned and commanded by a Pole. An international cast of characters enhances the plot which revolves about the ship and its mysterious cargo.

Other stories contained in this anthology are as follows:

1. **Punkt równowagi** (Point of Balance) - this deals with the recovery of a Catalina-type plane from a Guatemalan swamp by an American and his Polish assistant.

2. **Spotkanie** (The Encounter) - in this story an American aviator-soldier of fortune has an affair with the wife of a Guatemalan cotton rancher. Introspection, flash-backs and other literary devices are masterfully employed by the writer.

3. **Spadek** (The Legacy) - this prize-winning tale is set in a Mexican port during the celebration of Holy Week. The story probes deeply into the human condition, revealing the author's extensive knowledge of the European and Latin American psychology.

Coco de Oro also contains an interesting essay on Joseph Conrad entitled "Biografia Wielkiego Kosmopolaka" (Biography of a Great Polish Cosmopolite). Bobkowski had been greatly impressed by Jocelyn Baines' critical biography of the famous writer (**Joseph Conrad** - London, 1960), and particularly his comments on possible analogies between Poland and the land of "Costaguana" in **Nostromo** (London, 1904). Bobkowski, a long-time enthusiast of Conrad, basically agreed with the analogies cited by Baines, and even went further. He said that **Nostromo** could be interpreted as a novel about Poland, even though ostensibly dealing with a Latin American country called "Costaguana". He stated that pre-war Poland must have resembled -

at least to observers in Paris and London - a large "Costaguana" in Eastern Europe.

Bobkowski had great praise for **Nostromo** and believed that Conrad's work offered a still-valid, penetrating psychoanalysis of Latin America and its people. His long-time residence in Guatemala had only strengthened his belief that **Nostromo** should be read by anyone contemplating traveling to or investing in Latin America. He categorically declared that it did not contain a single error of factual material, and that Conrad's feeling for and penetration of this specific world bordered on the miraculous.

Bobkowski believed that Conrad was a typical specimen of a Polish cosmopolite, belonging exclusively to neither Polish nor English culture. He asserted that Conrad was not the only outstanding figure in the history of Polish cosmopolitanism, and that this subject should be probed in depth. Bobkowski expressed the hope that the younger generation of émigrés would turn out many more Polish cosmopolites, for he felt that they played a significant role in the propagation of knowledge about his beloved Poland.

In accordance with Bobkowski's interpretation, the term "Kosmopolak" can be readily applied to a number of Poles living abroad whose literary and scholarly contributions have helped to spread knowledge of Poland in areas where Polish culture is little known. I am personally acquainted, for example, with the work of Dr. Edmund Urbanski of Washington. He has written numerous works in both Spanish and English dealing with Poland, the Slavs and Latin America. Dr. Urbanski has traveled throughout Latin America on passports issued by three countries. I feel that he would not be unduly upset by being labeled a "Kosmopolak", although he makes no claim to comparisons with Conrad.

Bobkowski's next literary work was **Czarny Piasek** (Black Sand), a play in three acts. This was Bobkowski's first attempt at playwriting. The drama deals with a group of European exiles and is set on the Pacific coast of Central America. It was published in the monthly **Kultura** (Paris) in 1959.

During his stay in Guatemala, Bobkowski became the Central

American correspondent for Radio Free Europe (based in Munich). He also wrote for "Panorama Dnia" in the radio series "Okna na Zachód". In these articles he covered such diverse themes as Indian customs, folklore, and music, as well as revolutionary history and climate.

Thanks to his dynamic creativity, Bobkowski also wrote essays of a literary and ideological nature on a wide variety of Polish and European themes. His contributions appeared in such journals as **Kultura** (Paris), **Horyzonty** (Freiburg), **Wiadomosci** (London) **and Związkowiec** (Toronto). He was also published in Poland: **Nowiny Literackie, Twórczość, Przemiany, Dziś i Jutro,** and **Tygodnik Powszechny.** Among his more interesting essays, were his responses to polls taken by émigré journals in London and Paris. In these Bobkowski stated his belief in the indivisible unity of Polish literature. He also warned against the identification of "Polishness" with "socialism".

Bobkowski's literary creativity was discussed by several well-known writers and literary critics. These include Józef Czapski, Czesław Miłosz, Tymon Terlecki, Kazimierz Wierzyński and Józef Wittlin. All are agreed that his most important work is **Szkice Piórkiem.** Czapski and Wittlin feel that this war-time diary is a realistic socio-political work by an author disappointed with Europe. Wierzyński thought that it revealed a great and dynamic talent. Miłosz saw in Bobkowski a perspicacious foreigner who is both enamored in France and simultaneously repulsed by the undignified behavior of its people.

Terlecki also praised Bobkowski's literary talent, stating that he had naturally-endowed gifts both as a novelist and dramatist. According to the critic, Bobkowski was strongly influenced by Conrad's adventures in exotic lands. This opinion is shared by Maria Danilewicz-Zielinska. She feels that Bobkowski's reading of **Nostromo** motivated his trip to Guatemala. It is interesting to note in this regard, that the identification of "Costaguana" has long eluded Conrad enthusiasts. It is only comparatively recently that Marcelo Segall, a Chilean historian, has ventured to suggest that Conrad's fictional land is, in reality, Chile.

Czapski and Terlecki were very impressed by Bobkowski's Guatemalan-based creativity. Czapski was particularly amazed by the writer's ability to faithfully record the sights and sounds of nature. Terlecki made a scholarly study of his works and concluded that Bobkowski was strongly influenced by an apparent existentialist philosophy of absolute freedom. The critic noted that most of the heroes of his stories belong to the class of "contemporary 'conquistadores'". These characters get ahead in life by their own efforts and achieve independence. The stories are characterized by a Central American background, exotic genre and the struggle for life.

In 1955 Bobkowski represented Guatemala in a flying model contest held in Stockholm. He also visited Paris, Munich, Geneva and New York. In 1961 he was accepted as a member of the International P.E.N. Club Center for Writers in Exile. Membership in this world-renowned organization - two months before his death - served to confirm his position in the field of literature.

Andrzej Bobkowski died of cancer on June 26, 1961, and was buried in the family grave of Dr. Julio Quevedo in the Cemeterio General. A journey which had begun in the wintry climates of Poland had now ended in the warm embrace of the Guatemalan sun.

General Krzysztof Arciszewski in Brazil (1629-1639)

Edmund S. Urbanski

General Krzysztof Arciszewski is one of the most controvesial Polish figures that were connected with the colonial history of seventeenth century Brazil. Brazilian, Dutch, and Portuguese historians often give his name as Christoforo d'Artischau Artiszewski, Artichofski, Arciszewski or even Artisoskius. In the period 1629-1639, he went three times to the then Portuguese colony as one of the commanders of the Dutch forces which conquered the northeast coast of Brazil and which occupied it until the year 1654. Arciszewski arrived there in the year 1629, at the outset with the rank of captain of musketeers, but after the conquest of Olinda in the year 1630, he advanced to the rank of major. When in the year 1634 he came to Brazil a second time, he already had the rank of colonel and commander of Dutch forces in this country. Whereas during the third expedition, undertaken to Brazil in the year 1638, he sailed from Amsterdam as a general and commander-in-chief of Dutch land and sea forces, which was the equivalent of the rank of admiral. That is why on his galleon "Groote Christoffel" there waved his admiral's flag. Just as Dutch sources praise him as an excellent strategist, so Portuguese - Brazilian sources consider him the leader of Dutch pirate expeditions. Nevertheless, neither one source nor the other denies him outstanding military abilities, intelligence, and courage (1).

Krzysztof Arciszewski was born in the year 1592 in Rogalin (Poznan province), as the son of Eliasz Arciszewski, the Arian courtier of Prince Krzysztof Radziwill. In the period 1621-1622, he fought in Radziwill's ranks in the war over Livonia, and also against

Brazil: A monumental 150 ft. high sculpture of Christ, the Redeemer, on the top of Corcovado Mt. adjacent to Rio de Janeiro, is the work of the Polish artist **Paulo Landowski** (1931). Several Polish painters and sculptors settled in XXth century Brazil, leaving compositions with Brazilian or Polish motifs, among whom the better known are **Grechinski Zeni, Górski, Danikiewicz, Kisiel-Kislanski, Lewandowski, Slesinska, Zagloba, Zawadzka-Różańska, Zamoyski and Żak** (Zaco Parana), the last two also serving as professors of fine arts.

the Tatars and the Turks. He possessed a humanistic education, and, besides the art of war, he also wrote poetry and memoirs. As an intimate of Prince Radziwill, he left for Gdansk in 1622 on his family business. On his return, Arciszewski continued to take part in battles with the Swedes and distinguished himself in the battle at Mitawa. In the year 1623 - as cited by M. Paradowska, according to Kraushar - Prince Radziwill sent him to Warsaw in order to examine the attitude of King Zygmunt III Waza to the Prince, and in the same year he took part in a royal trip to Gdansk and was entrusted with the construction of city walls in Puck. While visiting his family in Smigiel, he became embroiled in the murder of a neighbor and in order to avoid punishment, he departed from Poland in the year 1624 and took refuge in Holland, where the Arians were popular. Taking advantage of Radziwill's aid, there he learned nautical skills, engineering arts, and the building of fortifications. With the passage of time his offense was forgotten at home, and, as a result of this, Arciszewski returned to Poland in the year 1625 and spent time at Radziwill's manor in Lithuania. He entrusted him with a certain political mission in France in the year 1626, which had, as it turned out, the support of the Polish magnate for Prince Gaston d'Orleans, the brother of Louis XIII, as the candidate for the Polish throne after the death of Zygmunt III Waza [2].

In the year 1626, Arciszewski already possessing satisfactory military experience, took part in the defense of the Dutch city of Breda, besieged by Spanish forces under General Espinola, who turned out to be the victor. Travels and military service for the Dutch occupied Arciszewski's life. And so in the year 1626 he participated in the siege of the French port of La Rochelle, the stronghold of the Huguenots, when Holland was giving aid to Prince Gaston d'Orleans. In these battles he (Arciszewski) distinguished himself by his gallantry, which gained the attention of the Dutch commanders, who at this time were searching for officers for their expeditions of conquest in Brazil. Arciszewski, who was fascinated by military matters and who sought fame, had the desire to return to Poland, which he wanted to serve with his arms. Unfortunately, the thing that stood in the way was the discovery of the already mentioned political conspiracy of Arciszewski on behalf of Prince Radziwill, who together with Cardinal Richelieu desired to place a Frenchman on the Polish throne. When Zygmunt III Waza found out about this, the supporters of the French candidate were not left in peace. In connection with this, warrants were sent for Arciszewski to Belgium, where he often stopped. As the historian Aleksander Kraushar rightly presumes, these circumstances determined that Arciszewski accepted a three year Dutch contract and toward the end of 1629 he departed with the rank of captain from Holland to Brazil.

Merchant Holland of the seventeenth century, seeing the enrichment of Spain and Portugal by trade with their respective American colonies, decided to compete with them. She therefore undertook the invasion of Brazil in order to transform her from a Portuguese into a Dutch colony. The Dutch were not discouraged by the fact that a similar French expedition failed in the year 1555. They were counting on the loosened relationship of Brazil and Portugal, which was then dynastically linked with Spain (1580-1640), which possessed her own colonies demanding particular attention. These circumstances and the small Portuguese - Brazilian military detachments simplified the seizure of small areas of the northeastern coast of Brazil for the Dutch in 1624. Yet, the escalating conquest produced long-standing battles between the Dutch and the Brazilians. With the aim of colonial exploitation, the Dutch created the East India Company in Amsterdam(3), whose task it was also the frequent dispatching of the military for the further conquest of Brazil. Arciszewski was recruited for one of these expeditions. (He came with the fleet of Admiral Long after the Dutch seizure of the town of Bahia, but on the eve of the invasion of Pernambuco, Olinda, and Recife, in whose taking he participated with his company of musketeers). Since the entrance of the port of Recife was blocked by its defenders with eight purposefully sunk ships, during the meeting of the war council Arciszewski proposed the project of disembarking the army to the north of Olinda and the attacking of the town from one of the sides that were not defended. The execution of this plan was a complete success, as a result of which the Dutch took Olinda after a short battle on February 16, 1630 (Nassau, Kraushar, Warsinck).

In consideration of the fact that Arciszewski was sent to Brazil a few times, there exists a certain divergence of dates, that historians cite, particularly in regard to the first period of his activity there. And so David Carneiro, who mainly relies on the English information of C.R. Boxer, makes note of Arciszewski's presence not until 1631 as the commander of Fort Oranje on the island of Itamaracá, from which further Dutch raids emanated. From this fort, according to Helio Vianna, an attack on Igaraçu began in the next year. In order to oppose him, count de Bagnolo placed a battery of cannons against this fort. Later, this battery was withdrawn because it turned out that its operation did not produce any results. It seems that the Dutch garrison, made up of 366 soldiers, was not sufficient for further Dutch expansion from the island of Itamaracá to the adjacent area. This island possessed a strategic significance to both sides. After Arciszewski's departure for Holland and as a result of Dutch incompetence, Itamaracá fell in the hands of the Portuguese. Not until June 1633 did Colonel von Schkoppe take it once again. After obtaining new reinforcements brought over by Arciszewski from Europe a new and decisive attack against Paraiba took place in November and December 1634. As Vianna indicates, the land force was then under the command of a German mercenary von Schkoppe and the fleet under Lichthardt.(4)

During this period the commander-in-chief of Dutch forces in Brazil was Colonel Waerdenburgh. By the mediation of its local so-called Council of Nineteen, which discharged its duties first in Olinda and then in Recife, the West India Company unfortunately circumscribed his authority, just as that of other officers, assigning them advisors who were merchants ignorant of the art of war. Because the pertinent protest of these commanders were being steadily ignored, Waerdenburgh as well as Arciszewski, as a sign of protest, left Brazil in March of 1633. The Pole remained at the time in Holland over a year. Jerzy Pertek, relying on the historical sources of Netscher and Kraushar, maintains that the West India Company in Amsterdam highly rated Arciszewski's activity in Brazil. The proof of this was his appointment as colonel and the proposition to take over military command in Brazil(5). This was the situation when on August 9, 1634 Arciszewski returned to Brazil with four ships, delivering 476 soldiers as reinforcements for Dutch garrisons. Meanwhile, after the departure of Waerdenburgh, Sigismund Schkoppe (Schoppe) took over the main command (considered to be a German, but descended from a Germanized family in Silesia and, even in Brazil, according to Netscher, was sometimes taken to be a Pole). So Schkoppe, also disgusted by his merchant advisors, contemplated the idea of leaving Brazil for some time. When receiving the news about the arrival of the newly appointed commander, he decided to leave for Holland. Arciszewski's decision kept him from doing this (Schkoppe undertook many military operations with Arciszewski, who in the name of the common good decided to relinquish his powers and serve as Schkoppe's subordinate). In reality, this was a duumvirate in which the topographical abilities of the Silesian were complemented by Arciszewski's strategic genius. As it later turned out, this duumvirate produced splendid results in many mutually undertaken military operations.

Thus, when the coasts of Itamaracá and Rio Grande, and later also Paraiba were being taken over by the Dutch, the surrounding area of Recife and Arraial also became battle terrain. In March, 1634, Recife (then already occupied by the Dutch) was attacked by Martim Soares Moreno, the conqueror of Ceara, coming with aid to Matias de Albuquerque. Taking advantage of the fact that he left the surroundings of Cabo, the Dutch besieged Arraial once again, however, they did not take it. In the year 1635 two attacks against Arraial, undertaken by the Dutch, were repulsed. However, taking into account "how effectively Arciszewski strengthened the Dutch occupation of the coast between Paraiba and Recife, nothing else remained for the Portuguese-Brazilian forces but to hold the territories located to the south of Arraial. The lack of new reinforcements kept Brazilian detachments from further maintaining these positions. Attacked in March by Lichthardt, Bagnolo lost Porto Calvo. Whereas in June, 1635, besieged in Arraial-Andre Marin, having no food or ammunition, surrendered to the Dutch commanded by Arciszewski." (H. Vianna, op. cit. p. 222).

The Brazilian historian Carneiro believes that the conquest of Arraial do Bom Jesus, in which the mulatto Calabar (who went over to the Dutch) took part, was a military exploit of great significance for Arciszewski. Similarly, the defeat of the Spanish detachments of Luis Rojas y Borja by Arciszewski's forces at Mata Redonda. Of no less importance was the taking by him of the Castelo Real, Porto Calvo, and Barra Grande, valiantly defended by the Brazilians. These victories strengthened the prestige of the Polish commander in Brazil in an unheard of manner, which unfortunately became a thorn in the side for the Dutch officers who fought there with mixed success. Some of them like Picard and Calabar, for example, experienced reverses at the hands of Matias de Albuquerque in the year 1637. This forced the Dutch to defend the territories already occupied in which they engaged in the production of sugar and the felling of timber. This work was done by Indians, mestizos (caboclos) and Negroes, oppressed by greedy Dutch planters. The Dutch authorities also burdened them with onerous contributions, which equaled slavery. The exception was the military districts under the command of Arciszewski, whose attitude towards the Brazilian natives was friendly. (Thanks to this attitude he was successful in attracting the Indians over to the Dutch side on several occasions) [(6)].

This situation did not change when Prince Jan Maurice de Nassau came from Amsterdam, sent by the Estates General of the West Indies in 1636 as the Dutch governor. On the contrary, it worsened! De Nassau was an intelligent person and generally tolerant, but politically ambitious, and surrounded by members of the so-called Council of Nineteen, who were people of a merchant mentality and desiring ever newer profits. As a result of this, the battles between Dutch "monopolizers" and Brazilian sugar producers sharpened, consequently the deliveries of sugar were confiscated several times by the Dutch or their native hirelings... Anonymous pamphlets appearing in the colony informed about this, in which certain Portuguese Jews, being the richest Brazilian growers, complained about their losses.

They also transpired the confiscation of properties. Carneiro underscores that Arciszewski criticized the Council of Nineteen, which was responsible for the shaping of local colonial politics, for these relations. It is almost certain that he discussed these thorny matters in Amsterdam with the directors of the West India Company in which he had a hearing and which for services rendered appointed him general and admiral of Dutch armed forces in Brazil in 1638. During his third voyage, Arciszewski arrived in Brazil with a squadron composed of nine ships on which there embarked 1600 soldiers. His unheard of indignation can be imagined when landing at Recife in January 1639, a Dutch shore battery ruined his admiral's flag with a well-aimed shot, which was preceded by the breaking away of two ships from his squadron on the high seas! This was a flagrant act of insubordination.

All this proved to be a plot of the Council of Nineteen and governor de Nassau for the purpose of not recognizing his military authority. In addition, the young, inexperienced, but conceited de Nassau began to believe himself to be not only the civilian governor, but also the commander-in-chief of military forces. This was a clear violation of the resolutions of the Company and an affront to Arciszewski! He intensely protested during a session of the Council of Nineteen, reminding it also of irregular deliveries of food, clothing, and ammunition for the military forces. While they were spilling their blood in the defense of Dutch merchants who were enriching themselves, they forgot about his soldiers. He also sharply censured the interference of civilian authorities in military matters, which came to the surface in the reshuffle of officers of units subordinate to him while he was in Holland. This stood out against the humanitarian relationship that characterized Arciszewski not only in the face of his soldiers, but also in the face of Brazilian Indians, since he treated everyone in a decent manner. His conduct, therefore, collided with the colonial and merchant rapacity of the Dutch, which was alien to his Polish nature.

As a result of the thorny situation it came to a sharp clash between the willful governor, supported by greedy merchants and members of the Council, and the military commander of the colony.

It ended with the arrest by deception of General Arciszewski by a trusted officer of Prince de Nassau and his return to Holland by a small sailing ship, about which it was maintained that it would certainly be lost on the way. After protracted investigations, the Estates-General of the West Indies rehabilitated and pardoned him in 1639. Estranged by the ungrateful conduct of the Dutch, Arciszewski broke off with them completely, although he still lived in Amsterdam a few years. After the departure of General Arciszewski from Brazil, the Dutch situation changed to their disadvantage, which to a large extent should be credited to the incompetent management of Governor de Nassau. The attempted incursion of the town of Bahia by him, which changed hands several times, met with an ignominious failure. The Pole foresaw it before. Carneiro maintains that it would have been successful if it were carried out by Arciszewski, who, faithful to his principles, never allowed his soldiers to rape women, which took place in the military campaigns of Governor de Nassau and which caused the growing hatred of the Dutch by the Brazilians. These facts did not escape the attention of certain historiographers of this period [(7)].

Another interesting detail and almost not mentioned by historians (with the exception of Dr. Carneiro) was the case of the Brazilian ransom for the freeing of higher Portuguese officers. The money of this ransom, instead of being divided among Dutch soldiers for sparing their (i.e., the Portuguese higher officers') lives, found its way to the pocket of Stauhouver, a rich merchant and prominent member of the Council of Nineteen... The same Stauhouver was later accused of the plunder of the property of a Portuguese Jew Pantalão Monteiro. This greedy Dutchman enriched himself not only by the trade of Brazilian sugar, but he also stole the money of the ransom of the aforementioned officer, swindling the Dutch soldiers! Yet he was the enemy of the Polish-Dutch general.

Simply uncommon for those times was Arciszewski's strategic postulate regarding the close cooperation between the navy and the infantry during the attack of sea fortresses. Dutch commanders of the seventeenth century believed their ships predominantly to be floating arsenals, also serving to transport the army. However, in his conception they (the ships) should serve as the intensified firepower potential during land-sea attacks. Our countryman applied this principle a number of times and because of this he postulated a one person command of Land-Sea forces, which became the strategic axiom of the twentieth century.

After his partial rehabilitation, bitter and lonely, Arciszewski lived in Holland for a few years. At that time he wrote the so-called **Apology** as a memorial about the disgraceful treatment of him by the Dutch colonial authorities. He sent this memorial to the directors of the East India Company as well as to Prince Radziwill and to Hetman Koniecpolski, who intervened in his case in Amsterdam, giving it an international character. Thanks to this, the Dutch changed their attitude toward the Pole. However, chroniclers do not mention him getting financial compensation. In the Dutch trade code there was no visible place for the total clearing of personal honor, which troubled Arciszewski the most. The same ingratitude of the East India Company was also met later by gen. Sigismund Schkoppe, another commander of the Dutch expeditionary forces in Brazil (1654), and before him by adm. Witte de With. The reason? Because they were beaten by more numerous Portuguese troops; they were even charged with treason [(8)].

Arciszewski returned to Poland in the year 1646. He had been summoned there twice by king Wladyslaw IV, from whom he obtained a nomination of royal general of the artillery, or as it was then called "Starszy nad armatą". At that time there hung over Poland the threat of war with Turkey, which had already occupied some of the Balkan countries. Arciszewski executed his military responsibilities scrupulously, pointing to the insufficient armament of the country, resulting from the lack of funds for this purpose. He generously worked in spite of the fact that he was barely paid a part of his back pay. He participated in battles with the Cossacks in the Ukraine in which he distinguished himself by courage in the defense of Lwów. He strengthened the fortifications of Zbaraz and the military camp at Zborów. However unable to agree to the ignominious Polish agreement with the Tartars and the Cossacks, in the year 1649 he resigned his commission and went to Hungary. He returned to Poland in the year 1650 and took up residence with his relatives near Gdansk (Danzig), where he died in the year 1656. His remains were carried to the Church of the Bohemian Bretheren in Leszno, where they were consumed by flames during the fire of this town.

Arciszewski wrote a **Treatise on Artillery** and **Memoirs from Brazil** in Latin. The latter entrusted to the Dutch scholar Gerhard T. Voss (in Latin: Vossius) disappeared, although some fragments were known to biographers. The aforementioned **Memoirs** contained, among other things, interesting information about the life of the Tapuya (probably Tupi) Indians, their customs and beliefs in demons, necrophage, and other cannibalistic practices. These written observations made him the first Polish and probably the first European contributor to Brazilian ethnography. Voss vel Vossius utilized this material in his own work(9). Fortunately, most of these notes were found later and published as **Pamiętnik Krzysztofa Arciszewskiego z pobytu w Brazylii** (Memoirs of Christopher Arciszewski From His Stay in Brazil), being compiled and edited by A. Danysz (Poznan, 1895). Polish biographers also mention some of Arciszewski's Brazilian letters to his patron Prince Radziwill, as well as the author of two poems "Krzysztof Arciszewski's Lament" (1637) and "Appeal from India to the Netherlands" (1638). Of Arciszewski's cartographic work **Map of the siege of Arraial** (1635) and the **Map of the Conquest of Porto Calvo** (1637) are known, victories in which he himself participated. They are adorned by his family crest "Prawdzic". They prove his experience also in the field of military cartography, an activity which then was reserved to professional cosmographers.

Walerian Kalinka gathered materials on Arciszewski in Holland, while Aleksander Kraushar published a two volume monograph in Polish entitled **Dzieje Krzysztofa z Arciszewa Arciszewskiego, admirała i wodza Holendrów w Brazylii, Starszego nad armatą za Władysława IV i Jana Kazimierza** (The History of Christopher from Arciszewo Arciszewski, Admiral and Commander of the Dutch in Brazil, General of Artillery Under (kings) Ladislaus IV and John Casimir), Petersburg, 1892. Further Polish biographies about him were written by, among others, Albertrandy, J.B. Rychlinski, Edward Raczynski, S. Serecki, and F. Sobieszczanski; also by Dutch authors J. Connelyn, L. Gerard, J. de Laet, Kronick, P.M. Netscher, Warsink, and H. Watjen. English accounts about him can be found, among others, in the works of C.R. Boxer and Robert Southley. Among contemporary authors, Stanislaw Fischlowitz devoted a monograph to him in the Portuguese language entitled **Cristóforo Arciszewski** (Rio de Janeiro, 1959). Whereas, Michal Rusinek wrote a novelistic trilogy about Arciszewski, from which the novel entitled **Muszkieter z Itamaryki** (Musketeer from Itamaricá) Warsaw, 1965, describes his stay in Brazil and Holland.

The Dutch struck a medal in honor of Arciszewski in the year 1637, while in Pernambuco they erected a monument to him as the Dutch conqueror of Brazil. The Dutch cartographer J. Blaeu placed Arciszewski's coat of arms "Prawdzic" on a map of Brazil in his **Geographia Blaviana**, vol. XI (Amsterdam, 1662). Arciszewski's portrait appeared in the collection of eminent European personages, in the famous album **Theatrum Europaeum** (Amsterdam, 1637), when the Polish-Dutch admiral and general was at the height of his fame. Even later encyclopedias devote much attention to him, among others, **Diccionario Enciclopédico Hispano-Americano**, issued by Segui Publishers (Barcelona-Madrid).

In conclusion, it can be said that General Arciszewski was a so-called "soldier of fortune", one of those who appear at all times in different countries. Maybe he was not so much concerned with fortune, which he did not attain, as with the realization of the art of war, in which he showed himself a master. In this light his other motivations pale to the advantage of humanitarian feelings that he demonstrated towards Brazilian natives and in the just treatment of his soldiers. However, he did not perceive the difference between Portuguese and Dutch colonialism of the seventeenth century. If he were in Portuguese-Brazilian service, he would probably be a good defender of Brazil against a Dutch incursion.

Finally, there are two questions about Gen. Arciszewski, which remain to be answered. The first deals with his unjustified treatment by the Dutch. Judging by his military record and three promotions, Arciszewski gained the complete confidence of the East India Company, which explains why he became the Commander-in-Chief of the Dutch colonial forces in Brazil. One may speculate that he could have been promised even the governorship of that possession. Suddenly in 1639 there occurred a political reversal caused by the nomination of De Nassau to this high office, a member of the prominent Dutch aristocracy. It was undoubtedly caused by a behind the scenes struggle between the Nassau family and the commercially-oriented East India Company, in which the Nassau possibly had a financial interest. In that internal struggle which ended in compromise, Arciszewski became a scapegoat instead of a hero. This assumption is plausible from the viewpoint of historic revisionism, when morality and honor are sacrificed for business or state considerations. Arciszewski's misfortune was, on the other hand, that he trusted Holland too much, while the Dutch betrayed him! Polish historians judge his foreign, strictly military exploits on the whole with sympathy. However, Janusz Tazbir, as asserted by Pertek, without depriving him of military bravery, possibly moved by political considerations, tries to separate Arciszewski from excessive heroic mythology, even though Voss and Boxer impartially recognize his prominent role in the Dutch colonial adventure in South America (10).

Also Arciszewski's tragic burial in Leszno needs clarification. The Poland of the Golden Age and thereafter, with its splendid cultural and political achievements, became a haven for thousands of religious refugees from various European countries (Czechs, Jews, Scotts). Among them were the so-called "Bohemian Brethren", a Czech Protestant sect persecuted in the Austrian empire. Headed by their patriarch-educator, Jan Amos Komensky, they settled in Leszno in 1628. Theologically somewhat close to the Arians or Polish Unitarians, they freely fostered their religious ideology in Western Poland(11), propagating there Protestantism among the Polish Catholics, and thus opposed the Counter-Reformation in the Polish Kingdom. Unbelievably, during the Swedish invasion and occupation of

Poland (1655-60), this Bohemian community, feeling religious kinship with the Swedes, joined forces with the Scandinavian invaders of Poland. They also intrigued against Poland abroad, while enjoying political hospitality. Thus, they antagonized the patriotically-minded Poles, who while throwing out the Swedes from their land, in an outburst of indignation, also burned down the city of Leszno, the stronghold of the "Bohemian Brethren". It was unfortunate that during that act, the remains of gen. Arciszewski were in the church awaiting burial, for they were consumed by flames then. Arciszewski, a Polish Protestant, in all his military activities was always faithful to his motherland, and for this he has to be commended. Henryk Sienkiewicz in his famous novel **Ogniem i Mieczem** (With Fire and Sword) had mentioned him several times positively. Above all, Arciszewski was praised by his biographers, whether Polish or foreign.

---

(1) Carneiro, David. "Grande figura de antagonista" (essay) in **Gaceta do Povo**. Curitiba, Parana. November 22, 1984.

(2) Paradowska, Maria. **Polacy w Ameryce Południowej**, pp.71-72.

(3) The East India Company was established in 1621.

(4) Vianna, Helio. **História do Brasil**, p.221.

(5) Pertek, Jerzy. **Polacy na morzach i oceanach**, vol. I, p. 421.

(6) Carneiro, David. Op. cit. passim.

(7) Carneiro, David. Op. cit. passim.

(8) Pertek, Jerzy. Op. cit. pp.442-443.

(9) Vossius, Gerhard. **De theologia et physiologia christana sive de origine et progressu idolatriae** (Amsterdam, 1642), in which the author quotes Arciszewski and defends his human attitude toward the Brazilian population, in contrast to that of the Dutch. According to M. Paradowska, Vossius' work was later translated into Polish (in indisclosed date).

(10) Pertek, Jerzy. Op. cit. p. 453 and passim.

(11) A propos the excessive tolerance of XVIth and XVIIthe century Poland of other religious ideologies and incoming foreign ethnic groups, one may wonder whether that unheard of then Polish liberalism, unknown in the still despotic Europe, was not one of the causes of future political misfortunes for Poland's downfall at the end of the XVIIIth century. A Polish historic writer, Jedrzej

Giertych, believes it was. This multiethnic society was a political novelty in Europe, hardly duplicated by other states. On the other hand, one should not forget that the variety of theological-social thought of Poland enriched its intellectual treasure. Thus, the radical Protestant view represented by Polish Arians or Unitarians, had influenced the views of philosophers Baruch Spinoza of Holland and John Locke of England. For they were avid readers of volumes known as **Bibliotheca Fratrum Polonorum** (The Library of the Polish Brethren), published in 1656 in Holland, where the Polish Arians settled after leaving Poland (Zieleniewicz, Andrzej. **Poland**, Orchard Lake, 1969, p. 52). Also in regard to Locke, in Giertych, Jerzy: **Jan Amos Komensky**. London, p.279.

Bibliography

Boxer, C. P. **The Dutch in Brazil 1626-1654**. Oxford, 1957. passim.

Carneiro, David. "Grande figura de antagonista" (essay). **Gazeta do Polvo**. Curitiba, 22 de Novembro de 1984.

Giertych, Jedrzej. **Jan Amos Komensky**. U źródeł katastrofy dziejowej Polski. London, 1964. Passim.

Vianna, Helio. **História do Brasil**. São Paulo, 1972. Chptr. "Os holandeses no Brasil" (pp. 219-250)

Paradowska, Maria. **Polacy w Ameryce Poludniwej**. Warszawa, 1977. Chptr. "Polski admiral w Brazylii" (pp. 67-93).

Pertek, Jerzy. **Polacy na morzach i oceanach**. Poznan, 1981. Vol. I (pp. 414-455, and passim).

Pyzik, Estanislao. **Los polacos en la Rep. Argentina y América del Sur**. Buenos Aires, 1966 (pp. 12-14).

Tazbir, Janusz. **Spotkania z historią**. Warszawa, 1979. Chptr. "Socynianizm w kulturze europejskiej", passim.

Inter-American Council,
Washington, D.C.

Educational and Political Activities of Dr. Józef Leonard in Central America (1880-1908)

Joanna Petry Mroczkowska

Dr. Józef Leonard was a Polish humanist, writer and educator engaged in cultural and political life in Spanish-speaking countries for forty years. He was born in 1841 in Hrubieszow. His father Anton came from Prussia and worked as a teacher of German. His mother was of French descendance and her name Bertholet, which Leonard sometimes added to his father's, in accordance to Spanish usage.

Józef studied humanities and law at Warsaw University where he received a doctorate. At that time he was involved in conspiracy against czarist oppression in partitioned Poland and took active part in the insurrections of 1863, fighting in the regiments of general Langiewicz and general Krukowiecki. As a captain of cavalry he took part in the successful battle of Zyrzyn.

After the collapse of the insurrection in 1864 he had to leave the country. He was not, like a few Poles, incorporated into the Austrian Legion sent to bring support to the fragile monarchy of archduke Maximilian Habsburg in Mexico. Nevertheless, his Latin American odyssey was meant to start several years later.

Leonard lived for a short time in Switzerland and France but it seems that he could not find a place in those countries. He had more luck in Spain although the beginnings were not without dramatic moments. In Spain where he spent twelve years, he was for a long time the editor of **Gaceta de Madrid** and wrote articles for other journals (ex. **Novedades**). He frequented meetings at the Ateneo which was a

UNIWERSYTET JAGIELLOŃSKI
INSTYTUT FILOLOGII ROMAŃSKIEJ

SKRYPTY UCZELNIANE
NR 413

JOANNA PETRY-MROCZKOWSKA

TEXTOS DE LITERATURA HISPANOAMERICANA

I. Poesía

Prof. E. Urbanski's
Polish-Latin-American
Book Collection

NAKŁADEM UNIWERSYTETU JAGIELLOŃSKIEGO
1981

A considerable role in diffusion of Latin American culture in Poland is being played by the Polish Universities, whose Departments of Hispanic Studies have a record enrollment, also by the publication of Spanish language textbooks. It suffices to mention here such recent works as **Antologia de la literatura hispanoamericana** (4 vols., 1975, 1979) and **Ameryka Łacińska w swej literaturze** (2 vols., 1979) by Prof. Grażyna Grudzińska, of Warsaw University; **Textos de literatura hispanoamericana: Poesía** (1 vol., 1981) by Prof. Joanna Petry-Mroczkowska, of Cracow University; **La parodia en la nueva novela hispanoamericana** (1991) by Prof. Elżbieta Skłodowska, of Poznań University, to mention just a few. This is complemented by over 1,000 Polish translations from Hispanic and Brazilian literature, which enjoys great popularity.

forum of liberalism and got acquainted with prominent liberal thinkers and politicians. Later, he was elected a member of the Real Academia Española and the Association of Writers and Artists in Madrid.

Between 1877 and 1879 Leonard taught Slavic literature and French at the Instítución Libre de Enseñanza in Madrid. As its name indicates already the purpose of the institute was to promote the humanities and sciences in a modern spirit, free from any restrictions of religious or political nature. This modernist trend was a variation of Krause's thinking in regard to secular education. Leonard transplanted this educational ideology to Central America where he resided for the rest of his life.

Dr. Leonard and Dr. Calderón y Arana, a natural scientist, were hired in Paris by the representative of the Nicaraguan government of President Joaquin Zavala who, by establishing in Leon in 1880 a college called Instituto de Occidente as a counterpart to already existing Instituto de Oriente in Granada, aimed at expanding the country's secondary education. Both professors taught previously at Instituto Libre de Enseñanza in Madrid and were known for their liberal views.

From 1880 to 1882 Leonard worked in Nicaragua as a professor of pedogogy, European history and literature in the Instituto de Occidente in Leon and later in the Instituto de Oriente in Granada.

This is when, in Leon, he had a considerable impact on Rubén Darío, the greatest modernist poet of Spanish language. In 1881 young Darío frequented the Colegio de Occidente in Leon where Dr. Leonard introduced him to the new currents of the European literature. He also tutored him in French. It seems that the relationship between the teacher and his student soon developed into a friendship. It is Leonard who encouraged Darío to write poetry and helped him publish his first collection "Poesias y articulos en prosa". When, as sworn advocate of freedom of conscience, Leonard became a target of criticism by conservative circles of Leon (and as was to be expected the government of President Zavala supported Leonard's position) young Darío was also on the side of his mentor, considering him a

Dr. José (Józef) Leonard
Rector of the University of Honduras
(1900-1903)

victim of obscurantism and for his defense used the pages of liberal periodical **La Verdad**. The friendship continued until the death of Leonard, in spite of the fact that their paths often diverged.

After resigning his position as director of the college in León Dr. Leonard moved to Granada (he taught there history and Spanish literature) and then to Managua where he became an advisor on educational matters to the President of Nicaragua and collaborated with **El Comercio** and **La Gaceta**.

After leaving Nicaragua in 1882 Leonard went to El Salvador where he was in friendly contacts with the President Rafael Zaldivar. He engaged in editing a liberal weekly **La República** which was published for a few more years. He was then sent on a diplomatic mission to Mexico and the United States as a representative of El Salvador. He accompanied the president on an official visit to Spain and France. The political downfall of Zaldivar and his government made Leonard go to Guatemala. This is where, while serving as a counselor to the President of Guatemala José María Reina Barrios, he resumed his friendship with Darío. It is also important to appreciate the link between Leonard and the propagators of the Federal Republic of Central America of which one of the most prominent exponents was President Barrios. Among others is quoted Dr. Salvador Mendieta, admirer of Professor Leonard and his former student at the University of Tegucigalpa. (History knows a precedent of this sort. In 1823 the region became autonomous under the name of the United Provinces of Central America. For almost 15 years the United Provinces existed as a political unit, despite strong Liberal-Conservatives battles).

In 1885, the year of conflict between Guatemala and El Salvador, Leonard went to France where he stayed one year, mostly in the circles of Central Americans. In Paris he helped Salvadorian General Samoya write his book **El Hombre Libre** which was a treatise on social and political matters.

In 1886 Dr. Leonardwas again in Guatemala. Shortly after he was sent to Mexico as Charge d'Affaires of Guatemala (1887-1888). He teaches in Instituto Nacional in Quetzaltenango and later in the capital, at the same, time collaborating with several periodicals (**El**

CENTRO-AMÉRICA.

LA VERDAD

Semanario de Política i Variedades.

ÓRGANO DE LA JUVENTUD.

Fundador Justo Hernandez. | *Editor responsable Justo Benito Hernandez.*

AÑO 4º.—TRIMESTRE 12º | LEON, JULIO 30 DE 1881. | NÚM. 103.

ADMINISTRADOR JENERAL— *Juan Mora [illegible]*

MODERNA LITERATURA POLACA

[illegible] KRASZEWSKI.

Conferencia dada en Madrid por

Don José Leonard

Señores:

Con la aparicion del cristianismo en Polonia empieza su historia, y con ella la de su literatura.

Reinaba en Cracovia Boleslao I. último monarca pagano, casado con la cristiana Dombrowka, princesa de Bohemia, que le dió un hijo inhábil para el gobierno. Mieczislao había nacido ciego. Un monje aleman, probablemente de la órden de los Benedictinos, promete á la desconsolada reina que el agua del bautismo infundirá luz vivificadora en los apagados ojos del tierno infante, y Dombrowka, madre como todas las madres, y creyente como los cristianos primitivos, obtiene del rey el permiso de bautizar á su hijo. En efecto, despues de la santa ceremonia, Mieczislao dirijió á la reina una mirada de ánjel, en la cual la afiijida señora halló copiosa recompensa por cuantos pesares y cuitas la habian aquejado antes, y el fraile [illegible] para vaticinar que, así como el heredero de la corona había visto la luz del dia, al recibir la del alma, así tambien, por obra suya, todo el pueblo lequita saldria en breve de las tinieblas del jentilismo.

[illegible] seria en estos tiempos [illegible] y críticos, en los dos sentidos de la frase, achacar á milagro la referida tradicion piadosa, ni tampoco entra en mis planes suscitar aquí cuestiones teolójicas: pero no es menos cierto que el reinado de Mieczislao fija en la historia de Polonia la transicion del paganismo á la fe del Crucificado, [illegible] la enseñanza y propaganda pacífica, sin derrame de sangre, sin [illegible] ni trastornos, cual cumplia á la doctrina de Aquel sublime mártir [illegible] todo amor, [illegible] y sacrificio.

Tal es, señores, el último detalle de la historia fabulosa de Polonia. El induce, seguramente, á que respetables investigadores de nuestro pasado confundiesen á veces, una y otra fuente, la tradicional ó hipotética y la escrita ó auténtica, de nuestra ora gloriosa, ora instructiva, pero siempre simpática historia.

Desde el siglo X empieza, pues, Polonia á marchar, mano en mano, con el resto de la culta Europa.

Diferenciándose poco en sus orijenes la lengua polaca, ó *lequita*, de la bohemia, ó *checa*, los primeros manuscritos son comunes á los dos paises. El de Krolodwor y el Salterio de la reina Margarita, figuran en ambas literaturas con títulos igualmente lejítimos. Pero á poco el pequeño reino de Mieczislao ha de adquirir gran incremento, y realizada la unidad nacional, bajo la dinastía de los Piast, ha de llevarse á cabo por el último de sus descendientes el peregrino hecho de la Confederacion de Polonia y Lituania, que alcanzará mas tarde, bajo el reinado de un Jaguelon, al Estado rusita de Halicz, á Gallitzia, Ukrania, Wolhynia y Podolia. Al casamiento de Ladislao Jaguelon con Eduvigis de Piast, y á la union de las dos monarquías, la polaca y la lituana, presidirá la misma idea que inspiró la conversion de Polonia, y la pagana Lituania doblará tambien la rodilla ante la cruz del Gólgota, y abrirá los ojos á la luz del Evanjelio, alentada por el amor de dos jóvenes soberanos, como antes su hermana mayor, la antigua Lequia, se habia abrazado á aquella cruz, conmovida por las lágrimas de una madre, contajiada por la gratitud de un monarca.

Desde el siglo XIV principia á hacerse cada vez más notable la influencia de estos dos hechos en la literatura polaca. Así se explica que entre los muy pocos pueblos católicos dotados de Vulgata nacional, figura Polonia con su Antiguo y Nuevo Testamento, traducido por el padre Wuyek en el siglo XVI. En el anteriormente [illegible], cardenales y obispos polacos asistirán á Concilios ecuménicos; Copérnico se anticipará á Galileo para robar sus secretos á la máquina admirable del universo; Wito Stwosz competirá en la catedral de Cracovia con los primeros maestros en el arte de la escultura, hasta que en el siglo de oro de nuestra historia literaria, siglo de los Sigismundos, surja una pléyade de escritores y eleve la lengua patria á tal grado de esplendor, que en lo sucesivo no cabrá en ella perfeccionamiento alguno. Pero estos maestros del habla como aquellos jigantes del saber [illegible] del arte, obedecerán siempre en sus trabajos á la idea eminentemente nacional, á la idea cristiana, que obligará al Estado á abrir sus dominios y recibir con hospitalidad, primero á los judíos expulsados de toda Europa, luego á los Husitas arrojados de Bohemia, y por último, á los protestantes flamencos, fujitivos ante los horrores de la Inquisicion, y que impondrá á los reyes polacos, en el acta del juramento, la promesa de velar por la paz y la armonía entre los disidentes en relijion: *Pacem inter dissidentibus fide conservabo*, era la fórmula inscrita en los *Pacta conventa*.

No puedo, señores, á riesgo de extenderme demasiado, daros ni siquiera una idea del estado floreciente de nuestra literatura en los siglos XVI, XVII y XVIII; no es esto mi objeto principal, y por otra parte, basta á mi intento consignar, que no ha ocurrido en Europa ningun suceso notable, ninguna digna manifestacion de la actividad humana que no tuviera eco en la literatura polaca. Al escolasticismo, al clasicismo y al enciclopedismo, cual todo el Occidente, pagamos nuestro tributo, sin perder, no obstante, cierta orijinalidad, y un pronunciado color local que distingue á nuestros pensadores de los de otros paises del mundo civilizado; y por este camino llegamos hasta la asombrosa época contemporánea, en cuyo bosquejo hemos de ocuparnos preferentemente.

Aquí ocurre, sin embargo, un cambio en la suerte y en las aspiraciones del pueblo polaco, cambio mediante el cual la literatura y el arte nacionales adquieren un ajente, ga-

Title page of the Nicaraguan weekly **La Verdad** of July 30, 1881, which contains an article on Polish modern literature by Dr. José Leonard. He was then director of the college-type Instituto de Occidente in Léon, where he also taught French and Spanish literature. Among his students was Ruben Darío whose ability he rocognized and therefore encouraged him to cultivate poetry, influencing his youthful poetic production. The grateful Darío composed even a few poems dedicated to Poland. Some of them appeared in **La Verdad**. When Darío later became the glory of Spanish American literature, he never forgot his Polish friend and intellectual mentor. He mentioned him several times in his latter works: **Semblanzas, Autobiografía, El viaje a Nicaragua e historia de mis libros** and **Crónica literaria.**

Bien Público, Diario de Occidente, Diario de Centro América, La Estrella, La República). Together with Cuban poet José Joaquin Palma and Salvadorian writer Francisco Castañeda among others he was invited to the jury of the contest for the Guatemalan national anthem.

Quite soon however, the political changes caused his moving to El Salvador where he worked for the Salvadorian Secretary of Education. He represented El Salvador at the first Pedagogical Congress of Central America which took place in Guatemala in 1893. The Polish educator takes the credit for reforming the antiquated reading system and for putting emphasis on civics in the general curriculum.

In Honduras where he resided afterwards he tried to carry out an unsuccessful project of colonization of two districts by Central European (Polish) farmer's emigration. Later, in Tegucigalpa he taught humanities in the liberal Colegio, "El Espíritu Santo" founded by President Policarpio Bonilla. Then he was chosen as a member of examination committee in Instituto Nacional and was offered a position in the Ministry of Foreign Affairs. He became an advisor to the President general Terencio Sierra.

Between 1900 and 1903 professor Leonard served as a Rector of the University of Tegucigalpa appointed by the Honduran president. Recognized as a prominent figure with broad experience in international affairs, Leonard was sent as an official delegate of Honduras to the Second Pan American Congress in Mexico in 1901 and represented Honduras in the Central American Tribunal of Arbitrage in Costa Rica between 1902 and 1903. He was also a General Consul of Honduras in San José.

After the political downfall of Sierra (Honduras suffered through three different administrations in 1903 alone) Leonard returned to Nicaragua. In 1906 he became partially paralyzed and could not work. The president José Santos Zelaya in recognition of his merits to the Republic of Nicaragua granted him a life pension. Immobilized Leonard enjoyed hospitality of an Italian architect Napoleon Re at his suburban residence and until his death received visits of his friends, including Rubén Darío, now full of glory as a celebrated father of the Modernist movement. Leonard died in April 1908, eighty years ago, and was buried at San Pedro cemetery in Managua, which suffered considerably from the earthquake in 1931. In consequence Leonard's bust from the mausoleum was placed by his friends in front of the masonic lodge El Progresso which he founded in Managua in 1882.

A dry account of Leonard's impressive activities in Central America of educational, journalistic and diplomatic nature, his involvement on the side of liberalism together with so many important figures of Central American intellectual life may still not give us a complete picture of this colorful personality. About Dr. Leonard's long-lasting influence write, besides Rubén Darío, such distinguished Latin American and Spanish figures as Nicaraguans: Dr. Manual Maldonado, Dionisio Martinez Sanz, Diego Manuel Sequeira, Francisco Castañeda from El Salvador, Spanish writer Vicente Pujol, Clodomiro Urcuyo - former Minister of Education in Nicaragua, Chilean literary critic Raúl Silva Castro and Dr.Rafael Heliodoro Valle, Honduran historian. Leonard, they all agree, anticipated his times by strongly believing in social justice, progress, fraternity, and freedom.

During his life, Dr. Leonard, son of Poland, demonstrated a full range of qualities in a somehow unusual combination. With his roots in so many cultures he found Latin American idiosyncrasy close to his Slavic background. His sharp intelligence, broad education, knowledge of several languages, eloquence and on the other hand a life-loving, out-going disposition, loyalty and readiness to help people won him so many Central American friends. Vicissitude of life forced him to live as a citizen of the world but he never stopped being a Pole, talked about Poland privately and in public and transmitted his love and concerns to numerous friends, including Rubén Darío who introduced Polish motifs to some of his early poems.

Leonard who cherished democracy, freedom, and was a fervent partisan of radical liberal ideas decided to live in Central America, the region where conservatism was still very strong, where often dictatorial governments and proverbial political instability reigned. Leonard's mobility until his more advanced age reflects his unusual intuition and Slavic adaptability. His active participation in Freemasonry seems to be proof of this, since this organization embraced the circles of Latin American high officials and provided an effective forum for spiritual and material solidarity and assistance to its members. His intellectual rationalism was mixed with idealism (Darío considers him a disciple of Hegel and Plato). His epicureism was complemented by occasional nostalgy and an often Voltaire-like mind did not prevent him from singing Christmas carols from the book his mother gave him when he was leaving to take part in the January insurrection of 1863.

---

* The biographic information about the figure of Dr. Leonard can be found in Prof. E.S. Urbanski's , "Dr. Jozef Leonard and his cultural-political activities in Spain between 1868 and 1880 (**The Polish Review,** no. 3, Vol. XII, NY 1967), "Rubén Darío's Teacher, Dr. José Leonard and his Franco-Spanish-Latin American cultural activities" (Papers on Franco-Spanish-Luso-Brazilian Spanish American Literary Relations, IMA. Conference 15, Chicago, 1967) and in the respective chapter of **Sylwetki Polskie w Ameryce Łacińskiej XIX I XX Wieku.** Stevens Point 1991.

Incredible Adventures of J. Fr. Waldeck, A Polish-born Maya Explorer in XIXth Century Mexico

Edmund S. Urbanski

In Mesoamerican archaeological history there are probably not many cases when a European explorer mistook a beak of a tropical macow bird for a head of an elephant, while doing pioneering exploration of the ancient Maya pyramids in southern Mexico. Such a surprising case which confused for many decades other Maya explorers, occurred in the early 1830's to Jean Frederic Waldeck, an artist-painter turned amateur archaeologist. During his previous stay in France and England, he was so attracted by the mysterious Indian civilizations of the New World that he decided at the age of 60 to come to Mexico, a country which fascinated him so much, that he remained there for twelve years (1825-1836).

Who was Waldeck? This was a rather enigmatic question for a long time. Because of encyclopedic inaccuracies, countries such as Austria, Czechoslovakia, Germany, and France dispute among themselves either his birthplace, citizenship or other affiliation. Most biographers place his birthplace in Prague, Paris or Vienna. However, the Mexican art historian, Federico Mariscal, found in 1941 in Waldeck's papers a letter in which he stated that he was born in the city of Przemysl, Poland, a fact reiterated by the Hondurian historian Rafael H. Valle in his **Bibliografía Maya** (Mexico, 1942). I verified this myself then as Prof. Mariscal's colleague at the National University of Mexico, and announced it later in a paper presented at the 37th International Congress of Americanists in Argentina (1966). Although the origin of Waldeck may be for many of secondary importance, it nevertheless unfolds a sad part of Poland's history when this country was dismembered by Russia, Germany and Austria at the end of the XVIIIth century. This caused an exodus of many Polish citizens. Among them was young Waldeck who left for France, where he soon assimilated to his new country, adopted French forenames and through his studies and other activities, considered himself a Frenchman and not a Pole.

Another difficulty in tracing Waldeck's nationality was that during his travels he used French, English and even Mexican documents. The orthographic examination of his personal diaries in over 100 small notebooks written in French confirms that it was not his native tongue. On occasions he also utilized correct German and Hebrew in marginal notes. This would suggest Waldeck's close association with either the German or the Judaic culture or the fusion of both. The latter was cultivated by the Ashkenazi people, a great number of whom settled in the past in Poland, fleeing from the Jewish pogroms in Germany.

Regardless of his national persuasion or spiritual affiliation, Waldeck's life was very exciting, although not devoid of events about whose veracity one may have serious reservation. This stems from the too colorful flow of encyclopedic information, which presents Waldeck's exploits like those of the legendary Don Quijote or Baron Münchhausen. If we are to believe this novelistic-like information, Waldeck at the age of nineteen enlisted in Paris in 1785 in the François Le Valliant expedition to the Cape of Good Hope in order to explore South Africa. In 1788 he returned to Paris where he studied painting and lithography at David and Prud'hon ateliers. In 1794, he enlisted in Napoleon's army and took part in the siege of Toulon, and again in 1799, he participated in the Napoleonic expedition to Egypt. When Gen. Menon capitulated there, not wishing to fall in English hands, he remained in the Black Continent and crossed Africa by foot from the north to the south in a company of four other soldiers. He later returned

Mexico: The Polish-born **J. Fr. Waldeck,** artist-painter by trade and the early explorer of Maya monuments in Mexico, whose incredible adventures may be compared to those of Don Quijote or Baron Münchausen.

via Madagascar to France, and again joined the famous Robert Surcouf expedition to India. In 1819 he went to Chile as a soldier of fortune with the mercenary British Admiral Cochrane to take part in its war of independence against Spanish colonial rule. On his way back to England he was allowed in 1820 or 1821 to disembark in Central America and utilized a period for archaeological visit of the Maya ruins in Guatemala. Except for the latter, the other facts are only hazily mentioned, if at all, in his notebook-memoirs, which makes us believe as Waldeck's literary fantasy, transmitted to the curiosity-seeking editors of the French Encyclopedia Larousse.

More verifiable data exist when Waldeck was commissioned in 1821 in London with the lithographic work for a book **Description of the Ruins of an Ancient City, discovered near Palenque, in the Kingdom of Guatemala in Spanish America: Translated from the original manuscript of Captain don Antonio del Rio etc.,** published in London in 1822. Del Rio was a Spanish officer who visited and described the Maya ruins of Palenque earlier and enclosed 17 sketches, transformed by Waldeck into illustrations which bear his initials. Thus, his name became connected for the first time with the Maya antiquities. Considering, however, some of those sketches apocryphal, Waldeck wanted to check on them "in situ" in Mexico. Thus, in 1825 he went to that country as a "mining engineer" contracted by a British silver mine in Tlalpujahua. It was obviously an excuse, because after several months work, he abandoned his position and settled in Mexico City. He led a truly Bohemian life there for a few years. Obsessed with Indian antiquities, he sketched the Aztec artifacts in the National Museum and various ruins in the Valley of Mexico, being sometimes praised for his artistic work in the Mexican press. As Mexico then was in a revolutionary turmoil, Waldeck took a precautionary step and deposited his collection of 129 drawings with their description at the British Legation in Mexico City. In order to survive, Waldeck dedicated himself to various activities. Thus, according to his own admission, he painted portraits of rich Mexicans, gave private lessons in drawing and piano, sang for one season as a baritone at the "Teatro Italiano" which presented a few operas, painted stage decorations for it, and for some time managed his own phantasmagoric show. He did not abstain from gambling, considered a favorite pastime in Latin America.

In the meantime he made contacts with some influential Mexicans, and thanks to them got a commission to make lithographic illustrations of Icaza and Isidro Gondra. It was published as **Colección de las Antiguedades Mexicanas** in 1827, and as his name was mentioned in the title page, it made Waldeck reputation in Mexican circles. Owing to this fact and promoting his own interest, Waldeck was able to inspire the Mexican **intelligentsia** with interest in the artistic achievements of the indigenous Mexican civilizations, especially in the Maya monuments of Palenque in the state of Chiapas. Consequently, a Society for the Exploration of Antiquities of Palenque, Peten and Chiapas was established in Mexico City in 1831, with the purpose of financing the publication of 200 plates and bas-relieves of Palenque in order to exhibit them in Paris and London. Thus, due to the Mexican funds and the patronage of the President Anastasio Bustamante and the Secretary of Foreign Affairs, Lucas Alaman, Waldeck, in order to accomplish these goals, went with an expedition in May, 1832, to Palenque, where he worked until the middle of March, 1834.

It was there that Waldeck faced the bas-relief of the so-called "Cross of Palenque" for the first time, a geometrically stylized figure of a cross, which for the ancient Mayas symbolized the tree of life, but which became a religious symbol of Christianity. On both sides of this ornament, two Maya Indians are standing in ceremonial attire, whereas above it a Guatemalan bird, the colorful quetzal, was perched. This unusual decoration must have puzzled Waldeck, who previously saw it in the Del Rio manuscript for which its sketch was made by the Guatemalan artist Almendariz, who presented both Indians with a severe face. Well, Waldeck did not like then the severity of their expression when he lithographed them in 1822 and therefore altering them, probably for esthetic reasons, presented their faces in a more gentle way. Fortunately, upon seeing the original bas-relief personally, restored to their original expression and other details. In this more acceptable form sold his drawings for Brasseur de Bourbourg's French work **Monuments Anciens du Méxique. Palenque et Autres Ruins de l'Ancienne Civilisation** (Paris, 1866), which also contains Waldeck's other archaeological drawings. However, some Maya hieroglyphs on the same bas-relief were reproduced by Waldeck inexactly, which could have been caused either by his artistic caprice or myopia. Thus, he imagined in some Palenque hieroglyphs an elephant's head, also when some details were lacking or disfigured by corrosion, Waldeck "reconstructed" them with his brush... An example was the case of a stucco sculpture known as "Beau Relief", which represented a king or a priest seated on a chair, sustained by two jaguars or tigers. In the original drawing made by Almendariz for Del Rio, the figure has a complete face but without an ornamental collar on his chest, which the Guatemalan artist could have forgotten to paint. Surprisingly enough, all these details appeared in Waldeck's unpublished original drawing, but disappeared in later drawings. Therefore, later explorers Stephens and Catherwood suspected that Waldeck, after painting the full face, disfigured it. In spite of this, the Waldeckian version of that beautiful bas-relief continues to be reproduced in archaeology books.

Waldeck's work in Palenque was very fruitful, for as he mentioned in his diary, he finished a good number of drawings and paintings there. In his Mexican passport he was described as a British subject, and was recommended to all the governors of states through which his caravan traveled. Waldeck found in Palenque many physical obstacles, for the archaeological ruins were covered with earth, tropical shrubs and trees, which had to be removed to make them accessible for artistic work. Strangely enough, after completing several drawings, the explorer-artist instead of sending them to Mexico City as it was agreed upon, remitted them to his friends in Paris, which was discovered by the Mexican authorities. This unfair behavior caused his disgrace among his patrons, who even suspected him of being a "British spy". Also his Mexican stipend was gone. All these circumstances brought to an end Waldeck's Palenque work. No wonder that on his way back the Mexican police confiscated a part of his sketches, while most of them were already deposited in Europe.

Not discouraged by such contrarieties, Waldeck continued with his explorations in Uxmal and other ruins in Yucatan, finding financial support of a British enthusiast of indigenous cultures, Edward King vice-count of Kingsborough. Knowing Kingsborough's quest to unriddle the mystery of the Twelve Lost Tribes of Israel and speculations about the possible Jewish origin of Amerindians, Waldeck shrewdly offered to the good lord to resolve it in the Mexican jungle! Curiously enough, he even drafted a profile of an Indian head which fits the contours of South America's geographic boundaries, as if they were shaped by his skull... He called it a symbolic drawing. It was one of his many fantasies. Waldeck was obviously not aware of the Mongolian origin of Indians, although he sometimes tried to relate them to Asiatic civilizations.

His ethnologic notion of pre-Columbian America was closely related to the then-prevailing French belief in the similarity of Egyptian and Mexican pyramids, which confused European scholars for a long time. No less erroneous was Waldeck's own idea when painting chopped off faces on Maya sculptures, he "reconstructed" them with Egyptian, Babylonian or Phoenician physiognomy... Some of his, thus, executed paintings with Maya motifs were later reproduced by other unsuspecting authors, and that even contributed to Waldeck's prestige! Also, unsuspecting French and American scientific societies, in their innocence, awarded him membership! We should, however, not forget that archaeology was then in an infant stage. Some early explorers did not initially know the name of the Mayas, as founders of that advanced indigenous culture of the New World, which rivaled only that of the Incas.

Let's now return to Waldeck's further wonderings, after he left Palenque. He traveled for some months in the states of Veracruz and Tabasco, until he reached the state of Yucatan, where in 1835 and 1836 he conducted his exploration of the fabulous ruins of Uxmal, which he painted with a doubtful degree of exactness. This refers especially to the frontal part of the pyramidal structure called "House of the Magician", over embellished, presenting it as if it were a quasi-

Roman palace... It was artistically speaking an esthetic wonder, but also an archaeological falsificate, for it also displayed a greatly diminished superstructure with addition in front of it of four sculptured figures which did not exist there originally. As we mentioned before, these figures had a Babylonian or Phoenician expression and attire, which have nothing in common with the ancient Mayas. Honoring his British benefactor, Waldeck named the "House of the Magician" - "Pyramid of Kingsborough", but this name never took root in American archaeology. Not surprisingly, Waldeck also mistook the sculpture representation of the Maya god Chac in Uxmal for a trunk of an elephant, even though he could not quite decide whether it could be a trunk of a tapir. He also imagined an elephant on the Stella B in Copan in Honduras.

However, perhaps we should not be too harsh with Waldeck since thirty years earlier, the Prussian explorer Alexander von Humboldt also thought that he saw elephants in the old Aztec "codices", although that animal did not live in Mexico during the historic times of the Aztecs and the Mayas. Humboldt insinuated its derivation from the worship of the god Ganesa of India, also represented by the elephant's head. Curiously, Waldeck criticized Humboldt for his unjustifiably low opinion of the Toltecs, whom he considered fine artists and builders, not knowing that they moved to Yucatan where they mixed with the Mayas and jointly continued to develop the Mayan art, as it was discovered in the XXth century. The Waldeckian "elephant theory" as groundless was later strongly opposed by experienced U.S. archaeologists Morley and Spinden, whereas it was defended by the British ethnologist, Sir Grafton Elliot Smith. When I spoke to Dr. Spinden in 1950 he was surprised that the already settled matter still finds some echoes, and with a big smile encouraged me to further research on Waldeck, whom he called an "old fox"...

In Waldeck's adventurous life there are a few events worthy of mention as they unveil his restless and frequently confused personality. While reading a few dozens of his notebook-memoirs, it was easy to find out that his intellectual "bagage" for his trip to Mexico, consisted mostly of French and German encyclopedias, lacking information on Spanish America, some books on the ancient Greco-Roman culture, others on philosophy and astronomy, **Gravures de Nuits Arabes** and an English dictionary. While in Mexico, he received from Kingsborough his IVth volume of **Mexican Antiquities,** and acquired a short manuscript on Palenque by Capt. Dupais, companion of Capt. Del Rio, two books on Guatemala and a map of Mexico. Logically, he could not lean back on this scant material and, thus, he was left to his own wits and investigation, without antecedents. This explains his fantasy-like approach to explored Maya monuments and confusing them with African-Asian structures. Some of his Maya drawings, if not architecturally altered, are artistically well finished. His paintings of live Indians, fauna and flora are also beautiful, which proved that Waldeck was a master in coloring and perspective, but with exaggerated architectural taste prone to magnifying old structures. All these elements are to be found in his French book **Voyage Pittoresque et Archéologique dans la Province d'Yucatan (Amérique Centrale) pendant les années 1834 et 1836** (Paris, 1838), dedicated to the memory of Viscount of Kingsborough, his intellectual patron.

In Waldecks collection located in the Chicago-based Newberry Library, I found an unpublished water color painting, representing a nude Indian of "mestizo" woman bathing near the Maya ruins in Palenque. Surprisingly, he painted her as a white lady à la Madame Pompadour... According to Waldeck's intimation, while doing his explorations there, she was his permanent companion and bore him a child. The explorer regretted that the boy would probably never meet his brother Gaston in Paris! This beautiful painting with all the graceful anatomic details worthy of a Goya, was a proof that Waldeck was a consummated portrait artist, who combined sex with explorations! It appears that in the latter he was guided by artistic fantasy rather than by archaeological accuracy! This reason must have also prevailed in Waldeck's drawing of the so-called House of the Nuns in Chichen Itzá in Yucatan. In the upper part of its doorway there were some decorative sculptures missing, consumed by erosion. In his artistic zeal he "restored" them and thus graphically beautified the outlook of the whole structure, instead of preserving its archaeological authenticity. Such "restorations" were Waldeck's obsession, although he naively believed them as his scientific or artistic contribution to unveiling the glorious indigenous past of the New World, disregarded or destroyed by the Spanish conquistadors.

After his explorations of Uxmal and Chichen Itzá, Waldeck's artistic adventures in Yucatan were not over, because some rumors were spreading about the mysterious mutilation or disappearance of some Maya sculptures and other objects from ancient ruins. This alerted the local press and authorities to watch his movements in Mérida as he was suspected of sending Maya archaeological artifacts abroad. On January 28, 1836, the mayor of Mérida confiscated Waldeck's sixteen drawings. The old fox previously sent, however, a few bundles of drawings, manuscripts and possibly other things under diplomatic protection, from Veracruz to England aboard the British ship "Pandora". He was notified about their safe arrival in London by the British Foreign Office on July 18, 1836, already in the United Kingdom's capital. It was approximately in that epoch that the British Museum was enriched with exquisite Maya archaeological objects. Curious about it, I asked the Museum about their origin one hundred years later, but surprisingly I never received an answer...

Now let's return to Waldeck's activities after his return to Europe. He lived for some time in England and later in France, which became his permanent residence. There, he divided his activities between professionally painting portraits and writing occasionally on Mexican indigenous affairs. He considered himself a "savant" and for his 1838 book on the antiquities of Yucatan, he received a gold medal from the French Geographic Society. It greatly enhanced his prestige in scholarly circles, and even caused in 1844 the academician Saint Priest to announce in Paris an appeal for a joint European scientific expedition to study Mexican pre-Columbian indigenous civilizations. Right or wrong, Waldeck was then their European promoter. He lived to the age of Methusalah and in 1872 when he was 106 years old, he published his second book **Le Sacrifice Gladiatorial. Histoire du Méxique vers le Fin du Regne de Montezuma II en 1509 Dix Ans**

Avant la Conquette par les Espagnoles (Paris, 1872). It contains varied information on Mexican history and civilization, based mostly on Spanish sources not always reliable, as Spaniards considered Indians as heathens and therefore untrustworthy. The book is illustrated by a number of drawings, some of which are quite peculiar. Thus, some Aztec idols have westernized faces, the Indian soldiers look more like Roman warriors, and king Montezuma II in spite of his native face, bears in his posture certain resemblance to a Venetian "doge". Curiously enough, one of the figures is portrayed with a Parisian hairdo! The only authenticity was retained by those Mexican natives whom he painted in their regional attire in the field. Reservation may also be made regarding his architectural drawings, even if they are imposing and artistically well executed. It looks to me that most of his paintings were made or redesigned in France a few decades after the artist left Mexico and his memory was somewhat dimmed. Or, maybe they were tailored to the esthetic taste of his Parisian publisher or readers! This artistic alchemy was probably unknown to many, including the American Antiquarian Society which bestowed membership upon Waldeck.

One may wonder whether Waldeck's artistic folly was a result of his intellectual confusion, misguided esthetic tendency to beautify everything or myopia, for the latter was also responsible for the famous El Greco's elongated figures in his Spanish paintings. Be that as it may with all of Waldeck's faults, one may recognize his pioneering exploration of the Maya ruins which encouraged U.S. and European explorers to similar tasks. Among them were J.L. Stephens, Catherwood, Barnum, Norman, Nebel, Baradère, Charnay and Friedrichstahl. Some of them inserted Waldeck's lithographs of Maya monuments in their works, presumably for their decorative value rather than scholarly reason. Surprisingly, Waldeck's controversial publications attracted even the attention of U.S. historians such as Prescott, Bancroft and Windsor, who, however, quoted him very cautiously if not critically. Very presumptuous and convinced about his wisdom, Waldeck defied any scientific authority in a field, in which he was really a novice. He regretted this attitude at his very advanced age, but afraid of losing his reputation, he never revoked his archeological errors in print. On the other hand, not many would believe Waldeck's boasting at the age of 70, that he crossed by foot the New World from the north to the south. It sounds like another of his fantasies.

Waldeck's other peculiarity was his self promotion as supposedly being of noble origin. While in Mexico he used his ordinary name, but after moving to France he added the word "de" in front of his family name, which also appeared in his first French book. Later on he changed to "Baron", whereas his second book was signed with the additional name of Maximilien and a title of "Count". One may speculate whether the latter was done while he painted more and more portraits of the French nobility, which thus made him feel more comfortable with real counts...

The Polish-Latin-American Collection of PIASA has a sizeable amount of documentation for researchers interested in Waldeck's enigmatic Americanist activities: seven folders with several hundreds xeroxed documents and ca. 100 reproductions of his drawings and prints; also several articles on Waldeck in English, Polish and Spanish. All this is catalogued as the "Waldeck Mexican Papers".

Bibliography

Waldeck, Frederick de 1825-35, 1860-66 Mmss. del diario personal, documentos, dibujos, pinturas y planes de... en la coleccion de la Newberry Library Chicago, en el British Museum, Londres, y en una colección particular en Mexico, D.F.

Waldeck, J. Fr. de 1829 Ms. **Description de 129 dessins d'idoles et costumes civils et militaires des Mexicains avant la Conquête.** Dessiné par... Mexico.

Waldeck, J. F. de 1834 Ms. **Premiers essaies des me idées sur l'Archéologie d'Amérique. Remplie d'erreurs et d'appréciation fausse mais envieux a consulter.** Palenque.

Rio, Antonio del 1822 **Description of the Ruins of an Ancient City,**

discovered near Palenque in the Kingdom of Guatemala, in Spanish America: Translated from the Original Manuscript Report of Captain Don Antonio del Rio, etc. 17 pl. London.

Icaza I. y Gondra I. 1827 **Colección de las Antigüedades Mexicanas que existen en el Museo Nacional, y dan a luz Isidro Icaza e Isidro Gondra,** litografiadas por Federíco Waldeck e impresas por Pedro Robert. 12 laminas. México.

Toussaint, Manuel 1934 **La Litografía en México. Sesenta y ocho facsímiles con un estudio.** Mexico, D.F.

Waldeck, Frederic de 1838 **Voyage Pittoresque et Archéologique dans la Province d'Yucatan (Amérique Centrale) pendant les années 1834 et 1836.** Par... Dedie a la memoire de feu le Vicomte de Kingsborough. 1 map, 17 planches, 3 plans. Paris.

Waldeck, Federíco de 1930 **Viaje pintoresco y arqueológico a la Provincia de Yucatan (America Central) durante los años 1834 y 1836.** Por... Dedicado a la memoria del difunte Vizconde Kingsborough. Traducción y prólogo del Dr. Manuel Mestre Ghigliazza. Merida, Yuc. México.

Brasseur de Bourbourg 1866 **Monuments Anciens du Méxique. Palenque et Autres Ruines de l'Ancienne Civilisation du Méxique.** Collection du Vues, Bas-Reliefs, Morceaux d'Architecture, Coupes, Terres cuites, Cartes et Plans, Dessinés d'apres Nature et Relevés par M. de Waldeck. Texte Rédigé par M. Brasseur de Bourbourg. Ouvrage Publié sous les Auspices de S.E.M. le Ministre de l'Instruction Publique. Paris.

Waldeck, J. Fr. Max. de 1872 **Le Sacrifice Gladiatorial. Histoire du Méxique vers le Fin du Regne de Montezuma II en 1509 Dix Ans Avant la Conquête par les Espagnols.** (Loisirs du centenaire) Paris.

Humboldt et Bonpland 1813 **Vues de Cordilleres et Monuments de Peuples Indigenes de l'Amérique. Atlas pittoresque.** 2 vols. Paris.

Kingsborough, E. K. 1831-1848 **Antiquities of Mexico: comprising fac-similes of ancient Mexican paintings and hieroglyphics, preserved in the royal libraries of Paris, Berlin, and Dresden; in the imperial library of Vienna; in the Vatican library; in the Borgian museum at Rome; in the library of the Institute of Bologna; and in the Bodleian library at Oxford.** Together with monuments of New Spain, by M. Dupaix, with their respective scales of measurement and accompanying descriptions. The whole illustrated by many valuable unedited manuscripts, by Lord Kingsborough. The drawings, on stone, by A. Aglio. 9 vols. London.

Stephens, John Lloyd 1841 **Incidents of Travel in Central America, Chiapas and Yucatan.** Illustrated by numerous engravings. 2 vols. New York.

Stephens, John Lloyd 1843 **Incidents of Travel in Yucatan.** Illustrated by 120 engravings. Two volumes. London.

Catherwood, Frederick 1844 **Views of Ancient Monuments in Central America,** Chiapas and Yucatan, by F. Catherwood, Archt. London.

Stephens, John Lloyd 1854 **Incidents of Travel in Central America, Chiapas, and Yucatan, 1841.** Revised with additions by Frederick Catherwood. London.

Smith, Grafton Elliot 1924 **Elephants and Ethnologists.** Woodcuts by A. Horrace Gerrard and K. Leigh Pemberton. Illustr., plates, bibliogr. London.

Thompson, J. Eric 1927 "The Elephant's Heads in the Waldeck's Manuscripts". **Scientific Monthly.** Vol. 25. New York.

H. I. B. 1929 "Baron de Waldeck's Journal". **British Museum Quarterly.** Vol. IV: 1929-30. London.

Castañeda Paganini, R. 1946 **Las Ruinas de Palenque. Su descubrimiento y primeras exploraciones en el siglo XVIII.** Guatemala.

Urbanski, Edmund S. 1945 "Juan Federíco de Waldeck y su obra exploradora de Yucatán". **Rev. Orbe,** Universidad de Yucatan. Merida, Yuc. Vol. III, No. 7.

Von Hagen, Victor W. 1946 "Waldeck, the life story of one of the most extraordinary personalities ever to follow the lure of lost civilizations, etc.". **Natural History,** Vol. LV, No. 4.

Cline, Howard F. 1947 "The Apocryphal Early Career of J. F. de Waldeck, Pioneer Americanist". **Acta Americana.** Vol. V, No. 4. Los Angeles-Berkeley.

Faustin E. Wirkus, The Marine Who Became "King" of La Gonave

Edward Kaminski

I first became interested in Faustin Wirkus when I read about him on July 2, 1977, in the **Nowy Dziennik.** The article was written by Jozef Dubicki and was entitled, "About Our Fellow Countryman Who Was A King". It was accompanied by a photo labeled: "Marine Sgt. Faustin Wirkus - King Faustin II". The article also included a humorous drawing of "King" Faustin being given a bath by two beautiful mulattos. According to Dubicki, these two women were descendants of the ill-fated Polish Legionnaires, and had been assigned to teach Wirkus the language and customs of the "Creoles". The reporter's reference to the Polish Legion struck a familiar note for I had long been interested in this chapter of Polish history.

Dubicki's brief, but very colorful account of the sergeant's life stimulated my curiosity. I decided to learn more about him. In the **N. D.** article it was stated that "... in 1945 Wirkus' body was disinterred from a Brooklyn grave and in a triumphal ceremony with the participation of 25,000 blacks, was buried in Arlington, Va. His grave marker bears the inscription: 'Faustus II King of La Gonave'." Reasoning that such an event would have received widespread newspaper coverage, particularly in the black press, I proceeded to check contemporary newspaper files in the N.Y. Public Library. The result was negative. An inspection of the famous Schomburg Collection of Negro Literature and the files of the **Amsterdam News** in the central Harlem Library revealed no reference to Wirkus. I then checked with

Marine Hq. in Washington. I was informed that "... there are no records indicating he was burried in Brooklyn and his body exhumed for reburial in Arlington National Cemetery." The Supt. of Arlington was kind enough to send me a photo of the grave. The simple inscription gives his name, rank and dates of birth and death. Apparently, Mr. Dubicki had engaged in some "poetic license".

Faustin Wirkus was born in 1896 in Pittsont, Pa., the son of Marcin and Anna Wirkus, immigrants from the Wilno region of Poland. He left school at the age of eleven and went to work in the coal mines as a breaker boy. Disheartened by his bleak prospects, he tried to join the Marines. The recruiters told him to wait until he was older. When he was eighteen he ran away from home and joined the Corps. The blond, square-faced marine was destined to find adventure and fame as have few others in the service.

After receiving basic training, he was shipped to Haiti with the first Marine outfit sent to restore order in that troubled country. It was the year 1915 and he arrived on board the U.S.S. Tennessee. He was an expert rifleman and had an excellent record. Later Wirkus was transferred to Guantanamo, Cuba, and promoted to sergeant in 1918. There he broke his arm for the second time and returned to the mainland for treatment.

In April, 1919, he returned to Haiti and was appointed a Second Lt. in the Haitian Gendarmerie. In January, 1920, he was posted to Arcahaie. On a visit to the remote village of Carzal, he discovered that the majority of its inhabitants - about 1500 people - were light-skinned, with kinky yellow hair. Many had blue eyes and some were freckled. He was told that it was their tradition that they were the descendants of a Polish regiments sent over by Napoleon to support Gen. LeClerc. LeClerc - Napoleon's brother-in-law - had been placed in command of about 58,000 troops whose mission was the suppression of the Haitian rebellion.

As an interesting sidelight to this paper, it should be noted here that Dr. Jan Pachonski, one of Poland's outstanding scholars on the Napoleonic period, has written extensively on the Polish expedition to Haiti. In 1979 he published a work entitled, **Polacy na Antyllach**

i Morzu Karaibskim (Poles in the Antilles and the Caribbean). In it he states that 5,280 Poles were sent to Haiti, including 260 officers. Of the latter group, about half survived bouts with rebels and yellow fever. According to Pachonski, about 4000 enlisted men and non-commissioned officers died principally from yellow fever and on the field of battle. Of the survivors, approximately 500 were incorporated into English units on Jamaica, and about 150 returned to their units in Spain. Others spent years in captivity on English prison ships. More than 200 Legionnaires fled to Cuba and others settled in the U.S.

Approximately 400 Poles were taken prisoner in Haiti. Gen. Jean Jacques Dessalines - leader of the rebels - magnanimously spared their lives and offered them citizenship in the newly-proclaimed republic. Dessalines felt that the Poles were victims of Napoleon, pressed into service against their will to make war on a strange people for whom they had no ill feeling. He said that they had been through troubles of their own which he had no desire to make worse. About 240 Legionnaires decided to remain on the island. The others were eventually repatriated to Europe. Many of those who remained intermarried.

Pachonski visited Haiti in the seventies and found some traces of the Polish presence in a number of surnames. He also came across some very old mulattoes who knew a few Polish words (e.g., "proszę", "przepraszam", "psiakrew") and who could even curse "... Do jasnej i ciężkiej cholery."

More than a century later - and by some strange turn of fate - Faustin Wirkus had come upon some of the Legionnaires' descendants in Carzal. He learned that the people of this village had mated mainly with mulattoes and octoroons. And by an equally bizarre coincidence, Wirkus bore the same name as that of a previous ruler of the island - Emperor Faustin Soulouque. According to an island legend, the emperor had vanished in 1848 with the promise that his descendant of the same name would return to take his throne.

In 1921 Wirkus asked to be sent to La Gonave, a voodoo-ridden island of 300 sq. mi., 40 miles north of Port-au-Prince. La Gonave is the only part of Haiti on which there were no colonial settlements. In pre-colonial Spanish days it was a pirate refuge. During the French domination it was a refuge for run-away slaves. Very few whites have been to La Gonave. When Wirkus arrived, he was appointed Administrator. He was responsible for the regulation of traffic, collection of taxes, enforcement of sanitary provisions and the prevention of smuggling. He spoke Creole fluently.

One day - after he had been there a year - the unofficial "queen" of La Gonave was brought to him as a prisoner. The voodoo priestess had been charged with "...endangering the authority of the government." When he announced his name, she was taken aback. She then told him about the legend of Emperor Soulouque. Wirkus told her that the French had probably brought the name "Faustin" to Haiti, and that they had the same holy names as those of "... my own Polish people." "Queen" Memenne was released on a promise of good behavior.

After a short stay on La Gonave, Sgt. Wirkus was assigned to other posts in Haiti. He distinguished himself in man-to-man bush warfare and once killed seven knife-wielding natives. He was particularly well-known for having killed the "caco" leaders Estraville and Olivier while leading patrols in the mountains.

On April 15, 1925, Wirkus returned to La Gonave as resident sub district commander. As a lieutenant in the Haitian Gendarmerie, he was also named Chief of Police. His duties were many and varied. The tough marine became the unofficial doctor, agricultural expert, tax collector, and general all-around adviser to the natives. He was the dispenser of justice, pills and instruction in sanitation. The people of La Gonave felt that he had certain mystical powers; that he could read their minds and foretell their futures. Wirkus felt that their belief in him was half the battle in helping them to help themselves. He protected them from graft, neglect and cruelty. He was a firm, but compassionate administrator. On his trips to the U.S. on leave, he would return to the island with clothing, shoes and tools for distribution among the natives. He even once made a trip to Port-au-Prince to get a book on the proper rearing of babies.

Soon he was summoned to the "royal domicile" of the voodoo queen. Ti Memenne was the Queen of the Congo Societies. She told him that the people felt that he had been sent by God to rule them, but that prior to his "coronation" he would have to undergo an initiation and ratification. In accordance with tradition, a rooster was sacrificed in his honor and its blood was used to mark his forehead and wrists in a secret rite. Following his initiation, a visit to the Wise Man of the sea cliffs sealed and sanctioned the belief that he was the reincarnated Faustin Soulouque.

He then returned to the voodoo temple for the installation ceremony. In an eerie atmosphere, marked by pounding drums and flickering candlelight, solemnly crowned and machetes were placed across his shoulders. He was immediately carried in his chair to greet the cheering crowd of about 10,000 Blacks.

After he was crowned, the marine was shown the mysteries of voodoo. He always maintained, however, that he was simply an observer, not a practitioner. On Feb. 4, 1928, an article entitled "King Leatherneck" appeared in **Collier's Magazine.** It was written by William Seabrook who had just returned from Haiti. Seabrook had heard about the "white king of La Gonave" and had gone to see him. The writer was greatly impressed by the marine and his accomplishments.

On March 7, 1928, the president of Haiti and Gen. Russell, the U.S. High Commissioner, arrived in La Gonave for an inspection. Soon after the visit, Wirkus went on leave and returned to Haiti in sixty days. In 1929 Seabrook wrote a book about Haiti called **The Magic Island.** In it he dealt more expansively on Wirkus' "reign". Unfortunately, he presented a highly romanticized and sensational account of the marine's activities. Shortly after the book appeared, Wirkus was deluged with letters from all parts of the world. The island was visited again by Pres. Borno and Gen. Russell. Ten weeks after the visit, Wirkus was relieved of duty and put in command of a gendarmerie company in the capital. He was reassigned supposedly to prevent the "ill-effects of prolong duty at remote stations." But the real reason for the transfer was the desire of Pres. Borno not to have a "kingdom" within the Rupublic of Haiti.

When his enlistment expired in 1931, Wirkus took a reserve

commission and left the service. He arrived in N. Y. and, according to the **N.Y. Times,** received a princely reception. He was quoted as saying that "... Queen Ti Memenne had done most of the ruling until he had been introduced as king." He expressed a desire for further adventures.

That same year, Doubleday, Doran & Co. published **The White King of La Gonave,** written by the marine and his collaborator, Taney Dudley. Wirkus then devoted himself to lecturing and selling securities for a Wall St. firm. In January, 1934, **Harper's Magazine** noted that he had visited Harlem and had supplied valuable information on voodoo and its practitioners to black researchers.

In March, 1937, he married Yula Fuller, a girl from Virginia. They had one child, Faustin E. Jr. In December of that same year the **N.Y. World Telegram** reported that Wirkus was planning a visit to Haiti the following year. He was apparently worried about the tense situation then existing between Haiti and the Dominican Republic. He blamed Dictator Trujillo for the death of 8,000 migrant Haitian sugar workers.

In December, 1939, the **N.Y. Times** noted that Gunnery Sgt. Wirkus had returned to the service in order to help to recruit 6,000 marines. He was placed in charge of recruiting publicity in Manhattan. In 1943, Warrant Officer Wirkus was transferred to the Navy Pre-Flight School at the Univ. of N. C. In 1945 - gravely ill with cancer - he entered the Brooklyn Naval Hospital. On December 8th - after a long and courageous struggle - he succumbed to the dread disease. The **N.Y. Times** and the **Nowy Swiat** - among others - devoted lengthy obituaries to the ex-marine.

Following his death, no further reference was made to Wirkus in the media, except for an article which appeared in the May, 1951 issue of **Coronet.** It was entitled, "The Yankee King of the Tropics", by J.P. Flinsbee. As a postcript to this paper, let me add the following:

Item 1 - Last year the **N.Y. Times** reported that John Wittek, an 86 year-old Polish American veteran from N.J., had finally received the Purple Heart decoration for wounds received in the Haitian Campaign.

His son, John, Jr., presented the award to his father who was confined to a nursing home. I immediately contacted the son with a view towards interviewing his father about possible contacts with and/or knowledge of Wirkus. Unfortunately, I was informed that Wittek was totally deaf and could not possibly be interviewed. I was sent, however, a xeroxed excerpt from the **U. S. Marine Corps Story** which briefly referred to Wirkus' stay on La Gonave.

Item 2 - Last month I learned that a Robert Virkus had recently resided in a building not far from mine. After some inquiries, I managed to contact him at his N. Y. office. The result was negative: he was **not** related to the marine from Pittston, Pa.

Faustin E. Wirkus left a legacy of good works on La Gonave. To what extent - if any - he has been memorialized is unknown. But there can be no doubt that his fame has become part of the island's folklore. And surely, too, for those who visit his grave in Arlington, the words "King of La Gonave" will always appear on the simple marker.

Curious Incidents During the Mission of Rev. Mateusz Matulski in Chile (1871-1894)

Edward Kaminski

The first incident occurred in 1876 in the small Chilean settlement of Punta Arenas, located on the coast of the Magellan Strait. At that time, Punta Arenas was the most southerly inhabited point on the globe. It served principally as a penal colony and place of political exile. It was administered by a civil-military governor with the aid of a small military garrison. There were also about 1200 civilians, consisting mainly of military dependents, craftsmen, fishermen and their respective families.

Punta Arenas was almost completely isolated, not only from the world, but from the rest of Chile. Communication was rare and often inaccurate. This state of events continued until an incident occurred which would not only deeply affect the local inhabitants, but would also have repercussions in the Chilean press and legislature. And directly involved in this curious episode was Father Mateusz Matulski, a Polish Franciscan missionary serving as both pastor and military chaplain.

Wiktor Matulski was born in Hrubieszow on March 26, 1841. He entered the Franciscan Order in 1859 and attended school in Warsaw. Deeply patriotic, he took part in the January Uprising of 1863. Later that same year, he celebrated his monastic vows, taking the name Mateusz. Following the Russian confiscation of the monastery, Mateusz - together with his fellow monks - went first to Austria and then to Italy, where he continued his theological studies. Holy orders were conferred upon him on November 27, 1870, and he celebrated his first Mass in a monastery in Frascati. Fr. Matulski felt called to do missionary work and left for Chile in 1871. There he was first assigned to the Colegio Apostólico situated in Castro. A year later, he was transferred to Punta Arenas as pastor of the local parish.

Fr. Matulski was a spry and jovial man, and was well-liked by his parishioners. This feeling, however, was not shared by the governor who was generally disliked for his severe dealings with both the military and civilian populations. Sgt. Major Diego Dublé Almeida was an agnostic, anti-clerical, free-thinker. This fact placed him squarely at odds with the religious, missionary zeal of Matulski. Gov. Dublé was also apparently irritated by what he called Matulski's "poor" Spanish. The stage was set, then, for an explosive encounter between the two men. And it was not long in coming.

One day in 1876 the fishing schooner "San Pedro" was enroute to its home port of Punta Arenas. Capt. José Nogueira was at the helm, skillfully maneuvering the vessel through the treacherous waters. The region was well-known for its frequent shipwrecks, and floating wreckage was a common sight. A clipper was shortly sighted lying on its side amidst juting rocks. Nogueira ordered a boat to be lowered to investigate the wreck. No one was found aboard, but the wreck has been stripped of all useful material. The only object which remained undamaged was the wooden figurehead of a woman, still attached to the remains of the bow. The figurehead showed a woman in a blue tunic, full of folds. Ruddy cheeks and eyes gazing into the distance were prominent features of the face. The head was covered with a crown decorated with flowers. The seamen from the "San Pedro" were transformed by the sight and concluded that it was a figure of a Virgin Mary which had been miraculously spared damage. They then detached the figurehead and brought it back to the ship. Two days later the "San Pedro" arrived safely in Punta Arenas.

As is usual in such isolated regions, the ship was greeted by many onlookers. The figurehead was brought to the landing area and placed on a tarpaulin. The crowd assembled around the figurehead, and Capt. Nogueira gave an account of its recovery. Soon news of the find reached Fr. Matulski and he quickly arrived at the scene. Nogueira repeated the story and then the Franciscan friar proceeded to examine the object very carefully. The spectators anxiously awaited the priest's decision. Who could be more competent in matters such as these? They did not have to wait long. Fr. Matulski announced that this was, indeed, the figurehead of the Virgin Mary! For the good friar and his parishioners the matter was settled. He immediately asked that the figurehead be brought to the chapel. Here it joined another Madonna - the Madonna of Carmen, patroness of the Chilean Army. Its fame and cult grew rapidly and it was soon referred to as the Madonna of the Tierra del Fuego. The faithful felt that at last they now had their own patroness of this storm-swept region. Soon it was rumored that favors and grace could be obtained through adoration of the Madonna. People began to consider the figurehead as a "miraculous" object.

Fr. Matulski decided to organize a Madonna brotherhood. The membership fee of twenty "centavos" was considered rather high at the time, but this did not deter the faithful. When Gov. Dublé learned of these developments, he was infuriated. Apparently he felt that his authority was being undermined, and that certain regulations had been violated. It is also possible that he believed that the priest was "taking advantage" of the trust and faith of the simple settlers. He decided, therefore, to personally inspect the figurehead.

Accompanied by his adjutant, he went to the chapel where he spent some time examining the object. He then returned to his office and inquired whether Capt. Nogueira had complied with the regulation requiring salvaged objects to be turned over to the local authorities. Upon learning that Noguiera had not done so, he immediately fined the Portuguese the considerable sum of fifty "pesos". Simultaneously, he ordered a detachment of troops to confiscate the figurehead and store it in the barracks. The figurehead was never to be seen again. Some believe that Dublé had also ordered its destruction. Others feel that it was probably used as firewood by the soldiers during some particularly cold winter.

Dublé then had Fr. Matulski brought before him. Although the pastor was also a military chaplain, the governor could not find any legal grounds on which to punish him. He limited himself to stating that the priest had acted "unjustly" in charging such a high membership fee from poor, hard-working people. The governor also told him that the figurehead - in his opinion and in that of many others - was that of Queen Victoria of England! Fr. Matulski left the office very upset and worried, but not disheartened.

Soon thereafter, a mail boat left for Valparaiso carrying correspondence and two articles relating the Madonna story. The articles were printed in the Catholic press and attributed to a certain "F.C.". There was speculation that the initials meant "Fiel Católico" (faithful Catholic) or were the initials of Francisco Cancaro who had been Matulski's predecessor in Punta Arenas. At any rate, the matter would not have gone any further if it had not been for the subsequent publication - with editorial comment - of one of the articles in "El Ferrocarril", a prominent Santiago daily. The matter was then brought to the attention of Fr. Matulski's superior, Bishop Francisco de Paula Solar. The bishop asked the friar for a complete report on the Madonna affair. Matulski complied and sent his superior additional information regarding Dublé's harassment. The bishop in turn sent the report to the Minister of Foreign Affairs and Colonization.

The minister sent the report, plus the article, to Gov. Dublé, demanding an explanation. Dublé sent an immediate reply, defending himself and attacking Matulski. Dublé's answer was then sent to the bishop, who once again sent all of the correspondence to Fr. Matulski, together with a note in which he expressed his regrets at the lack of understanding between the governmental and church authorities in Punta Arenas. He also proposed that the Polish friar be replaced by someone more agreeable to the governor. An amicable resolution of the embarrassing situation seemed near. Unexpectedly, however, two Catholic deputies brought the matter up again with the minister, demanding the removal of the governor. Several Congressional sessions were also devoted to the subject. A detailed report was compiled in the Official Daily, and, as a result, the Madonna incident became a part of Chilean history.

Fr. Matulski was relieved of his position as local pastor and preparations were made for his departure from Punta Arenas. But before he could leave, another, more serious incident occurred, which would place him once again in direct conflict with Sgt. Major Dublé.

The military garrison in Punta Arenas - particularly the enlisted ranks - had long been restive under the harsh rule of the governor. He was also disliked by the exiles and their families. His administration - although progressive in some respects - was marked by severity and acts of cruelty. In a letter to his religious superiors, Fr. Matulski accused Dublé of ordering the deaths of twenty starving Indians for the theft of government-owned cattle. He also declared that the governor had given or sold two Indian children to the British. It was quite apparent that festering conditions in the settlement had reached an intolerable stage. The eruption was not long in coming.

In November, 1877, the garrison mutinied. The exiled were given arms and a number joined the mutineers. A group of prisoners also managed to seize weapons. In the bloody fighting that ensued, more than fifty people were killed or wounded. Public and private property damage was very extensive. The chapel, however, was not touched. Gov. Dublé was wounded, but managed to escape and return with reinforcements. After a brief struggle, the mutineers were overwhelmed and their leadership fled to Argentina.

The governor immediately ordered the imprisonment of forty two suspected conspirators, including Fr. Matulski. The priest was put on board the "Magallanes", a Chilean corvette. There he would remain imprisoned for twenty two days. Seemingly, two circumstances motivated the incarceration of the priest. Firstly, he had been seen talking to Cpl. Riquelme prior to the rebellion. Riquelme was one of the principal instigators of the mutiny. Secondly, the governor considered it "highly unusual" that Matulski's chapel and quarters had been spared destruction. Needless to say, these circumstances did not constitute evidence proving the priest's complicity in the mutiny. Indeed, a number of inhabitants declared that he had hidden in the nearby woods for fear of his life. And according to some accounts, the very same Cpl. Riquelme had ordered his execution!

Dublé was well aware of Fr. Matulski's popularity among the

soldiers and exiles. Additionally, the chapel was reportedly used as a sanctuary during the rebellion. The fact of the matter is that the governor's personal animosity towards the friar had led him to take such an unjust, drastic step.

A military tribunal was convened and Fr. Matulski was found innocent of all charges. Only nine of the accused were found guilty. The minutes of the proceedings clearly reveal that Dublé had intended to implicate in the mutiny innocent people whom he personally detested. It was noted that Dublé had governed imprudently and severely, if not to say cruelly. Shortly after the conclusion of the trials, the governor tendered his resignation and left Punta Arenas.

On March 23, 1878, the Chilean daily, "El Mercurio" of Valparaiso, lauded the Polish priest for the manner in which he had accompanied the nine condemned to death. He was highly praised for his humanity and spirituality. The paper strongly recommended that - as an act of justice - he be restored to his former position. This, unfortunately, did not come about.

Father Matulski's mission to the penal colony had been marked by controversy and personal conflict. The two incidents in which he had been involved had left him spiritually and physically exhausted. He therefore decided to request reassignment. In late 1878 - after a six-year stay in Punta Arenas - the Polish Franciscan left for Valparaiso to recover from his ordeals. Following his recovery, he was given various assignments. These included missionary work among the Araucanian Indians.

On April 22, 1894, at the age of fifty three, Fr. Matulski passed away in the monastery of Osorno. His death was duly recorded in the May issue of the Franciscan journal, "El Misionero Franciscano". The editors noted that the Polish friar had left behind "...the memory of good, industrious and apostolic friar." No further historical reference to Matulski would be made until 1969 when Armando Braun Menéndez described his role in **Pequeña História Magallanica**. This publication was followed by **Los Pioneros** (Vol. 2, 1984) by Enrique Campos Menéndez. The Polish priest was frequently and favorably mentioned in both of these works.

Hispanic Reflections on Edmund Urbanski's Work *Od Wikingów do Indian*

Janina J. Kusielewicz

My topic today "Hispanic Reflections on Dr. Edmund Stefan Urbanski's Polish book **Od Wikingów do Indian** is more than just a discussion on the merits of the work or a typical review of a book. It is actually an account of a man's life: of his perceptions, observations and reflections upon the world he studied and influenced. In 1979 our esteemed chairperson Dr. Edmund Urbanski established at the Polish Institute of Art and Sciences this forum for those interested in the esoteric field of Polish-Hispanic studies. Dr. Urbanski's sojourns throughout the world, his personal circumstances and his life's work combined with a strong Polish cultural heritage have made him a pioneer in this realm and led to the creation and perpetuation of today's panel "New Perspectives in the Polish-Latin American Studies". Just as some may question what possible connection could exist between Poles and Hispanics, so too would some say of the connection between Vikings and Indians. The apparent opposition and lack of correlation between these seemingly disparate topics is exactly the misconception that many of Urbanski's comparative works attempt to destroy.

Dr. Urbanski's book **Od Wikingów do Indian: Wspomnienia Wojenne i Powojenne za Skandynawii, Hispanoameryki i USA** is a series of vignettes documenting four distinct periods in his life: Pre-WWII Poland, Scandinavia, Latin America and the USA. In classical terms the autobiographical and the historical in literature were consid-

EDMUND S. URBAŃSKI

OD WIKINGÓW DO INDIAN

WSPOMNIENIA WOJENNE I POWOJENNE
ZE SKANDYNAWII, HISPANOAMERYKI I USA

ARTEX PRESS

This Polish book *From Vikings to the Indians* (1987, 1994) describes **Dr Urbanski's** travels in Hispanic America, combined with essays on Indians, Mestizos, Creaoles and Negroes. It is now being translated into English and Swedish.

ered nearly the same. Such a definition of autobiography lends itself well to Urbanski's anectdotaly journalistic, historical, chronological collage. Witold Balinski says of this piece that Urbanski:

> "*W swych wspomnieniach pokazuje nam sylwetki ludzi ze wszystkich warstw społecznych, od prostaków do uczonych, od zajmujących się swymi przeciętnymi, codziennymi troskami do znanych działaczy politycznych, piastujących najwyższe stanowiska. Jak w kalejdoskopie przewijają się w książce prof. Urbańskiego całe zastępy takich ludzi i ma się wrażenie że wyczucie autora przenika ich na wylot, że kultura ich stanowi dla niego otwartą księgę, której hieroglify są dla niego łatwo czytelne.*" (Baliński)

This book presents a myriad of persons from all walks of life: authors like Teodor Parnicki, Elena Poniatowska and Rafael Muñoz; scholars like Professor Bronisław Malinowski and Professor Seweryn Cyronberg; government officials like the President of the Republic of Costa Rica Lic. Teodoro Picado Michalski, or Cuban senator Dr. Nuñez Portuondo; artists; businessmen; journalists. The kaleidescope of topics personal, historical, humorous and dramatic springing from Urbanski's path from Poland to the USA is as rich and diverse as its background. Dr. Antoni Mantykowski expressed that Dr. Urbanski's writing weaves the facets of this work, from the reflections on Mayan and Aztec civilization to dramatic episodes evading the SS in Norway, into a very readable, entertaining tapestry.

In a review of "**Od Wikingów do Indian**" for "The Polish Review" Joachim Baer discusses the books appeal of Polish adventursomeness in a land that he considers "distant from Poland and lacking (any) cultural links with Poland other than the connection through Roman Catholicism" (Baer). I agree with Baer's regard for this work as "more than a scholarly book" with a pervasive "spirit of Polishness." But I disagree with his narrow view discounting anything more than common religion as a link between these two worlds. Baer's comment perpetuates the very dichotomy between these cultures that Urbanski himself challenges. The chronicle begins with our "protagonist's" experiences as a journalist in pre-WWII Gdansk and

Gdynia and moves quickly to his time in Sweden and Norway. Finding himself pursued by SS and Nazi supporters, he is forced to follow the path of the Vikings and go by ship to the New World - Latin America. As early as his second vignette about Mexico entitled "Początkowa penetracja kulturowa Meksyku" Urbanski notes not only linguistic similarities between Polish and Spanish, due to many related Latin roots, but also something more. Urbanski arrives with doubt, fearing that moving from a Slavic past, with just a short "intermezzo" (Urbanski, 29) among Scandinavians, to Latin American culture might be difficult due to the common preconception of a lack of any similarity between their cultures. He soon states, however, that "*przekonałem się jednak, że kultura słowiańska ma pewne wspólne cechy psychiczne z hiszpanoamerykańską, zwłaszcza w zakresie zamiłowań humanistycznych i pewnych manifestacji uczuciowych*" (Urbanski, 29). It is my belief that this psychic, humanistic and emotional connection that Urbanski so expediently detected, is a direct result of the common histories of oppression and revolution historically associated with both Slavic and Latin American countries. The struggle for freedom inevitably leads to the fiery, passionate nationalism endemic to both Poland and many Latin American countries. A connection often discounted by scholars but brought to the forefront here.

It is his other scholarly works such as **Hispanic America and its Civilizations, Spanish Americans and Anglo-Americans**, published by the University of Oklahoma in 1978, that we see the academic fruit of Dr. Urbanski's life long observations and labors chronicled in **Od Wikingow do Indian**. The main premise of **Hispanic America and its Civilizations** is that each Latin American ethno-culutural group (e.g. mestizos, Negroes etc.), thanks to their individual historical experiences and biology, manifest their own particular styles of living, modes of behavior and idiosyncracies, all of which are based in unequal economic structure and disparate cultural levels perpetuating social disorder. The evolution of his thoughts for that topic is evidenced here in the book **Od Wikingow do Indian** as early as the vignette entitled "Veracruz i moje pierwsze

Among **Dr. Urbanski's** ten books dedicated to Hispanic-American matters, the first one was **Studies in Spanish American Literature and Civilization** (1964), 1965, W.I. Univ. Press), whereas the second one was **Angloamerica e Hispanoamerica. Análisis de dos civilizaciones** (1965, Madrid, Studium). Both works were utilized by U.S. and Canadian universities, and as pioneer works enouraged other Latin Americanists to publish books on similar topics.

kroki meksykańskie" (Urbanski, 27). From his first moments on Latin American soil Urbanski's investigative eye was gathering information. His vivid description of the languid movements of the Indian and Mestizo dock hands in Veracruz seems to be the seen that would later lead to scholarly investigation in the aforementioned book. Later recollections such as "Indianie Nahua i ich zwyczaje" (Urbanski, 37) where he discusses the customs of the Nahua people; "Gdzie jest kolebka cywilizacji indo-amerykańskiej?" (Urbanski, 174) referring to his analysis of contemporary anthropological theory about the birth of Indo-American pre-Columbian civilization; "Prekolumbijskie powiązania kulturowe Ameryki z Azją" (Urbanski, 178) recounting the controversial presentations at the 35th International Congress of Americanists; and "Metysi w obronie swego dziedzictwa indiańskiego" (Urbanski, 185), where he refers to Octavio Paz's analysis of Mestizo mentality, these among other vignettes, continue to trace the development of Urbanski's ethno-anthropological interests and studies.

Another recurring theme in **Od Wikingów do Indian** that corresponds directly to a future work of Urbanski's, is that of Polish cultural influences upon and influential Poles in Latin America. In the section entitled "Ślady Polaków w Meksyku, Ameryce Środkowej i Hiszpanii" (Urbanski, 82) we see beginnings of what is Dr. Urbanski's latest work **Sylwetki Polskie w Ameryce Łacińskiej XIX i XX wieku** which is a compilation of biographies of influential Poles in Latin America spanning two centuries. This is more than autobiographic compilation, rather the sequence of vignettes in **Od Wikingów do Indian** documenting the path of Dr. Urbanski's scholarly life and serves the starting point for most of his academic achievements. Although Urbanski mentions by name several of his individual works (for example **Angloamérica e Hispanoamérica: Analisis de dos Civilizaciones** (Urbanski, 208) and **Studies in Spanish American Literature and Civilization** (Urbanski,178,208) as they correspond with his "life chronology", if one follows his work, nearly every book, article and essay can find its origin in one of the many reflections and recollections chronicled in **Od Wikingów do Indian**.

The cultural variety of the previously mentioned books that

were born from Dr. Urbanski's experiences and studies, as recounted in the multitude of section in **Od Wikingów do Indian**, reflect one of the main themes underlying many of Urbanski's works: cultural pluralism. (How well such an attitude serves and fits today's academic institutions from the culturally pluralistic grade school to the politically correct institution of higher learning). Half way through the book we come across a statement "Moja nowa teza o pluralizmie kultury hispanoamerykańskiej" (Urbanski, 191). This new thesis on the cultural pluralism in Latin America appears to be the central ideology, not only of this book, but of much of Dr. Urbanski's body of work. As he himself states within these pages, the wide cultural variety (not without its similarities) of his experiential life journey, a man of three fatherlands, according to some, or four cultures, according to others, has created his interest in civilization. With commentary such as this, it becomes difficult to determine if Urbanski's work acts as a reflection of his life or if his life is a projection of his work. The broad differences in pluralistic Latin American culture were at the time of his proclamation, groundbreaking and controversial. This cultural pluralism reflects not only society, but the components of this man's life.

Given this broad range of cultures and topics, what is it then that joins Poles to Vikings? "Co łączy Polaków z Wikingami?" Well, in this case it seems to be Urbanski himself.

> *"Wspomnienia moje, przeplatane refleksjami historycznymi, kulturowymi, społecznymi i politycznymi, nazwałem* ***Od Wikingów do Indian****. Odbyłem bowiem podróż tranatlantycką śladami Wikingów, docierając do Ameryki, której autochtonami byli i są Indianie, choć ich poważnie wytrzebiono. Nie była to wyprawa zdobywcza, lecz podróż po części naukowa po części emigracyjna. Podobnym szlakiem, choć w historycznie odmiennych warunkach, podążyli tu w przeszłości inni Polacy..."* (Urbanski, 257)

And so Dr. Urbanski discusses Vikings, sailing, Poles and Latin America. Perhaps that is what connect these disparate peoples: travel, exploration, adventure and the sea. Ending with commentary on a Polish team as champions kayaking across South America, Urbanski brings his tale full circle: *"Tym razem Polacy nie płynęli szlakiem Wikingów..., lecz w odwrotnym kierunku, do Oceanu Atlantyckiego, który łączy Amerykę z Europą."* (Urbanski, 259)

Co łączy Polaków z Wikingami? What do Vikings have to do with Indians? What could possibly necessitate Polish Hispanic studies? The answer to the first of these questions was already provided. The second question can be answered on the path of the explorer or the adventurer, but in this case lies in the life journey of a scholar. As for the third, well, the answer begins with the myriad of cross cultural connections made every day and continues within the work of each and every one of us in this room.

Concluding these observations I would like to say that Dr. Urbanski considers himself to be a modest intellectual who avoids publicity. And yet, whether he likes it or not, his fifty years (as chronichled here) of Indo/Ibero/American activities, with sixteen books, on various topics, in three languages, is an undeniable fact which must be recognized.

Works Cited

Baer, Joachim. "Review of Edmund S. Urbański, **Od Wikingów do Indian**" in **The Polish Review** No. 3-4, 1990, N.Y.

Balinski, Witold. "Nowa książka Prof. Edmunda S. Urbańskiego" in **Lud**, July 2, 1988, Curitiba, Brazil.

Mantykowski, Antoni. "Review of **Od Wikingów do Indian**" in **Gwiazda Polarna** January 7, 1987, Stevens Point, WI

Urbanski, Edmund S. **Od Wikingów do Indian: Wspomnienia Wojenne i Powojenne ze Skandynawii, Hispanoameryki i USA.** Artex Press, 1987, Stevens Point, WI.

Reception of Spanish-American Literature in Contemporary Poland

Elżbieta Skłodowska

What we should bear in mind when evaluating the presence of Latin American literature in contemporary Poland is that the reception of literature — especially foreign literature — is not a self-contained phenomenon. Readers operate inside specific — and often complex — political contexts and they have been educated within powerful systems of values which often breed misconceptions and prejudice about foreign cultures.

The very project of providing a strategy for cross-cultural translation or representing "other" peoples' discourses is, obviously, an unsettling one even though it has been pursued at least for over a century, since the birth of anthropology as discipline. But what is disturbing in the case of Polish reception and perception of Latin American letters is that anthropological thinking — with its concern for the politics and ethics of representing the "other" — has not permeated our modus operandi. The problems I have just raised elicit a complex array of answers. In the following pages I will attempt to entertain some of them.

In the 1970, as Poland was opening up to the Western world and entering what at that point looked like an era of economic prosperity, Polish cultural establishment became increasingly aware of the aesthetic, political and commercial possibilities of a local version of the so called Boom of Latin American literature. Translators were undoubtedly the most knowledgeable — if not the most powerful — initiations force behind this phenomenon. In 1971 they joined forces with the publishers of the Cracow-based Wydawnictwo

Literackie (Literary Publishing House) in order to set up a mechanism which soon proved to be the most important force in the reception of Latin American literary works: the so called **Seria Prozy Ibero-Amerykańskiej** (Ibero-American Prose Series). With its hundred plus titles published over twenty years. the series is generally considered to have shaped the Polish version of Latin American literary canon (Elbanowski; Kalicki; Kaniowa; Marrodán-Casas; Mickiewicz-Sklodowska), even though both the quantity and the quality of translations launched by other publishing houses, such as "Czytelnik" and PIW (Polish Publishing Institute) should not be underestimated (cf. Rymwid-Mickiewicz).

Originating from the intersection of political and economic thaw, with dissatisfaction about the lack of studies in the field of Hispanic and Ibero-American cultures, a number of area studies programs were created throughout the 1970 in major universities all over the country (Warsaw, Cracow, Wroclaw, Poznan). The Department of Iberian Studies at the University of Warsaw — inaugurated in the Fall of 1972 — soon became besieged by scores of candidates seeking master's degree in its emergent interdisciplinary program that combined fields as diverse as linguistics, literary criticism, history, geography and anthropology of the Hispanic and Luso-Brasilian world.

Regardless of whether we consider Polish reception of Latin American literatures as an original phenomenon or a mere imitation of what had previously happened elsewhere — particularly in France, given the francophile inclinations of Polish intellectuals (Molloy: 183; Luchting: 82) — the fact of the matter is that even today, twenty years after the emergence of Latin American studies as academic discipline, dissatisfaction with literary criticism in this area is prevalent.

My story of what happened and why between Latin American books and their Polish readers is a personal, subjective tale with no claims whatsoever to "represent" Polish specialists in the field of Latin American letters. As a graduate of the Katedra Iberystyki in Warsaw, I quickly realized that whereas my practical knowledge of

Spanish and my understanding of at least some Latin American contexts were beyond reproach, I was lacking the most basic tools of a contemporary literary critic even though I was able to produce an extensive M.A. thesis on the subject of "Lo real-maravilloso americano." Language was for me a vehicle of communication — transparent, monosemic, homogeneous — and it was not until Ph.D. studies in the United States that I caught a glimpse of a wider range of interpretive possibilities often referred to as post-structuralist. Upon receiving my doctorate and returning to Poland, I managed to implement my freshly acquired expertise while teaching Latin American literature and directing scores of M.A. theses at my Polish **alma mater**, whereas virtually all of my scholarly publications continued to appear abroad in journals such as **Hispamérica, Chasquí, Plural, Revista Iberoamericana**. As a beginning scholar in a new discipline, I simply could not find in Poland an adequate outlet for my critical writings.

Without trying to justify or legitimize the approaches of Polish literary criticism to Latin American writings, I would like to become a spokesperson on behalf of Polish critics and underscore the fact that the basic premises of their critical activities were preconditioned by the expectations of their real and potential readers. What were these expectations? As is natural in a country with no significant legacy of inter-cultural encounters with Latin America, the focus of Polish critical studies dealing with Latin American literatures has been by large informative. Our readers demanded interviews with the "stars" of the boom, they appreciated lively anecdotes, capsule summaries of biographical data on individual writers and essential background facts on their respective countries of origin. So, in scores of reviews, articles and prefaces devoted to Latin American letters the critics were asked to provide conceptual framework for beginners, for an audience that was not conversant with recent literary theories and that was not willing to give up their assumptions about Latin American culture. The very format of these publication was, obviously, very restrictive and didn't allow for analytical or highly specialized insights. Even the most sophisticated essays — published in such academic journals as **Kwartalnik Neofilologiczny, Estudios Latinoamericanos** or **Hispánica Posnaniensia** — share an affinity with more "popular" critical discourses: they all seem to resist literary theory.

Polish reading public is by large well educated, demanding and curious but — as Edmund Urbanski has noted in his well researched and incisive article — the unprecedented popularity of Latin American literatures in the last three decades is largely due to its perception as being alluringly exotic, magical and "different." Following these expectations, the most diverse works were lumped by the critics and journalists under the rubric of "magic realism," a somewhat dangerous operation which instead of increasing the awareness of the diversity of Latin American cultures tended to homogenize them. Most of the critics did not dare to challenge preexisting stereotypes. Those who did, published in highly specialized, somewhat elitist journals, that had a limited educational impact. To my knowledge, only some of the curricula —mainly in the Polish Language Departments at the university level — have been slightly revised in the light of the increasing presence of translations of Spanish and Portuguese-writing authors.

The perspective of Polish critics — even those who were privileged enough to have traveled throughout Latin America — remains fully European: they privilege alterity (especially in the guise of "magic realism") without truly challenging the eurocentric paradigm of cultural difference. This attitude is exemplified by Jerzy Kuhn's collection of essays **Ojcowie i ojcobójcy** (Fathers and Parricides) and Roman Samsel's journalistic **Bunt i gwałt** (Rebellion and Violence).

Of the practitioners of Latin American literary criticism in Poland, Rajmund Kalicki is undoubtedly one of the most knowledgeable and incisive. A monograph on Borges written by this leading critic and translator attracted general interest from Polish readers and it could easily compete with similar introductions published in other European countries, had it appeared in English, Spanish or French. In the arena of Polish literary studies on Latin American letters, Kalicki's book — a decade after its original publication — remains the liveliest, most readable and thoroughly researched original monograph.

Despite the fact that a few generations of specialists in these areas have graduated over the past fifteen years, there has not been a single comprehensive overview of Latin American letters. Unlike our colleagues historians — who managed to produce a three volume history of Latin America under the inspiration and guidance of the late Tadeusz Łepkowski — we have lacked energy and imagination to tackle a collective project of such dimensions. So far the only primer of Latin American letters available to Polish readers is the classic but somewhat outdated — both in the historical and methodological sense — **History of Spanish American Literature** by Enrique Anderson Imbert.

At this point, to adopt a stance of advocacy for original Polish criticism of Latin American letters would be entirely unrealistic. It is true that no more do we have to translate works and write critical commentaries that clearly fit within the limits established by political orthodoxy, but it is also true that a proliferation of third-rate books in the free-market economy has been so overwhelming that publishing houses, translators and critics committed to high-brow — or even middle-brow — literature have been forced to alter their taste in order to survive. Latin American literature in Poland can survive only by magic. Unfortunately, the socio-economic reality is far from breeding miracles.

Bibliographic References

Elbanowski, Adam. **Proza iberoamerykańska w polskiej krytyce literackiej.** Literatura na Świecie, 1978.

Kalicki, Rajmund. **Algunos aspectos sobre la recepción de la literatura iberoamericana en Polonia.** Cuadernos hispanoamericanos 358 (1980): 172-78.

Kaniowa, Maria. **En torno a 18 Serie Prosa Iberoamericana.** Estudios Latinoamericanos 4 (1978).

Marrodán-Casas, Carlos. **Narrativa o cultura? Apuntes sobre las traducciones de narrativa latinoamericana en Polonia.** Estudios Latinoamericanos 4 (1978).

Skłodowska, Elżbieta. **El libro hispanoamericano en Polonia 1945-1984.** Warszawa: Wydawnictwa Uniwersytetu Warszawskiego, 1986

Skłodowska, Elżbieta. **La parodia en la novela hispanoamericana 1960-85.** Purdue Monographs in Romance Languages. Amsterdam-Philadelphia: Benjamins, 1991.

Urbanski, Edmund Stephen. **Latin American Studies and Bibliography in Poland.** Latin American Review 15.3 (1980: 175-79).

The First Congress of Polish Communities In Latin America Held in Buenos Aires in 1993

Mariano Kawka
(Brazil)

The First Congress of Polish Communities in Latin America was held on November 11-16, 1993, in Buenos Aires (Argentina) and Punta del Este (Uruguay). The program and the discussions of the meeting were centralized on the following objectives:

1. To look for a closer approach among the Polish communities in Latin America to the effort of developing a common activity in every significant area, aiming at their progress and development.

2. To favor and enhance their relations with the local authorities through appropriate legal representatives elected for that purpose.

3. To stress the contribution of the Polish Nation in general and of the Polish communities and individuals abroad in the field of culture, science, arts and work in all countries of their residence.

4. To consider the possibilities of co-operation among the Polish communities in the area of educational, social, artistic, scientific and sporting activities.

5. To co-operate with the Polish authorities searching for the development of a common action for the benefit of the Polish Nation.

6. To promote biannual congresses, in rotatory seats and biannual authorities elected in the seat countries, with coordinating commissions in specific areas (cultural, social, scientific, artistic, sporting, etc.)

7. To express through the Congress — as their legitimate representative in Latin America — the recognition and the grateful-

ness of these communities to the countries where they met with such a generous reception.

Course of the Congress in Buenos Aires

The date of November 11, Poland's national holiday, was chosen and recognized as a symbolical date for the opening of the Congress. The meeting was also embellished by the presence of the following Polish authorities: Dr. Andrzej Stelmachowski, president of the **Wspólnota Polska;** Bishop Zygmunt Kamiński, vice-president of the **Wspólnota Polska;** Prof. Andrzej Zakrzewski, delegate of the chancellery of Poland's President Lech Wałęsa; Dr. Adam Struzik, chairman of the Polish Diet; Prof. Aleksander Łuczak, vice-president of the Cabinet Council; Iwo Byczewski, vice-minister of Foreign Affairs; Senator Jan Sęk, chairman of the Senatorial Commission for the Affairs of Poles Abroad; Deputy Leszek Moczulski, chairman of the Parliamentary Commission for the Affairs of Poles Abroad; Dr. Witold Kozinski, vice-president of the National Bank of Poland; Andrzej Arendarski, president of the Polish Board of Foreign Trade; Elzbieta Janiszewski Kuropatwa, director of the Board of the Cabinet Council; Anna Szklennik, director of the Senatorial Office for International Contacts; Jerzy Żołnierkiewicz, Boleslaw Polak and Zdzislaw Dromlewicz, directors of the Polish Diet.

The Congress was prepared and conducted by an organizing committee composed as follows: chairman Jan Kobylanski, president of the Union of Poles in Argentina and Poland's honorary Consul in Punta del Este (Uruguay); directors: Jan Bieles vice-president of the Union of Poles in Argentina, Leopold Bilozur, president of the Union of Ex Servicemen and vice-president of the Union of Poles.

Official delegations from several Latin American countries came with the following number of delegates: Argentina - 56 delegates; Brazil — 40, Uruguay — 9, Chile — 3, Costa Rica — 2, Ecuador — 2, Guatemala — 2, Paraguay — 1, Peru — 1.

A special attention is due to the presence of Dr. Zygmunt Szkopiak, president of the Polish Organizations in Great Britain.

The first day was destined to the opening of the Congress and the first plenary assembly, The assembly was conducted by president Jan Kobylański. The participants listened to the reading of messages sent by Pope John Paul II, by President Lech Wałęsa and other authorities. Then an address was delivered by Prof. Andrzej Zakrzewski, delegate of Poland's President. The speech was related to the date of November 11 and presented an account of the happenings that made possible the recovery of Poland's independence after World War I.

After the inauguration assembly the participants went to the Recoleta cemetery, a kind of Argentinian historical monument, where Bishop Zygmunt Kamiński blessed the Polish Pantheon with mortal remains of three prominent Polish generals dead in Argentina.

In the afternoon a mass was said in the cathedral and a bouquet was deposited on the Plaza de Mayo. In the evening the solemn inauguration of the Congress took place at the San Martin Theater. The ceremony began with an artistic show and was performed in the presence of Argentinian authorities, with distinction to Dr. Jorge Luis Maiorano, Minister of Justice and representative of President Dr. Carlos Saul Menem.

On the following day, November 12, began the activities of the several specific commissions. There were seven commissions with the following topics presented for discussion:

1. Juridical Commission: problems of double nationality.

2. Industry and Trade Commission: projects and suggestions for the enhancement of industrial and commercial exchange between Poland the Latin American countries.

3. Pastoral Commission: the role of the Catholic activities of the Polish communities and the religious education of the new generations.

4. Educational and Cultural Commission: problems related with schools, libraries; cultural, artistic and sporting projects; cultural exchange in Latin America; scholarships; perspectives for the press and publication of books.

5. Humanistic and Historic Commissions: the union of the

Polish community in Latin America and its relations with Poland; contacts with the Polish community in Latin America and in the world, as well as means of communication and forms of information.

6. Ex-servicemen and Scouting Commission: the preservation of the traditional links of ex-serviceman outside Poland; the education of the youth in the Polish spirit and the family as chief fountain of education.

7. Social Welfare Commission: the problem of the aged people, the new Polish emigration law and the relationship of the Polish community with this problem; possibilities for emigrants in Latin America.

On November 13, important decisions were taken, especially the creation of the Union of the Polish Communities in Latin America (in Polish USOPAL — Unia Stowarzyszeń i Organizacji Polskich w Ameryce Łacińskiej) and the foundation of the Federation of Polish Boards of Trade in Latin America (CABIPAL).

Second part of the Congress in Uruguay

With the closing of the activities in Buenos Aires the delegates traveled to Uruguay, where the second part of the Congress would be fulfilled. The activities in Uruguay began with the celebration of a mass in the cathedral of Maldonado by Bishop Zygmunt Kamiński, with the participation of other priest delegates from various countries.

In continuation a bouquet was deposited on the monument of General Jose Gervasio Artigas and then followed the solemn inauguration of the Congress in Uruguay, with a speech of President Luis Alberto Lacalle Herrera. In his brilliant address the President gave evidence of his excellent knowledge of the Polish problems, as well as of his affection for the Poles.

The delegates moved to the residence of Jan Kobylański, which is also the seat of the Honorary Consulate of Poland in Punta del Este. In the Consul's superb residence the guests were presented with an artistic show of Uruguayan and Polish folkloric dances, the latter performed by the **Nasz Balet** (Our Ballet) from Buenos Aires, an ensemble the delegates had already had the opportunity to applaud during the inauguration of the Congress in that city.

In Punta del Este the delegates of the different countries had a chance for a closer acquaintance and exchange of ideas. This human contact is one of the important results of the Congress. Such a knowledge tightens national and international links and provides at the same time a valuable exchange of experiences and information about the life of the communities in different countries.

An important decision in Punta del Este was the election of a seat for the Second Congress, which will be held in Curitiba, Brazil, since this city shelters one of the major Polish communities in Latin America. In Punta del Este were elected the two vice-presidents for the Second Congress, representing the two chief and sometimes antagonistic Polish organizations in Brazil, both with their seats in Curitiba: Anisio Oleksy — president of the POLBRAS and Rizio Wachowicz — president of the BRASPOL. The president of the Second Congress should be elected in Curitiba, within the next six months.

On the last day, November 16, there was the celebration of a mass and the blessing of a chapel of Our Lady of Czestochowa in Montevideo. The mass was said by Bishop Zygmunt Kamiński, with the assistance of the priest delegates and of the Nuncio in Uruguay.

Results of the Congress

The most important result of the Congress was undoubtedly the creation of the above mentioned Union of the Polish Communities in Latin America, among whose functions remains the care for the preparatory works related with the Second Congress in Curitiba. Here is the direction of the USOPAL/Union: president: Jan Kobylanski, vice-presidents, Roman Tustanowski (Uruguay) and Andrzej Zablocki (Chile), secretaries Witold Ptasznik and Maria Brzezinska (Argentina).; advisers: Alicja Olszynska (Argentina) — president of the Polish Club and Miecislau Surek - editor of the fortnightly newspaper **Nowy Lud** (Brazil), presidents of the work commissions: Aldred

Podrez, Rev. Stanisław Grzymkowski, Stanisław Farkas, Leopold Bilozur and Roman Tustanowski.

During a meeting of the USOPAL/Union in Buenos Aires on December 11, it was decided that a publication will be created for the Polish community of Latin America. The name of the bulletin, which will be published in Polish, Spanish and Portuguese, will be **Głos Unii/Voz de la Unión/Voz da União** (Voice of the Union).

Another important consequence of the Congress was the establishmnet of the Federation of Polish Boards of Trade in Latin America (CABIPAL), with its seat in Buenos Aires, whose aim will be the concentration of all promotions, information and exchange between Poland and the Latin American countries.

The *representatives* from Argentina, Brazil, Chile, Perú and Uruguay established a Founding Commission for the Confederation of Binational Boards of Trade in Latin America, with the following direction: presidents Prof. Jozef Skowron — Polish-Argentinian Board of Trade, 1st vice-president: Miecislau Surek — Polish-Brazilian Board of Trade; 2nd vice-president: Danuta Madej — Polish-Peruvian Board of Trade; Counselors: Rudolf Watroba — Polish Uruguayan Board of Trade and Jan Taylor — Polish-Chilean Board of Trade.

Conclusion

The idea of uniting in an organized form the Polish communities in Latin America became a reality after the realization of the first Congress in Buenos Aires and Punta del Este.

Congregated in an international congress, the Poles and their descendants in this part of the world came to the conclusion that without a central organization and direction they do not represent a real, decisive and important force in the present international arena, and they do not have the political and social presence and influence proportional to the significant number of the Poles and their descendants in the whole world. If united and organized, however, they may constitute a force whose voice will be heard and respected. And this awareness is all the more significant because a good part of the delegates were young people whose enthusiasm and temper foretell interesting perspectives for the Polish communities in Latin America.

This congress was a historical and unprecedented happening in the life of the Poles and their descendants who live and work in Latin America, but for various reasons were unable to congregate and form a solid organization with the purpose of living together, thriving and collaborating with Mother Poland and with the countries of their present residence. Now this day seems to be in view.

Recent Polish and Polish-American Contributions to Hispanic American Humanities

Edmund Stephen Urbanski

The Polish and Polish-American contributions to Hispanic American scholarship are very significant, as judged by the diversity and quality of publications in this specialized field. They are carried out by about thirty university professors-specialists in various branches of Hispanic studies, although many times that number is engaged in teaching the Spanish language and literature, as well as Hispanic American literature and civilization. This random survey embraces only the best known and accessible works published in the United States and abroad, in English, Spanish and Polish. The topical variety is astounding. Most of these scholarly works embrace Ibero-American literary criticism and anthologies, linguistics, anthropology, sociology, economics, law, biological sciences, and even Amazonic explorations. Chronologically they cover mostly the XXth century, when waves of Polish and Polish-American scholars worked in Spanish- and Portuguese-speaking America. Many of them later relocated to the United States and Canada where they took university appointments. Some of them, however, remained in various Ibero-American countries and joined forces with local scholars and are actively engaged in a variety of research.

This essay is limited to literary, civilizational and linguistic matters of Hispanic America which makes us divide these works into various thematic groups. It is noteworthy that the subject which caught the earliest attention among US. scholars was civilization, the key to the knowledge of cultural phenomena of any country, especially sensitive and sometimes controversial in the case of bilingual or multilingual Iberian America. According to linguists, in this multiethnic part of the New World, in addition to Spanish or Portuguese, about five hundred Indian languages are still spoken. This attests to the distinctive multicultural character of the Ibero-American civilization, the scope of which extends far beyond our topic. This very fact, however, compels us to call some of them Indo-Ibero-American civilizations.

The Polish interest in Ibero-American civilization goes back to the middle of the XIXth century, and is represented by two scholars who lived in South America for a considerable period of time. One was Dr. Ignacy Domeyko, who during his fifty years sojourn in Chile combined university teaching with geological exploration of the Andes, and who for sixteen years discharged the duties of President of the University of Santiago (1867-1883). One of his works **La Araucania** (Santiago, 1845), which was also issued in French and Polish, contains myriad observations not only on the Chilean but also the Araucanian-Indian civilizations. Another Polish scholar, Prof. Jozef Siemiradzki, after three extensive sojourns in various South American countries, published a Polish book **On the Edges of Civilization** (Na kresach cywilizacji), Lwow, 1896, in which he vividly described reflections on Ibero-American culture and customs with which he had become acquainted. His observations on this civilizational complex were made from the European perspective. Domeyko and Siemiradzki presented both the "ups" and "downs" of the Hispanic American culture, which balances, and makes credible their observations.

In the XXth century the Central European, including the Polish interest in Iberian America increased, which accounts for a good number of intelligent travelers and even explorers who visited that part of the New World.

They left vivid impressions of their sojourns in the various Hispanic countries, extending from the Mexican Rio Grande to the Antarctic Tierra del Fuego. They described not only their population, but above all their culture, mentality and behavior. Among the most notable titles in Polish are **The Land of the Holy Cross** (Ziemia Świętego Krzyża), Warsaw, 1929, by Jerzy Ostrowski; **Brazil, the Country, the People and the Internal Relations** (Brazylia, kraj, ludzie, stosunki), Warsaw, 1930, by Franciszek Łyp; **From the Amazon to the Tierra del Fuego** (Od Amazonki do Ziemi Ognistej), Warsaw, 1956, by Mieczyslaw Lepecki, also the author of books, describing Argentina, Bolivia and Brazil; **Peru, My Not-So-Promised Land** (Peru, moja ziemia nie obiecana), Wrocław, 1974, by Feliks Woytkowski; **Chile** (Chile), Warsaw, 1925, by Kazimierz Warchałowski; **Ten Years in Guatemala, 1893-1902** (Dziesięć lat w Gwatemali, 1893-1902), Sopot, MS, 1950, by Antonio Wiatrak; **Argentina-Paraguay-Bolivia** (Argentyna-Paragwaj-Boliwia), Warsaw 1929, by Mieczyslaw Fularski; **Urugayan Sketches** (Szkice urugwajskie), Curitiba, 1925, by Wladyslaw Wójcik and **Santa Rosa, a Polish Settlement in Mexico** (Santa Rosa, polskie osiedle w Meksyku), London, 1967, by Alfons Jacewicz. The reader will notice that most of these books are dedicated to Argentina and Brazil which also became the **foci** of Polish immigration.

A major feat accomplished by a Polish writer and film maker, Antonio Halik, who after thirty years of residence in various Latin countries, was capturing the Latin people in an ethnographic film called **180,000 Kilometers of Adventures,** also published in a book form as **180,000 kilometrów przygody** (Warsaw, 1975). It covered Halik's transcontinental trip from Tierra del Fuego to Alaska. This work was warmly received in three continents and made Halik a confirmed champion of Hispanic America.

A more detailed and systematic analysis of the Ibero-American civilization is found in the works of S. Andreski, T. Szulc and E.S. Urbanski, professional Latin-Americanists, who spent considerable periods in Spanish-Portuguese America. Among the works of Stanislaw Andreski, of the British University at Reading, the most significant is **Parasitism and Subversion: The Case of Latin America** (London, 1966) which describes its socio-political make-up from historical perspective. Whereas, Tad Szulc, a professional writer-journalist, wrote several books among which **Twilight of Tyrants** (New York, 1959) and **Winds of Revolution: Latin America Today and Tomorrow** (New York, 1963) stand out, because of the directness and open-mindedness with which he exposes rather complex problems. Both Andreski and Szulc, while engaged in analyzing the Hispanic-American idiosyncrasies, cultural achievements and social behavior, are mostly concentrated in political customs of traditional ideology. A different approach is taken by Edmund S. Urbanski, who after lecturing at Mexican, Brazilian and U.S. universities, adopted an anthropological-cultural method in evaluating the Latin civilizational phenomena, with certain psychological accents. Thus, his books such as **Angloamérica e Hispanoamérica. Análisis de dos civilizaciones** (Madrid, 1965) or the bilingual **Hispanoamérica, sus razas y civilizaciones** (New York, 1972) contain an extensive historic-anthropological analysis of that culture. Its logical interpretation merited the adoption of these books by U.S. and Canadian universities.

All three authors, Andreski, Szulc and Urbanski expose many idiosyncratic Hispanic "taboos", rarely mentioned if at all, by other scholars. Contrary to the belief among some Latinamericanists about the spiritual cohesion of the Hispanic American civilization, Urbanski introduced within it a division in various subcultures, which thus justifies new terminological terms: Hispanic-Creole, Hispanic-mestizo, and Hispanic-Negro civilizations as a parallel to the long-ago recognized Amerindian Civilizations. This civilizational plurality has been accepted by most Latinamericanists, with the exception of a few so-called "nativists", who deny any Iberian roots in Hispanic American culture, even though, they use the Spanish language.

Tremendous strides in recent years in Hispanic studies in the United States are due to the increased popularity of the Spanish language as well as by the tremendous thematic variety of Hispanic American literature. These circumstances permit the reader to better understand his southern neighbors, - their mentality and customs - and thus avoid making the kind of social and political mistakes that litter the history of U.S.-Latin American relations. Thus enlightened idea was since 1970 championed by the quarterly "Hispania" and found several U.S. univeristy followers, who instead of treating Hispanic American civilizations as a monolithic abstraction, compare it more and more with our own Anglo-American civilization, showing some of their ideological similarities and unavoidable idiosyncrasic differences. This comparative approach is visible in Urbanski's **Hispanic America and Its Civilizations. Spanish Americans and Anglo-Americans,** (1987, 1981), followed by David Suárez-Torres' **Contrastes culturales** (Lexington, 1981), where the Hispanic American culture is compared with the Spanish culture, or by Frederic B. Pike's **The United States and Latin America** (Austin, 1992), whose subtitle "Myths and Stereotypes of Civiliazation and Nature" explicitly explains its contents. In following the comparative trend, they display a conceptual similarity. These are a few examples of the comparative approach, also adopted by other authores.

Perhaps even richer is the Polish American output of works covering various phases of Hispanic American literature, literary criticism and anthological editions, the authors of which sometimes also deal with the Castilian "belles-lettres". Scholars representing these fields include the following: De Chasca, Debicki, Dobrowolski, Kaminski, Landowski, Kicza, Lisowski, Petry Mroczkowska, Sarnacki, Sklodowska, Swietlicki, Tannenbaum, Sosnowski, Stanislawski, Ziolkowski and Ziomek. In this academic "playade", Debicki and Ziomek, produced the greatest number of quality monographs on a variety of subjects, which assured them an outstanding place among U.S. Hispanics.

From among Andrew Debicki's thirteen works, five are dedicated to Hispanic American literature and eight to Castilian literature. Not counting over sixty critical essays on various Hispanic topics, Debicki's most important publications are **Estudios sobre poesía española contemporánea** (Madrid, 1958), **Poetas hispanoamericanos contemporáneos** (Madrid, 1976), **Antología de la poesía mexicana moderna** (London, 1977) and **Studies in Twentieth Century Literature** (Madrid, 1990). Henryk Ziomek also published thirteen books, entirely dedicated to the Castilian drama production of Spain's Golden Age, also one co-authored on

The Warsaw-born actress and signer, **Milica Korjus vel Kurcjusz**, who appeared in a few Mexican movies made during WW II in Mexico City. Here Milica plays a leading role in a Spanish-language film "Cavalry of the Empire", based on the story of a short-lived Mexican Empire (1864-1967), for which Napoleon III, manipulating Mexican politcis, sent and seated on the throne the Austrian Prince Maximilian. He and his supporting French Expeditionary Army were finally defeated by President Benito Juárez. Daughter of a Polish colonel, Milica changed her family name from Kurcjusz to Korjus, for easier pronunciation. After her movie career in Mexico, Milica moved to Hollywood, where she also played in a few American movies.

Hispanic American biography. Some of his salient books are: **Reflexiones de Quijote** (Madrid, 1971), **Lo grotesco en la literatura española** (Madrid, 1983), **A History of Spanish Golden Age Drama** (Lexington, 1984), and **Compendio de la literatura española** (Warsaw, 1986), also over forty articles and essays, and ca. 150 abstracts of a variety of topics in English, Spanish, French and Polish in various American and European magazines.

Among the nine original or edited books on Hispanic-American topic by Saul Sosnowski, the most important are: **Julio Cortazar: Una búsqueda critica** (Bs. Aires, 1973), **Borges y la Cabala** (Bs. Aires, 1986), **La orilla inminente: Escritores judios argentinos** (Bs. Aires, 1287), and **Realismo y naturalismo** in Vol. 12 of **Literatura hispanoamericana en imágenes** (Madrid, 1983), also over fifty articles and essays on similar South American topics. A significant value have the five works of Edmund de Chasca (Trzaska) on the critical evaluation of the medieval Castilian poem **Cantar del mio Cid,** published in Spanish between 1972 and 1978 in Spain and the U.S., as well as a monograph on the Renaissance dramatist **Pedro de Alarcón's El sombrero de tres picos** (New York, 1965), also numerous articles on the Castilian and Hispanic American literature.

Elzbieta Skłodowska has to her credits two monographs: **La parodia en la nueva novela hispanoamericana** (Amsterdam-Philadelphia, 1991) and **Testimonio hispanoamericano: historia, teoria, poética** (New York, 1992), also about forty essays on a variety on Hispanic-American literary subjects. Another Latinoamericanist, Joanna Petty Mroczkowska published **Antología de la poesía latinoamericana** (Cracow, 1982), and translated from Spanish or French into Polish several books on Hispanic American topics by M. Rojas González, M.A. Asturias, Carlos Fuentes, Alejo Carpentier and J. Supervielle; she also wrote introductions to many more books by Hispanic authors, which were published in Poland. An interesting study **El concepto de motivo en literatura** (Valparaiso, 1972) was issued by Sophie Kalinowska during her scholarly sojourn in Chile. In addition to several articles, Gerald J. Langowski is credited with a monograph **El surrealismo en la ficción hispanoamericana** (Madrid,

1982). Like Julian Dobrowolski, Joseph A. Chrzanowski, interested mostly in literary criticism, covered in his scattered essays a large-territory from Mexico to Argentina. He also heralded the role of women writers in Latin America. The traditional Polish attraction to literary criticism is undoubtedly responsible for appearance in Colombia of an analytical work by Bogdan Piotrowski titled **La realidad nacional colombiana en su narrativa** (Bogota 1988), which was used as a university manual there. During his voluntary, political exile in Colombia, Piotrowski also published a book **Infierno político de Polonia 1942-1981** (Bogota, 1981), which as an anthology of twenty-seven angry Polish poets, is a strong condemnation of German-Soviet domination of their motherland, where seven million Poles were killed.

As incredible as it may seem, the surging Polish post-WW I interest in Hispanic American literature was also responsible for the increased curiosity in Castilian "belles-lettres", even though the Polish translation of Don Quijote was made in the 18th century. The promoter of this trend was Jozef D. Morawski, author of the **History of Iberian Literatures** (Historia literatur iberyjskich), Warsaw, 1931. It was followed by such works as **Spanish Mysticism** (Mistycyzm hiszpański), Cracow, 1938, by Stefania Ciesielska-Borkowska, **The Spanish Theatre of the Golden Age** (Teatr hiszpański wieku złotego), Warsaw, 1948, by Kazimierz Zawanowski, **Cervantes** (Cervantes), Warsaw, 1954, by Zofia Szmydtowa, and **History of Spanish Literature** (Historia literatury hiszpańskiej), Wroclaw, 1966,. by Maria Strzałkowa, to mention only a few works. Nowadays, they are appearing by dozens, some of them published in Spanish, and on Brazilian literature sometimes in Portuguese.

An interest in the religious-mythological aspects of the Peninsular literature among the Polish-American Hispanists, is displayed in the following works: **Spanish Christian Cabala** (Univ. of Mo. Press, 1986) by Catherine Swietlicki, and **The Sanctification of Don Quijote: From Hidalgo to Priest** (University Park, 1991) by Eric J. Ziolkowski.

Not only literary but also other cultural aspects of Hispanic

America attracted Polish or Polish-American Latinamericanists, as proven in **Studies in Spanish American Literature and Civilization** (WIU Press, 1964, 1965) by Edmund S. Urbanski, who also authored over fifty topical essays on various cultural aspects of Hispanic America. Of a general cultural-historical scope are the following publications: **Unity and Diversity in Colonial Spanish America** (New Orleans, 1989) by John E. Kicza; **Cronología, Latinoamárica y el Mundo** (Caracas, 1986) by Leszek Zawisza; **En el campo de Mexico** (Mexico, 1969, 1978) by Witold L. Langrod; **La pampa** (Warsaw, 1985) by Jan Krawczyk; **Diario argentino** (Bs. Aires, 1968) by Witold Gombrowicz; and **The Anatomy of Eleven Towns in Michoacán** (Austin, 1950) by Dan Stanislawski, who also penned a few works dedicated to early Lusitanian problems, to mention just a few examples.

No less significant are the Polish contributions regarding the Spanish and Portuguese languages and related complex problems of indigenous linguistics of Latin America. This specialized field attracted such scholars as Druszcz, Filipak, Kawka, Kozlowski, Lipski Staczek, Tempski and Wieczorek. Not long ago the Brazil-based Francisco Filipiak published two works: **Dicionário dialetológico do Paraná** and **Dicionário toponímico aborigene brasileiro,** which as their titles indicate, are closely related to ethnolinguistic problems of Brazil. These studies were preceded by two other research works: **Os brasileirismos do dialeto polono-brasileiro** (UCP, 1982) by Mariano Kawka, and **O bilngüismo em Araucaria. A inferencia polonesa na fonologia portuguesa** (UCP, 1983) by Arlindo Druszcz. Kawka, a multilingual expert, also published **Dicionário Português-Polones** (Curitiba, 1984), which earned him high marks among academic linguists. Another scholar, Edvino Donato Tempski, after arduous research and countless field trips, penned **Vocabulário e noções gramaticais da lingua Caingang** (Curitiba, 1982), published by the local Academy of Literature and Sciences.

The Indians of the Caingângues tribe, who formerly inhabited Southern Brazil, are rapidly disappearing. Thus, their cultural heritage has been preserved.

The Spanish Language, Rules and Grammar (Bs. Aires, 1949) with Polish explanations was issued by Tadeusz A. Kozlowski, who spent many years in Hispanic America and is fully acquainted with the intricacies and charm of Cervantes' native tongue. Unique of its kind is John J. Lipski's book **The Language of the Isleños** (Baton Rouge, 1990), which examines the Spanish-creole dialect brought from the Canary Islands to Louisiana in the late 1700s, where it was modified by the local English influence. His other research work is **The Spanish of the Negroes Congos** (Philadelphia, 1989), which analyzes the Spanish-African dialect spoken on the Panama's eastern coast. His research study "The Chota Valley Afro-Hispanic Language in Highland Ecuador" (LARR, 1987), still spoken on the Ecuadorian maritime province of Esmeraldas, is of similar exotic flavor.

Of similar importance are three university manuals on comparative linguistics edited or co-edited by John J. Staczek, dean of Georgetown University.They are entitled **On Spanish, Portuguese and Catalan linguistics** (Washington, DC, 1988), **Perspectives on Bilingualism and Bilingual Education** (Washington, 1985) and 1974 **Colloquium on Spanish and Portuguese Linguistics** (Washington, 1975), which broke ground for further investigative work in this scholarly field. Staczek also devised a method for bilingual education and authored ca. thirty articles on multilingual problems, related to Hispanic linguistics. A similar topic of investigation has been undertaken by Joseph A. Wieczorek, who in his frequent articles shows interest in Spanish dialects, inter-language analysis and morpho-phonemic problems in Hispanic linguistics. Wieczorek is the author of a manual **The French and Spanish Pronunciation** (Baltimore, 1987).

It appears that applied linguistics had fascinated Polish scholars and professionals already in the 19th century. An indication of this is the fact that a Polish-born physician practicing in Brazil Piotr Czerniewicz (better known as Pedro Chernoviz) prepared and published in Portuguese a **Dicionário da Medicina Popular** (Rio de Janeiro), which dealt with the treatment of various diseases and was the first of its kind ever published in South America! The author received for it a high Brazilian decoration, while his work six times reissued in Brazil, was later translated into Spanish. Its new thirteen editions appeared in Hispanic America, where they achieved its greatest popularity in Mexico and Colombia.

Linked to linguistics, but in an elaborate philosophical meaning of words and related to epistemology is the semantic science. It was founded by the prodigious Alfred Korzybski, a Polish philosopher, whose scientific exposition excited linguists as well a humanists. As an important branch of linguistics, semantics is concerned with the identification and differentiation of the true meaning of words. Numerous semantic institutes now encircle the whole globe, particularly the Spanish- and Portuguese-speaking countries, which is no mean feat. Speaking of linguistics, it would be negligent to omit the inventor of the composite language with Latin roots, called **Esperanto**. It was invented at the end or the XIXth century by a Pole, Ludwik Zamenhof, for intercontinental communication. Esperanto is being utilized now by a few million people in international meetings and literature, also in Spanish- and English-speaking America.

In addition to these humanistic disciplines, strong Polish-American contributions are made to various sciences and technology in Spanish-Portuguese America, but they are beyond the scope of our article. Instead, we have concentrated on literary and pedagogical works, which enhance the Ibero-American image through its cultural and natural diversity in Central Europe. This has been accomplished in two ways: by the publication of books by prominent Ibero-American writers in Polish translation, and by the descriptive works of Polish explorer-scientists who visited various Hispanic countries. As to the former, John Sarnacki in his bibliographic survey **Latin American Literature and History in Polish Translation** (Port Huron, 1973) listed about 800 entries, which after twenty years probably doubled, because of the popularity of Latin works among the Polish readers.

Irena Rymwid-Mickiewicz and Elzbieta Sklodowska published interesting article in Spanish, "La recepción del libro hispanoamericano en Polonia (1945-1985) in the Warsaw-based review **Estudios Latinoamericanos** (1989). These authors revealed an extensive list of Ibero-American writers and poets whose works became popular in that Slavic country, mentioning especially those who became known through the so-called **literary boom,** such as García Márquez, Fuentes, Cortázar, Vargas Llosa, Carpentier, Paz, Asturias, Cardenal and Neruda. Among the Polish publishing houses, the Cracow-based publisher "Wydawnictwo Literackie" established for this purpose a series called "Ibero-American prose", which alone issued over 200 titles. Similiarly active were two Warsaw-based publishers: P.I.W. and "Czytelnik", interested mostly in fiction. Whereas, among P.W.N. Hispanic publications a good number was concerned with scholarly subjects.

Also, the Ibero-American Studies departments of Polish universities with surprisingly large student enrollement, contribute to the surging interest in Hispanic matters. Frequent news coverage of events from that part of the New World in the Polish press cannot be discounted either, as well as occasional visits to Poland of Latin writers. In this regard, along with sympathy, the Polish intellectual curiosity is mixed with exotic bewilderment, so typical for Europe.

The strongest supporters of Hispanic American multicivilizational and environmental variety were, however, Polish writers-explorers and traveling authors, who after spending considerable time in Iberian countries, recorded their impressions in various works. One such book is the scholarly **La naturaleza en la América Ecuatorial** (Lima, 1955) by Witold Szyszlo. It combines scientific-ecological aspects with cultural observations on Peru, Bolivia, Brazil, Ecuador, Colombia and Venezuela. Besides being quoted by other authors, it displays the Polish predilection for the mysterious Amazon Basin, also shown by entomologist Arkady Fiedler. He is the author of several Polish books such as **Bichos, my Brazilian Friends** (Bichos, moi brazylisjcy przyjaciele), 1931, **Fishes Sing in Ucayali** (Ryby śpiewają w Ukajali), 1955 and many others. Because of interesting topic. most of Fiedler's works were translated from Polish into other European languages, which reached about ten million copies! **Mato Grosso** (New York, 1946) by Waclaw Korabiewicz, was published in bilingual Polish-English edition, while Ann Zulawski's forthcoming work on **The Colonial, Social Differentiation and Ethnicity in the Andean Countries**, covers Bolivia, Peru and Ecuador. Joseph Lisowski's **Caribbean Perspectives** (New Brunswick, 1991) describes the cultural and ethnic variety of the Antilles, and **Poland-Mexico** (Polska-Meksyk), Wroclaw, 1980, by Tadeusz Lepkowski, great part of which is dedicated to Mexican civilization, history and customs. These are just a few examples of in-depth Polish scholarly incursions into Spanish- and Portuguese-speaking America, which have pushed beyond the New World conventional boundaries.

A group of Polish writers who were the **emigré literati**, and escaped the horrors of World War II in Europe, found refuge in Hispanic America, and compose another distinct category authors focusing on Latin themes. There, they continued their professional activities, in which they frequently utilized Iberian fabulary motives. Their number was not large, but the literary output considerable. Of fifteen notable authors, six lived in Argentina, four in Mexico, three in Brazil, one in Uruguay and one in Guatemala. Those who mostly utilized Ibero-American literary motives were: Andrzej Bobkowski in Guatemala, Elena Poniatowska, Edmund Urbanski and Juan de Wyskota Zakrzewski in Mexico, Jerzy Kossowski and Bohdan Pawlowicz in Brazil, Witold Gombrowicz, Antonio Halik, Janina Surynowa Wyczolkowska and Jozefa Radzyminska in Argentina, and Czeslaw Straszewicz in Uruguay.

Bobkowski's a three-act play **The Black Sand** (Czarny piasek), Paris, 1955, is based on the native Indian and mestizo motives from the Central American West Coast, as his collection of short stories **Coco de oro** (The Golden Coconut), Paris, 1970, interwoven with fictional tale on U.S. pilots and Polish sailors, set against the tropical background of the Pacific. In Mexico rose to prominence, the Paris-born, Polish-Mexican Elena Poniatowska, author of several outstanding books such as **La noche en Tlaltelolco** (Mexico, 1970) on the severe governmental suppression, of the Mexican student riots in 1968, in which her brother died, **And Hasta no verte Jesús mío**

(Mexico, 1969). The latter, in spite of its religious title, is a secular novel describing Mexican native beliefs and customs still prevailing in that Aztec country. Beautiful Mexican legends which are rich in Indian-Mestizo folklore, are found in a collection of stories, scattered in various magazines, by Juan de Wyskota Zakrzewski. Whereas, Edmund Urbanski's scholarly experience are recorded in his work **From the Vikings to the Indians** (Od Wikingów do Indian), Stevens Point, 1987, in which the creole, mestizo and Indian civilizations of Mexico and other Ibero-American countries are explained, a vital factor indispensable for understanding the multidimensional aspects of their culture.

Witold Gombrowicz, Janina Surynowa Wyczolkowska, Jozefa Radzyminska and Florian Czarnyszewicz, who for a few decades resided in the creole atmosphere of Argentina, have produced works that compose a different social vein. This may be seen in Gombrowicz's several volumes of his **Diarios argentinos**, covering the period 1938-1962, with a variety of reflections on his sojourn in the European-culturally-tinged Buenos Aires. Closely related to Argentina through her family ties was the seasoned writer Surynowa Wyczolkowska, who left a few Polish novels in which fiction is combined with personal experience.

These socially conscious novels, published in Paris or London (1950s-1970s) include the following: **Gringa** (Gringa), **The Summer of Gringa** (Lato Gringi), **The Autumn of Gringa** (Jesień Gringi) and **Theresa, the Unfeign Child** (Teresa, dziecko nieudane), which describe the psychological dichotomy of Polish-Argentine intermarriage, also the mentality of the "porteños" and "provincianos" i.e. inhabitants of this largest River Plate country. Another type of author was Radzyminska who in her writings praised the glorious pages of Argentine history. She also published a book **Fourteen Years of Darkness** (Czternaście lat mroku), Bs. Aires, 1978, which due to her maladjustment, refers to her uneasy personal life in her adopted country, made her unpopular among her compatriots there. More straightforward are the works of Florian Czarnyszewicz, particularly his book **Stepchildren** (Pasierby), Paris, 1958, which narrates his forty-year life experience in the Argentine lower and middle-class milieu with all its "ups" and "downs". The usage of a Polish-Argentine **lingo** gives his story a somewhat exotic flavor. Another writer was Czeslaw Straszewicz who, on the basis of his twenty-year experience in Uruguay, published a novel **Men From the Stork's Nest** (Ludzie z bocianiego gniazda) Paris, 1953, which while describing the fate of Polish sailors-refugees in Montevideo, who escaped from communist-dominated Poland, paints vivid pictures of various phases of Uruguayan life.

Likewise, realistic descriptions of Brazilian life and culture are to be found in the narratives of Jerzy Kossowski and Bohdan Pawlowicz. Both produced works on the life of Polish immigrants in Brazil, which also gave them the opportunity to present the civilizational background of the adopted country. They do it "sine ira et studio", which assures it a good degree of veracity.

Concluding our remarks, it is obvious that writings of all these authors, in addition to satisfying the narrative curiosity of readers, also had an intellectual value, which allowed them to get acquainted with fabrics of the multidimensional import of Ibero-American culture. Our Hispano-Americanists should take it into scholarly consideration especially, since some of the above mentioned works were translated from Polish into various European languages. Thus, they became an effective vehicle of cultural dissemination of Latin America in Europe. A Polish Ibero-Americanist, Maria Paradowska, published a Polish book titled **Polish Gontributions to the Civilizational-Cultural Development of Latin America** (Warsaw, 1992), which enumerates the variety of ways Poles participated in its growth and expansion, not only in Humanities but also in Sciences and Technology, frequently related to university teaching.

Author of many other works, Dr. Paradowska is one of the leading researchers of Hispanic American and Indianist affairs in contemporary Poland.

One may wonder about the source of the Polish interest and even attraction toward Latin American matters. The explanation for this are certain intellectual bonds existing between the Latinos and

Western Slavs, proceeding from similar Latin-Roman cultural roots and some idiosyncratic features. Visible among them are emotionalism and a predilection for fine arts, literature, music and dance. These factors account for mutual understanding and common sympathy among these two diverse ethno-linguistic-civilizational groups.

Bibliography

Anais da Comunidade Brasileiro-Polonesa. Curitiba, 1970-1972.

Barreto, Abellardo. Bibliografía Sul-Riograndense. Rio de Janeiro. 1973-75

Bukiet, Albert. **Materiały do bibliografii polskiej Ameryki Łacińskiej.** Buenos Aires, 1975.

Enciclopedia Universal Ilustrada Europeo-Americana. Madrid, 1945.

Filipak, Francisco. **Antología do Valle do Iguaçu.** União da Vitória. 1976.

Fredecensis. **A Polonia na literatura brasileira.** Curitiba, 1927.

Gez, Juan W. **Historia de la provincia de San Luis**. San Luis, 1930.

Jawrower, Otokar. Ed. **Polonia en el Uruguay.** Montevideo, 1945.

Kochanek, Kazimierz. Ed. **Los polacos en el Peru.** Lima, 1979.

Kula, Marcin. **Ameryka Łacinska w relacjach Polaków.** Warszawa, 1982.

Łepkowski, Tadeusz **Polska-Meksyk 1918-1939** Wroclaw 1980.

Paradowska, Maria. **Polacy w Ameryce Południowej.** Wrocław, 1977.

Paradowska, Maria. **Wkład Polaków w rozwój cywilizacyjno-kulturowy Ameryki Łacińskiej.** Warszawa, 1992.

Reclus, Elisee. **Géographie Universelle.** Paris, 1910-1914.

Pyzik, Estanislao. **Los polacos en la Republica Argentina y America Sur desde el año 1812.** Buenos Aires, 1966.

Retinger, Jozef H. **Polacy w cywilizacji świata.** Warszawa, 1937.

Sarnacki, John. **Latin American Literature and History in Polish Translation.** Port Huron, 1973.

Schlesinger, Hugo. **Polonika brazylijskie.** São Paulo, 1948.

da Silva Carneiro, David. **Galeria de ontem.** Curitiba, 1963.

Skowronski, Tadeu. **Paginás brasileiras sobre a Polonia.** Rio de Janeiro, 1942.

Urbanski, Edmund S. **Hispanic America And Its Civilizations. Spanish Americans and Anglo-Americans.** Norman, 1987, 1991.

Urbanski, Edmund S. **Od Wikingów do Indian.** Stevens Point, 1987. Ostrow Wlkp., 1994.

Wojcik, Jan K. **Bibliografía brasileiro-polonesa.** Porto Alegre, 1960.

Encyclopedic **Who's Who Notable in Mexico,** Mexico, 1972.

Zakrzewski, Juan. **Los intelectuales polacos en Mexico** (Época), Mexico, 1943.

Zielinski, Stan. **Słownik pionierów polskich kolonialnych.** Warszawa, 1932.

Yaben, Jacinto. **Biografías argentinas y sudamericanas.** Buenos Aires, 1931

Polish-Latin American Book Collection and Archives in P.I.A.S.A., New York.

Valle, Rafael H. **La Cirugía Mexicana del siglo XIX.** Mexico, 1942.